A FIELD GUIDE TO
INTERNATIONALIZING
BUSINESS EDUCATION

A FIELD GUIDE TO

INTERNATIONALIZING

BUSINESS EDUCATION

EDITED BY

Robert F. Scherer

Sarah T. Beaton

M. Fall Ainina

Jeffrey F. Meyer

James Thomas, Editorial Director

Published by
the Center for International Business Education and Research
at the University of Texas at Austin

Acknowledgements of other bibliographic works cited in the text are fully annotated in *Chapter Reference Notes and Additional Resources* at the back of this book.

The paper in this book meets the guidelines for permanence and durability of The Committee on Production Guidelines for Book Longevity of the Council on Library Resources.

This book is intended to promote the exchange of ideas among researchers, practitioners, and policymakers. The views expressed within are those of the individual authors and are not necessarily those of the U.S. Department of Education, nor do they express U.S. Department of Education policy.

This book was supported with funding from the Business and International Education and the Center for International Business Education programs administered under Title VI of the Higher Education Act of 1965 as amended. These programs have supported hundreds of U.S. institutions of higher education improve the academic teaching of international business education, particularly since 1983.

BOOK COVER & BOOK DESIGN BY TAMMY BRAZEL

The following may be contacted for more information:

Robert F. Scherer, Wright State University, Raj Soin College of Business, 3640 Colonel Glenn Highway, Dayton, OH 45435; Tel: 937.775.3718, Fax: 937.775.3545, E-mail: robert.scherer@wright.edu

Sarah T. Beaton, U.S. Department of Education, Branch Chief, International Studies Team, International Education and Graduate Program Service, 1990 K Street, N.W. Washington, DC 20006; Tel: 202.502.7621, Fax: 202.502.7859, E-mail: sarah_beaton@ed.gov

Library of Congress Cataloging-in-Publication Data

A field guide to internationalizing business education / edited by Robert F. Scherer…[et al.].
    p. cm.
  Includes bibliographical references and index.
  ISBN 0-9678682-0-3
    1. Business education—United States—Curricula. 2. International business enterprises—Study and teaching. 3. Business education—Study and teaching—United States. I. Scherer, Robert F., 1955-

HF1131 .F54 2000
650'.071'173—dc21

00-022646

Travel is fatal to prejudice, bigotry and narrow mindedness, and many of our people need it solely on these accounts. Broad, wholesome, charitable views of men and things cannot be acquired by vegetating in one corner of the earth all one's lifetime.

Mark Twain

Contents

Preface

Sarah T. Beaton

In his book review of Thomas Friedman's *The Lexus and the Olive Tree*, Lester Thurow observes that, once started, globalization cannot be turned off because it is not driven by trade—which governments can control—but rather by technology, which governments cannot control. In order to win in trade, it is not the hardware of globalization that counts (telecommunications and transportation systems) but the software, which Thurow defines as "a well-educated work force ... the honesty, transparency, and legal systems needed to support global capitalism." That is today's challenge for American capitalism, says Professor Thurow, to which we would add the need for a globally conscious and culturally aware citizenry: a challenge that has to be translated by the American educational system into action. This book addresses one such challenge; how to internationalize business education so that graduates and others will have a better understanding of the global marketplace.

In 1958, the U.S. Congress realized that the nation's defense, security, and welfare were inseparably linked to education and enacted the National Defense Education Act (NDEA) under which Title VI legislation was authorized with the goal of increasing U.S. knowledge of languages and area studies. Twenty-five years later, recognizing that the marketplace had far-reaching global effects and that the nation needed to prepare for the next generation of business professionals, Congress expanded the Title VI legislation to include the Business and International Education Program (BIE). Since 1983, the BIE program has provided funding to universities, four-year colleges, and community colleges to better educate and prepare students and businesspeople through the active and interactive study of international business.

The need to internationalize the business curriculum has long been recognized by AACSB—The International Association for Management Education (the principal such accrediting institution in the nation.) As early as 1974 AACSB issued a mandate for schools to become more globally competent and provided guidelines for them to follow. The Congressional action under Title VI, along with the AACSB mandate, provided a welcome and needed impetus for many business schools to apply in greater and greater numbers for BIE grants with which to internationalize. Institutions not pursuing accreditation also began to take note.

In the early 1980s only thirty-six bachelor degree programs in international business existed in the United States. Our business schools were far behind their European and Asian counterparts in teaching about international trade. Moreover, very few U.S. business students, graduate or undergraduate, studied a second language or world region. Most faculty and students believed then that a sound foundation in a traditional business discipline was sufficient to secure a top level management position, and that further international training and sensitivity could be acquired abroad on the job.

Today, this mindset has changed radically. In 1997, for example, there were in place 195 bachelor degree programs in international business, a fivefold increase over 1983, and 352 business schools had received AACSB accreditation. Exhibit 1.1 in Chapter One shows the current number of existing international programs in the business and economics disciplines. The proliferation of these programs in the short span of just fourteen years is remarkable and reflects vividly the existence of a burgeoning demand. Many of these programs incorporate and emphasize the study of a second language, world region, and area studies. Several programs require or recommend a period of study abroad or an internship with a non-U.S. company.

Since 1983, the BIE program has supported over 300 U.S. institutions of higher education with approximately $35 million. The program's goals are two-dimensional: (1) to improve the academic teaching of the international business curriculum, and (2) to conduct outreach activities to local businesses that assist them in the international marketplace. Each grantee must conduct at least one activity that addresses each component of the legislation.

Past recipients of BIE funding are two-year and four-year private and public institutions at all levels of internationalization. These schools are quite diverse in nature, and the subsequent changes effected are likewise very different.

Changes may occur subtly and may have an implicit and systemic (rather than explicit and immediate) impact on individual programs and departments at larger institutions. At smaller schools the same type of changes may, at the same time, ignite a flurry of activity and promote long-lasting systemic change.

The impact of the BIE program is difficult to quantify because of the variety of results it produces. However, what has clearly resulted is a vast body of knowledge about how to internationalize a business school. Many business schools may not be aware of the wealth of information already available from the forerunners of internationalization. This book is, in part, an attempt to gather and present some of that early experience and information—a field guide for identifying strategies and techniques with which to transform colleges, schools, and programs from a local, regional, and national orientation to an international—global—orientation. The authors have written from trials, tribulations, practice, and commitment to transforming their business schools and colleges into international business education leaders. The following chapters outline what we believe the U.S. business school should look like now in the twenty-first century and how to get there.

Our intention is to provide the reader with a guide to wade through the complex and muddy waters of internationalization. While no two schools are alike, there are some common tools that can be used to internationalize both the larger public state institution and the smaller private college. Internationalizing can be a messy, difficult, and very time-consuming affair. However, once you recognize the possibilities and see the effects on your students, faculty, staff, and institution, you cannot derail the vital energies that you have unleashed, energies far more powerful than traditional business education. When you take a group of students to the Yucatán or Rajasthan, or set up a faculty exchange program with China, you will realize that you are engaged in activities more profound than developing a marketing formula. You are not only engaged in the exchange of ideas, about commercial trade relations and negotiations, but also in the exchange of cultural values and systems with *people*, the most priceless commodity driving the world economy today.

Foreword

Rishi Kumar

Today, businesses and citizens are more interlinked globally than ever before, and our move toward a world without borders continues to progress at an astounding rate. This borderless world functions in a fiercely competitive business environment where customers' expectations are barely met by manufacturing capabilities, and suggests an immediate future where today's excellence will be a minimal requirement to stay in the game.

This rapid change is rooted in the technological sphere. The spectacular growth in technology, a consequent revolution in the telecommunications industry, and a broad-based spread of e-commerce (both business-to-customer and business-to-business) have led to a paradigm shift in the ways organizations—businesses as well as universities—manage themselves. For instance, the transformation of the telecommunications industry is creating an infrastructure that allows both consumers and businesses to communicate through voice, data, and video transmissions safely and speedily anywhere in the world. The advent of e-commerce has meant that consumers are ever-more knowledgeable and sensitive to the availability and quality of products globally. In this new world of technology, it is a risky strategy to presume that corporations alone will dictate what to produce, and where and on what terms to sell—it is much more likely that consumers themselves will determine, if not dictate, how corporations operate, develop, produce, and sell within a global economy.

The emergence of an inextricably-linked international marketplace for goods, services, capital, and investment is a fact that can neither be denied nor ignored—and it is a concomitant certainty that the complexity and competition in that market will only grow in magnitude and scope. Thus, globalization is a revolution-in-progress, the central storyline of the twenty-first century, with major consequences within as well as between nations. The borderless world is a place of mixed blessing—with impacts of that revolution producing both winners and losers. And while it can be successfully demonstrated that the benefits of growth in international trade and investment far exceed the costs, it would be folly to disregard those costs. What is particularly fortunate, however, is the reality that globalization is a phenomenon over which we can exert control, and thus enable us as nations to choose policies that maximize the net benefits.

The case for globalization which depends on falling barriers to trade and investment—the twin engines for growth and prosperity—is simple and compelling. International free trade, whether rooted in comparative advantage or scale economies, is a powerful and positive force. Trade stimulates economic growth, creates jobs, raises incomes, expands both choice and competition, improves product quality, and lowers prices. The fact that most of the countries of the world willingly participate in some form of international free trade is evidence that they see it in their own best interest. Further substantiating this is the widely held belief that it is a lack of trade, investment, and freedom which keeps the world's poorest economies in poverty and environmental degradation.

Huge benefits of globalization notwithstanding, trade among nations still remains contentious. Some of the sources of contention against international free trade are frivolous and without solid empirical support. "Low-wage competition," "environmental destruction," and "undermining national sovereignty" are examples of these less well-considered objections, while in fact there are far more serious issues which require resolution in order to preserve any real gains from globalization. This list includes the asymmetrical impact of increased trade and investment on different social groups, the undermining of domestic norms and traditionally accepted social institutions, and erosion of a government's ability to provide social safety nets for those citizens who suffer losses due to the massive shifts in economy.

Globalization bestows enormous gains on the owners of capital, workers with high and specialized skills, and professionals able to move their talent as dictated by demand. Those who lose include unskilled and semi-skilled workers, and most middle managers. The latter group, workers in particular, experience reduced earnings due to erosion of their bargaining power as well as greater instability in earnings due to fluctuating demand for their services. This loss is further accentuated by the reduced role that governments now typically play in terms of providing some sort of social insurance against shocks experienced by workers. The hostility toward international free trade, particularly in the rich, advanced countries, is further nourished by the fact that globalization seriously undermines the prevailing institutional norms, including working conditions in the factories, legal rules, and social safety nets. Workers usually consider this a betrayal of their trust by government and businesses.

Clearly, the economy of today is materially and markedly different from the economy of yesterday, and business leaders must confront the key challenges emanating from international free trade, forward-thinking government agencies, and multinational corporations, while ameliorating some of the adverse effects. That burden appropriately falls on institutions of higher learning. Hence, the need for the internationalization of business schools. The challenge of designing a new and creative curriculum which incorporates issues of international trade in their multi-faceted dimensions is an awesome responsibility, but unavoidable. Indeed, the very survival of business schools hinges on producing business leaders of tomorrow who do not just survive in this new and complex business world, but flourish in it.

It has been rightly said that "great organizations change before they have to. Lucky organizations are those which eventually catch up. All the other organizations are history." Let us hope that U.S. business schools can be lucky, if not great, organizations.

Acknowledgements

Publication of *A Field Guide to Internationalizing Business Education* is the result of our collaboration with many business education professionals whose mentoring, organizational, and writing skills have yielded many important contributions to the field. Ralph Hines, Susanna C. Easton, and Donald N. Bigelow of the United States Department of Education have been instrumental in shaping international education for over twenty-five years. Their dedication to strengthening and improving international education in the United States is the inspiration behind this book. Ed McDermott, of the United States Department of Education, contributed his research skills in assisting to bring this book to fruition. Arthur A. Iwanicki, of the United States Department of Education, deserves special recognition as professional mentor and friend.

Through financial support for the publication of this book, the Centers for International Business Education and Research continue their leadership in advancing international business education. In addition, we offer our greatest appreciation to all of the contributing authors without whom this project would not have materialized. Their vision and perseverance have resulted in relevant and practical material for their international business colleagues.

The production of the book was made possible through the efforts of our colleagues at the University of Texas at Austin, Center for International Business Education and Research. Robert Green, Linda Gerber, and especially Diane

Wilson provided expert guidance and support during all phases of the project. At Wright State University, Susan Davis and Kathi Dye prepared the text and figures in a professional manner and with a positive approach; Todd Trickler, Carmen Gloria Muñoz, Elizabeth Luloff, and Gustavo Frêne performed research that assisted in the preparation of resources and a number of the exhibits in the book. Tammy Brazel was responsible for the cover and interior design which effectively complements the theme of the book. Byron Crews line-edited and proofread the entire manuscript to ensure appropriate syntax, as well as grammatical and mechanical accuracy. Our editorial director, James Thomas, crafted the book—massaging format, organization, and text—from the first page to the last, utilizing his experience with the bookmaking process.

We acknowledge the support and encouragement of our families whose inspiration was the foundation and cornerstone of this book: Ian and Kelton Rhys Beaton Williams, Lisa Russell, Evan, Bernard, Helene, Douglas, and Renée Scherer, Alexandra Robles, Jackie Annes, Judy and James Rose, Khairata and Cheikh Ainina, Laynae and Rylie Meyer. Finally, we acknowledge our professional friendship, which sustained us throughout this project.

R.F.S.
S.T.B.
M.F.A.
J.F.M.

[**Editors' Note:** Acknowledgements of bibliographic works cited in the text are fully annotated in *Chapter Reference Notes and Additional Resources* included in the back of this book.]

The generous support of the following CIBERs, made this book possible.

Brigham Young University/University of Utah
Columbia University
Duke University
Florida International University
Georgia Institute of Technology
Indiana University
Michigan State University
Purdue University
San Diego State University
Texas A&M University
Ohio State University
University of Memphis
Thunderbird - The American Graduate School of International Management
University of California at Los Angeles
University of Colorado at Denver
University of Connecticut
University of Florida
University of Hawaii at Manoa
University of Illinois at Urbana-Champaign
University of Kansas
University of Michigan
University of North Carolina at Chapel Hill
University of Pittsburgh
University of South Carolina
University of Southern California
University of Texas at Austin
University of Washington
University of Wisconsin

For a complete listing of CIBER sites, with addresses,
please see pp.291-295.

CHAPTER ONE

The Future is Now

Robert F. Scherer

Sarah T. Beaton

M. Fall Ainina

Jeffrey F. Meyer

Imagine a university without borders: degrees granted by international consortia, business professors teaching in the United States, Europe, and Latin America simultaneously; students taking courses on multiple campuses across the globe, culturally savvy, and fluent in at least two languages; and businesses participating in the development and delivery of courses which incorporate the most recent technological advances. While this vision may seem years away, those business schools embracing the future are implementing programs with these components today.

We can no longer teach our students with classroom examples extracted from templates of domestic manufacturing industries. We can no longer stay within the walls of our classrooms, borders of our states or regions, and hope to produce graduates able to compete with their Asian, Latin American, and European counterparts. Research conducted by sending questionnaires to a local U.S. business community and then extrapolating and generalizing the results to similar industries and business practices throughout the world is no longer advantageous or appropriate. In order to survive we need to travel abroad ourselves as faculty, develop relationships with colleagues internationally, and engage our students in practical work experiences on at least two continents before graduation.

In order to understand the future of U.S. business education which includes a true global perspective, we need to understand the factors that have catalyzed into an awareness of its importance today. Exhibit 1.1 shows the growth of international business degree programs in the United States from 1972 to 1999. Going back further, the slow growth in global business education drifted over the previous twenty years, with even well-known and respected colleges of business not developing programs. Thirty years ago, however, a breeze began to blow, and this small fleet of programs (thirty-five) began to increase—and in the past decade (there were 163 in 1989) grew to a 420-strong armada by 1999.

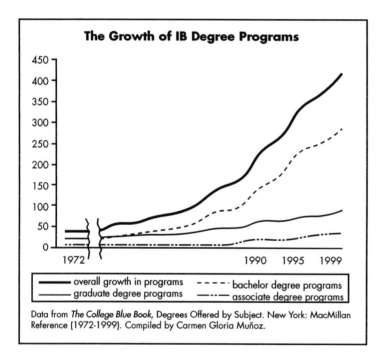

The Growth of IB Degree Programs   **Exhibit 1.1**

Legend:
- overall growth in programs
- graduate degree programs
- bachelor degree programs
- associate degree programs

Data from *The College Blue Book*, Degrees Offered by Subject. New York: MacMillan Reference (1972-1999). Compiled by Carmen Gloria Muñoz.

This slow growth is in part a function of the great prosperity the United States enjoyed for thirty-five years following World War II. We were on top in the manufacturing, electronics, agricultural, and financial service sectors of the global economy. Prosperity led to complacency, and the isolationist point of view that every other nation would buy from the U.S. and look to the U.S. as the leader in world trade. However, as we continued to rely on our massive ability to manufacture goods and grow food, the U.S. economy started to change. Little by little—industry by industry, and farm by farm—our economy shifted from manufacturing and agrarian-based to service and technology-based. As this process slowly evolved, the business schools evolved even more slowly.

M.B.A. enrollments slowly climbed in the 1960s and 1970s, as did undergraduate business enrollments, both in the United States and abroad. Yet our business schools rode the wave of academic success and did not navigate through the crest of international business education. Instead, curricula were charted through a traditional and uniform course across business schools as accreditation demanded, while in Europe and around the globe business schools began to change. Programs were put in place in Europe allowing students mobility among various universities of a multinational consortium; second-language learning was mandatory for graduation in many Latin American business schools; and international students flooded the United States only to learn our business practices and take them home where, with modification, they might apply and take advantage of them.

Although there was nothing inherently poor about the credentialed quality of the business faculty or the academic qualifications of our undergraduate and graduate business students, as the time came to play catch-up with the rest of the world, the sluggish and sometimes haphazard nature of development in U.S. business schools made for slow progress. What then, now, are the necessary elements for international business education to catapult itself into the future? How must business schools of today change to make international business education a focal point of relevancy for the hallmarks of tomorrow's university: teaching, scholarship, service? How do we create and implement even newer and more relevant programs in order to prepare students to participate in a global economy and world culture?

Building a Foundation

The aim of this book, and our summary here in this first chapter, is to discuss the components required to answer those questions. How do you go about developing an international business education program that is not only relevant today but has a built-in capacity for relevance over time, a sustainable system in which the curriculum can respond lightening fast to business needs, faculty initiatives, as well as student interests, and still meet the muster of accreditation reviews? To develop such a sustainable and renewable system of development and implementation we must develop a model which is interdisciplinary, multi-method, and outcomes-oriented.

Exhibit 1.2 provides a schematic overview of the model, which encourages interdisciplinary cooperation among academic units on campus, embedded in the mission of the business school. The model, while recognizing formal (and, to some extent, informal) disciplinary boundaries, draws faculty together from several traditionally separate colleges within a university. These distinct disciplines provide the formative matter to shape international business programs through a jointly developed curriculum, ongoing faculty development and renewal experiences, and linkages to universities and faculties throughout the world. These developmental activities in turn drive the implementation of programs via technology, study abroad, practical experiences, and outreach to the international business community to achieve a set of internationally-focused outcomes for students, graduates, business, faculty, and programs. Finally, the outcomes are checked against the mission to determine the degree of congruence and to make any revisions to the mission based upon the university's interface with its external stakeholders in the international business community. The objective is students with a growing global outlook and awareness.

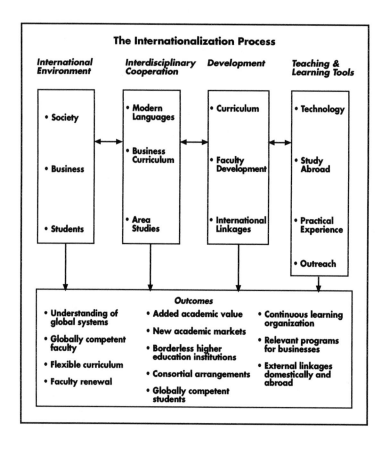

Exhibit 1.2

The Internationalization Process

International Environment	Interdisciplinary Cooperation	Development	Teaching & Learning Tools
• Society	• Modern Languages	• Curriculum	• Technology
• Business	• Business Curriculum	• Faculty Development	• Study Abroad
• Students	• Area Studies	• International Linkages	• Practical Experience
			• Outreach

Outcomes

- • Understanding of global systems
- • Globally competent faculty
- • Flexible curriculum
- • Faculty renewal

- • Added academic value
- • New academic markets
- • Borderless higher education institutions
- • Consortial arrangements
- • Globally competent students

- • Continuous learning organization
- • Relevant programs for businesses
- • External linkages domestically and abroad

Mission Development

Mission—or, when stated properly, *purpose*—is derived from an assessment of and interaction with all the stakeholders of a given entity, whether university, governmental, or business entity. Colleges of business are uniquely positioned to connect with the business community and serve as bridges of learning, understanding, and cooperation. But with distance-learning technology driving growth opportunities in higher education, the business school's mission can no longer focus on interaction with the community within the immediate fifty-mile radius of the campus. Even a "metropolitan" or "regional" business school must include some statement in its mission about the need to prepare its students for effective participation in the global economy.

In the past, business schools were bound by tight and rigid accreditation requirements, which constrained the curriculum and preparation of their faculty and students. Uniformity was the force driving reaccreditation. However, AACSB-The International Association for Management Education no longer requires the same methodical consistency among business schools in their undergraduate and graduate curricula. To replace the "one size fits all" mode of approval, the organization has moved to a "mission-driven" approach. Thus, the dean and faculty now have much greater freedom to set the direction of the business curriculum and programs by aligning resources and developing programs that fit the specific situation of the college and its student and business constituencies.

Interdisciplinary Cooperation and Planning

Once a mission statement has been developed among the business school faculty, the new vision of international business education requires extending the reach beyond the school's borders. A "future" orientation requires an invitation to colleagues across campus to participate in the design and development of programs. This approach, while alien to many business schools, includes the involvement of modern languages and international studies faculty which have long been involved in international education.

The Business Core

To be globally competent, the academic skills required of undergraduate and graduate students must include a solid core grounded in fundamental business disciplines. Being able to grasp traditional business concepts such as financial statements and supply and demand curves remains fundamental to the business education process. Against this backdrop the student is ready to study international business topics.

A typical business curriculum includes some elective courses with the word "international" in front of them, such as "International Accounting" and "International Marketing." The student progresses through a series of seemingly independent survey courses. Once completed the student has a "major" in international business and is presumed to be "globally competent." Unfortunately, students miss the linkage between theory and practice because they have not had opportunities to apply the text to the real world. Elementary case studies, reports based on library research, and in-class role-playing exercises are no substitute for hard experience. Students leave the university with a degree in international business, but lack the essential skills to be effective.

International business is a dynamic discipline, with some aspects as variable as international politics. New courses need to be developed that encourage the student to integrate marketing, finance, and management. International business logistics must include perspectives regarding transportation, customs operations, and trade networks. Transcultural management focuses on the integration of language, culture, and business. These integrative courses spin webs of information and understanding that allow students to see the dependencies among disciplines and think holistically, rather than compartmentally. While universities are not trade schools, they can teach an application-oriented academic trade, complete with language skills and real experience abroad.

Business students traditionally did not go abroad to study or work because there was little flexibility built into the degree requirements. Nor did students typically gain business degree credit for second-language competency. University business courses were not integrative. Curricula were rigid and course equivalencies from non-U.S. universities to domestic universities were scrutinized rigidly for purposes of accepting transfer credit. A student needs applied theory and integrative experiences in order to become globally competent. Universities must accept liberal transfer credits and equivalencies for courses taken at an overseas university, for credit internships which are a valued and required part of the degree program, and fewer required credit hours in traditional business courses in order to provide essential simulative experiences.

These tasks necessitate reciprocity agreements between the U.S. university and non-U.S. universities and colleges. Colleges highly effective at delivering international business education will model the flexibility, adaptation, integration, and dynamism of international business for their students and for other U.S. business schools. Achieving these qualities requires the identification of core business competencies, followed by new integrative course development, the establishment of exchange agreements which allow the student to make progress toward graduation while working and studying abroad, and collaborative projects with colleagues in other disciplines outside the business school.

Modern Languages

"English is the language of business" has long been the mantra of business education in the United States. Although this statement remains true in the sense that English is still the single most widely used language in international commerce abroad, to do business effectively graduates should be able to communicate in at least one second modern language. Vast numbers of individuals in the United States already speak a language other than English as their primary language, further pointing to a future that is multilingual. To do business internationally means being able to navigate and communicate in the language of the country in which business is being done. Fluency is the principle means to increase trust and foster understanding, and students who only speak English will not be as marketable or as competitive as their counterparts.

The lack of U.S. interest in studying a second-language is evident in the primary and secondary schools, where there is little exposure until the ninth grade (at which time it is almost too late to acquire fluency), and no more evident than at the doctoral level in business administration. Today, the majority of business doctoral programs have opted to allow additional quantitative courses in lieu of even a reading knowledge of a second-language. By contrast, liberal arts programs require at least one additional international language, and sometimes two, before awarding a Ph.D.

The disciplines of business and modern language have been at crosscurrents for years. Business curricula have not incorporated mandatory second-language training because of a perceived absence of demonstrated need. Modern language instructors are typically well-read in literature, but not business communication. The net result is that the two disciplinary worlds have collided continually, pushing each other further away over time. Certainly it is vital for business students to be trained in basic grammar and conversation in target international languages. Knowing the literature of another country assists in knowing the culture, people, and society, which in turn assists in conducting business. Yet, we must go beyond the basics. The key is to be able to communicate verbally and nonverbally, and our current curricula are not structured to meet this objective.

A dialogue between business faculty and modern language faculty must begin immediately. The dialogue must include discussions of what skills and abilities students need to communicate in the business language of other countries. This change in thinking will require new courses, business faculty who can communicate in a second language, and modern language faculty who know the technical terms used in business and have some experience in the international arena of business.

The result of international business curriculum revision in the area of second-language acquisition needs to be, at the very least, a business language track at the undergraduate and graduate levels which requires students to complete language courses through the fourth year of study with a mandatory internship or applied experience, which requires them to use the non-native language studied. Basic courses can be designed with the business professional in mind. Literature and grammar should be included as well as business communication, correspondence, etiquette, and conflict resolution.

Courses could, ideally *should*, be team-taught by business and modern language faculty. Such an approach provides students with the best of both worlds: faculty who have the technical skills to teach second-language acquisition, and faculty who can communicate in the international language and know the technical language of business. During the third and fourth year of study, students should be able to study principles of management and international economics in a second-language so that language and business are integrated.

Area Studies

Similar to modern language education, changes need to occur in the design of area studies courses. The globally competent graduate needs to have a solid understanding of at least one specific region of the world outside of the United States. Area studies courses should be incorporated into the business program as a set of complementary courses. For example, students studying Spanish as their second language can complement their education with foundation courses on Latin American history, anthropology, economics and trade, contemporary politics, and culture, while more advanced level courses can focus on doing business in Latin America, including specific issues of labor relations, working conditions, transportation, and related commercial topics. Again, business faculty and area studies faculty should partner to design courses that include the necessary content. Courses in which a student must apply the learning gained in business settings abroad and at home should be obligatory.

Development

Changes desired to move the business program into the future *today* require thinking that is radically different from what we are traditionally used to seeing in the curriculum revision process. It is not uncommon for business faculty to disagree on what the content of a "good" business education looks like. Such disagreement is healthy and can lead to productive change as long as it does not devolve into disputes regarding the number of quantitative courses versus "soft" courses to be included in the curriculum. The focus should be on how to integrate all of the different courses and experiences necessary to teach the skills needed by international business.

Funding *is* available to create the future, from a variety of sources not the least important of which is the U.S. government. These funds can be used to design curricula, establish partnerships domestically and abroad, and assist faculty in the development of their international business tool kit. Any higher education institution willing to make the effort can apply and compete for funding. In this way the international business pump can be primed. The hard part, however, is sustaining the momentum to develop a program in which the curriculum includes both basic business courses to teach the fundamentals, and module courses that can be modified, adapted, and changed to meet the continuously changing and dynamic needs of international business.

Equally important, deans and their faculties can create the future by being bold and reallocating resources within their colleges for development purposes. Faculty need to move beyond disciplinary parochialism to ensure a truly integrated curriculum. The contemporary international business degree should shift the number of credits in business administration courses to less than fifty percent of the degree, and include required courses in modern languages, area studies, and applied experiences such as internships. Integrating the curriculum using concepts such as "non-English language across the business curriculum" can be a method to afford coverage of business content and international language. Business schools should encourage students to obtain international experiences for which they are given credit counting toward their degree. Faculty should likewise be encouraged to teach abroad for periods of time in order to achieve cultural and business fluency in another country as part of the overall program development.

Practical Constraints

Resources are scarce and require careful allocation and reallocation. In developing the future-oriented international business program, the college and university cannot cover the world. It is not reasonable to assume that a university can provide language training in ten or more international languages. In the change assessment process, faculty need to first identify the areas of expertise already in their skills bank of second-language acquisition, area studies, and business specialties. For example, if there is a strong Spanish language faculty, and faculty resources in Latin American studies, then a strategic thrust of the business school should surely be to develop a program centered in Latin American business studies. Some schools will be able to do more than others, but in all cases the task entails cross-campus collaboration between business, modern languages, and area studies disciplines.

Future-oriented international business programs must build upon existing strengths and resources to graduate students with competence in specific regions. In the long run such programs promote sustainability, and also reduce programmatic redundancy from university to university.

Teaching Tools

What are the methods that can be used in the development, implementation, and maintenance of international business programs? The answer includes newly-refined methods including the utilization of cutting-edge technology, extensive student study abroad programs, intensely practical internship experiences, and outreach programs that truly "reach out." While these methods may not seem that radical, they are clearly the fast lane into the future. The problem is that many business schools are in the middle lane or, worse, stuck in the slow lane. To be sure, computer labs abound, and organizations such as international trade and small business assistance centers can be found on campus—but in order to get up to speed, these educational resources require a new, different, and much expanded utilization.

With Internet-based technologies, we can deliver courses on e-commerce to our students while they are studying or fulfilling an internship abroad. Business schools can conduct virtual classes in real time in several regions of the world simultaneously using current Internet technology, satellite, and compressed video. Finally, by providing credit for international business internships and applied experiences, our students can profitably study and work abroad. For those students who simply *cannot* travel abroad—for reasons of work, family, or health—authentic business practice and commercial language experiences can be provided by leveraging the resources on campus and in the community.

Traditional methods for teaching business include lecture, discussion, case studies, and homework assignments. These pedagogic tools, while passive at best, cannot prepare students to be leaders in the global economy. Reading a book and listening to a professor who is a content expert is appropriate for transmitting basic information. However, the globally-competent graduate requires an education that includes active learning strategies including the use of new technology, and field experiences which afford multiple opportunities to communicate and hone new skills. For example, online courses encourage students to interact with their counterparts domestically and abroad, communicate with international business professionals, and help develop research skills. These methods are widely available, but not yet widely used. Technology's benefit is in enabling distance-learning and promoting a sense of global proximity, while providing great flexibility in instruction and fostering performance-based outcomes.

Final Note

Why should we consider embarking on this arduous international journey? What are the reasons to promote change in business education when the resistance can be so strong, the resources seemingly nonexistent, and the rewards only internal? The reason is that if U.S. businesses are to continue to thrive in the new global market place, *all* business students must be exposed to more than a simple textbook chapter on international trade, and a *significant* number must graduate from specialized and diversified programs which equip them to enter the global marketplace ready to compete. Those schools and faculty able to adapt will receive their share of graduates courted by the top organizations. Although many *schools* are not yet aware of the need for internationalization of the curriculum, *employers are*—and will provide resources to those schools that have taken the initiative to rejuvenate their curriculum to meet the challenge.

As with all changes or innovations there are early and late adopters. To continue the trend indicated in Exhibit 1.1 and achieve the outcomes shown in Exhibit 1.2, business schools will require concerted effort from individual faculties in charting unnavigated interior waters. In fact, internationalization of business education does not just mandate change, it requires a transformation. The passageway toward institutionalization inevitably follows a route in which faculty must test the waters. In this stage there are one or a few individuals who teach an international business course ("champions" of international business education), take students on a study tour, or become involved in joint research projects with colleagues at an overseas university. Once experienced, this small group of professors may develop a series of courses in international business that may culminate in a major or certificate program. Still further along the journey, the faculty involves its students in research projects, international internships, or even tries teaching a course over the World Wide Web or satellite that includes students on two or more continents. It is at this point where the momentum (or "critical mass") has grown strong enough that organizational policies can either work to institutionalize the international programming, or sink it as faculty become disenchanted with the support from the college and university-level administrations.

In order to stimulate new learning and usher in the future, universities must institute incentives for faculty such as reduced teaching loads, extended working and teaching assignments abroad, internships, and rewarding pay for teaching-skills acquisition. The selection of administrators, deans, provosts, and presidents who have the vision and are willing to take calculated risks, and to allocate or appropriate resources to develop international programs, is essential to these teaching incentives. Universities must change reward systems, improve communication, and foster a positive culture that will support international business education.

Strategic alliances across campus and around the world must be created. Partnerships with globally competent businesses will need to be developed to produce globally competent faculty and graduates. Business school professionals will need to see the linkage between formal classroom training and work. The faculty role will evolve from teaching to facilitating. The curriculum for an international business program, at the undergraduate and graduate levels must be a model of flexibility and practicality. The program must include a systemic approach to the design and implementation of that curriculum. Finally, the university must prepare its students to (1) communicate in at least a second language, (2) experience at least one actual international trip, (3) gain insight into one other culture or region of the world, and (4) demonstrate a minimum level of competency in the practice of international business. Universities that set their sails to this course will chart the future.

Imagine a university without borders; multiple campuses around the globe, degrees granted by international consortia, business professors teaching regularly outside their own cultures, in person or electronically; language-equipped graduates taking positions which can greatly enhance their employers' understanding and marketability in the complex global economy. Imagine the future. The future is now.

CHAPTER TWO

Charting
Your
Course

Joseph Ganitsky

You have looked ahead and seen what the future can be for your students, faculty colleagues and staff, and yourself. The future includes internationalization of academic programs, internships abroad, faculty development, and research in other countries. Now you only need a map to help chart the course and provide direction for your efforts. You need a strategic plan.

Your strategic analysis (see Exhibit 2.1) should start by identifying your school's internationalization experiences, both past and present. Your school, like all others, has made explicit and implicit decisions since its inception and will continue making decisions through time that lead to different positions within the internationalization experience-commitment spectrum, from "none whatsoever" to "very significant."

Your strategic analysis should continue from specification of your current situation to your desired future situation, an analysis of your relative competitive position, and identification of the key players in the possible process of program transition. Estimating the impact of technological, social, regulatory, and competitive changes should permit you to visualize a new set of opportunities and challenges relevant to these key players, the field of international business (IB) education in general, and to your school in particular. This visionary exploration should also yield a creative estimate of your school's international business imperatives and strategic options. Such preliminary conclusions will permit you to reach a carefully considered balance between what your school might be, can be, should be, and wants to be in the future (see Exhibit 2.2).

Exhibit 2.1

Strategic Analysis for Your School's Internationalization Process

	Past	Current	Future
International Business Education Field		2 ←→	2, 3
Your School	1 ←→	1 →← →	↓ 4, 5, 6

Strategic Issues

1. **Your school's internationalization experiences (*past* and *current*).**

2. ***Current* and most likely *future* scenarios, competitive positions, and interrelationships of key players in IB education.**

3. ***Future* opportunities and challenges. Impact of ongoing trends and forces upon IB's key players in general, and your school in particular.**

4. **Your school's *future* global imperatives and strategic options.**

5. **Your school's desired *future* expertise, competencies, resources, and relationships.**

6. **Best evolutionary path and supporting processes to get from your school's *current* to *future* competitive positions.**

The emerging strategic plan for your school's internationalization should specify the distinct expertise, competencies, resources, and relationships that it needs to develop in the foreseeable future to meet its goals. It should also include the simplest, most expedient, and most viable path to get there, as well as identification of the relevant supporting processes and systems to be utilized, and specification of benchmarks along the path. Because no school can afford to wait for a "perfect" internationalization strategy before beginning implementation, the key elements for long-term success are carefully-crafted and well-integrated and supported processes and systems. These, when properly conceived and executed, facilitate and encourage continuous adjustment.

Each school's internationalization strategy will be unique. A thorough review

Exhibit 2.2

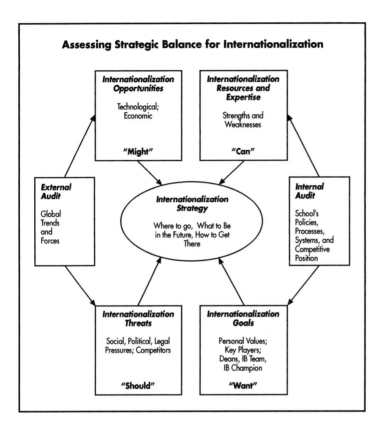

Assessing Strategic Balance for Internationalization

Internationalization Opportunities
Technological; Economic
"Might"

Internationalization Resources and Expertise
Strengths and Weaknesses
"Can"

External Audit
Global Trends and Forces

Internationalization Strategy
Where to go, What to Be in the Future, How to Get There

Internal Audit
School's Policies, Processes, Systems, and Competitive Position

Internationalization Threats
Social, Political, Legal Pressures; Competitors
"Should"

Internationalization Goals
Personal Values; Key Players; Deans, IB Team, IB Champion
"Want"

of other schools' approaches and experiences will reveal valuable points of reference for your school, but cannot serve as a replicatable model. These reference points should allow you to develop a broad and comprehensive perspective with which you can objectively check your intuitions, assumptions, and options. This data, when weighed against your school's resources, priorities, and values, will yield the most viable and desirable strategy to follow. More significantly, the participants in this analytical process will strengthen their confidence and commitment to the options and process they choose to pursue. Exhibit 2.3 shows indicators for a business school with a high level of commitment.

Some schools may even conclude that internationalization is not for them, or at least not now. But if this is the case, the analysis will nonetheless allow the school to identify the major hurdles inhibiting it, and allow it to take appropriate corrective actions if it chooses.

Your school's internationalization strategy must fit its specific goals and particular circumstances. It will be *unique* because the combination of your school's opportunities, resources, commitments, values, and expectations from key constituents (faculty, administrators, students, and businesses—both local and global) is unique. For each school, this combination of internal strengths and external opportunities will differ.

Exhibit 2.3

Some Indicators of a Business School's Internationalization with High Program Commitment

Involvement of

Constituents	Indicators
Faculty	Most teach and do research in IB subjects and programs
Students	More than 20% from diverse nationalities
	Most learn international business concepts
	A significant number attend programs abroad
	Obtain, on average, high scores in international component of exit-performance exams
Administration	Invest significant resources to develop programs and expertise
Alumni	Worldwide presence, many working with multinational enterprises
Business community	Multinational enterprises and international-minded executives support school's international business programs
Supporting agencies	Track record of successful international grants completed

Other U.S. entities and government agencies	Conduct joint international teaching and research programs
Other U.S. universities	International consortia
Universities abroad	Network of faculty and student exchange programs
Business community	International executive education programs
	Active in school's governance (international advisory board)

Setting the Stage for Internationalization

U.S. business schools need to create appealing environments and incentives if their strategies are to succeed: environments where internal and external players will be motivated both to contribute their ideas and to commit their efforts and expertise. Unfortunately, this has not been the case at many business schools.

Historically, these complex and heavily-politicized educational organizations have had difficulty managing even their *domestic* goals (such as financial stability, formal teaching and research, executive training, and being a catalyst for local economic development). Their service to the business community has been weakened by a variety of problems, including excessive education regulation, local school rivalry, and the unintended and unfavorable consequences of tenure. Hence, compared to other more competitive service industries, their managerial practices have been less market sensitive, their allocation of resources less efficient, and their faculty and staff less accountable. To avoid or circumvent these difficulties, the leaders of the most successful business schools have empowered their key players to formulate and implement strategies that creatively match their vision with each school's internal resources and most attractive external opportunities.

Due to increasing global complexity, program internationalization requires a more careful and more creative allocation of resources (time included) than domestic program management (including new initiatives). Yet, in order to be viable, any international strategy must be simple and easy to implement—and especially responsive to local conditions. These apparent paradoxical requirements explain why in the past many U.S. business schools preferred to (1) ignore their international opportunities, (2) shortchange the value of their services, or (3) greatly limit their growth potential. Given today's unprecedented and all-encompassing global economy, and the growing competition in IB education, continuing on this short-sighted path could be suicidal for many business schools.

The following eight *guidelines* can help academic leaders avoid the disappointment, if not failure, that can result from designing and implementing internationalization strategies based on old paradigms and practices, and instead move most quickly and effectively to an up-and-running program:

- Form an ever-expanding team interested in your school's internationalization.

- Start small, think BIG, remain flexible, and do not lose sight of your goals.

- Identify an IB champion or champions, then share opportunities, responsibilities, and rewards.

- Develop key relationships while assessing your school's IB potential.

- Prepare project proposals and an ongoing summary of your school's IB goals.

- Develop an assessment process that fosters learning and entrepreneurship.

- Prepare a timetable outlining key activities, deadlines, and budgets.

- Assess your performance regularly and take corrective actions as needed.

Form an ever-expanding team interested in your school's internationalization.

International business program initiatives usually begin with faculty members informally discussing their common interests, goals, and concerns. The value of these discussions increases as focus and depth intensifies and as the diversity of participants grows, depending on such important factors as discipline and background. As discussions progress, participants may agree to shape a more formalized IB team, or committee, that shares a common goal. Remaining open to everyone (including student and business community representatives) is essential to the IB team's eventual success. Staying isolated for long may make the team appear as another small "special-interest group." If so, the team will be unable to capture the imagination and appreciation of many colleagues. At worst, colleagues might perceive the IB goals as a threat to their own power, and argue against the allocation of the school's scarce resources.

Without the support of the majority of the business school faculty as well as the liberal arts language and area studies departments, it will be difficult to succeed in the internationalization process. Therefore, one of the team's *permanent* goals should be to continuously welcome new members from incoming faculty, as well as to reach out to those who in the past did not embrace IB goals. Likewise, the IB team should solicit and encourage all established departments to include international goals in their plans, and provide support in every possible way to achieve such goals.

Start small, think BIG, remain flexible, and do not lose sight of your goals.

During the initial deliberations of the IB team, its members should show great empathy for various individual and collective expectations, goals, expertise, and potential contributions. These discussions should give proper recognition to the agendas and priorities of *all* of the school's constituents (see Exhibit 2.3), whether internal (students, administration, and department faculty) or external (business community, alumni, potential institutional partners, regulatory, and supporting agencies). The team's emerging plan should coherently integrate the goals, activities, resources, and opportunities to be gathered, developed, and allocated. This comprehensive perspective will allow the IB team to identify and convincingly communicate the benefits, costs, and risks associated with its initiatives.

The IB team can increase its chance of reaching its long-term goals if its initial goals represent relatively modest and acceptable changes rather than heavily ambitious undertakings. Examples of small, yet feasible, undertakings are "next hires will include IB competencies," or "organize an open-lecture series with invited IB guest speakers." In contrast, many constituents may perceive as overly ambitious such initial goals as "redefine the school's mission" or "revise the school's curricula."

Regardless of scope, the activities initially agreed upon should be realistic. Whether lecture, course, or trip abroad, they should be informative, challenging, and exciting. If the IB team can maintain motivation through its early and easier tasks, then the school's other key internal constituents will be more receptive to other, more ambitious initiatives—even if riskier or not fully detailed. In this way, the IB team and the school's other players will gradually engage in a constructive dialogue that will identify new challenges and opportunities, some even requiring detours. The team must remain flexible and willing to adapt to emerging conditions. Detours (characteristic of the incremental and flexible approach advocated here), successfully navigated, can in fact strengthen the team's confidence and credibility, and, paradoxically, allow them to reach their goals more expediently.

Identify an IB champion or champions, then share opportunities, responsibilities, and rewards.

The most typical problem with IB teams is that *none* of the members will be capable (or willing) to invest the time, expertise, and energy demanded by a comprehensive internationalization agenda, particularly during its humble but crucial inception and very early stages. Although team members could conceivably cooperate and coordinate their efforts to achieve their shared goals, if just one falters their collective effort may be jeopardized. Therefore, two crucial responsibilities of all members of an embryonic team are to acknowledge their own limitations, and to discuss their priorities with the school's other constituents. If they can agree on the potential of IB programming for their school, and on a set of specific priorities, they are equally capable of overcoming their limitations and moving to the next step.

An effective response to the lack of time and expertise among team members is for the entire faculty to support the identification and development of one or more internal IB champions. If the internal process is perceived as too cumbersome and uncertain, an alternative is to hire at least one champion from outside the organization.

Although there are no two identical internationalization champions, the successful ones seem to share some qualities which ideally can be combined into their profile. Champions require an appropriate and complementary mix of competencies in planning, organizing, leadership, communication, and innovation. However, in many instances these qualities can only be found by integrating the qualities of two or more individuals, which also helps explain why so many business schools prefer to maintain a leadership team rather than to identify a single IB champion.

The primary responsibility and mandate of the IB champion is to work with all of the school's internal and external constituents to advance the internationalization agenda. Success will come more easily if both the champion and all of the school's constituents exhibit patience in understanding each other and in integrating their work and potential contributions. Neither the team nor the champion can get it done alone. An essential element for success is that all parties are listened to, recognized, challenged, and rewarded in the continuous execution of their shared IB strategy. In fact, numerous business schools have failed in their attempts at internationalization after assigning most responsibilities and rewards to the champion and only two or three peers. The key to success seems to be sharing opportunities and rewards as rapidly and widely as possible, with an expanding group of colleagues willing to take on new tasks, and being extremely supportive of those individuals and their uniquely personal internationalization agendas.

Develop key relationships while assessing your school's IB potential.

The champion, on behalf of the team, must understand the nature of the school's strengths, and the threats to it. In doing so, the champion must gain institutional support and commitment to the goals and programs that might emerge from such analysis. Therefore, the auditing process includes both gathering information and developing valuable relationships and trust among all parties.

The champion should start by identifying the current competitive landscape of the IB discipline, and the trends and forces shaping its future. By visiting websites of leading business schools (a good place to start is with those operating CIBERs which can be found in the *Chapter Reference Notes and Additional Resources* section at the back of this book), the champion can develop an initial sense of relevant external points of reference and determine what internal information-gathering might be of highest priority.

Given that the school's most crucial internal constituent is its dean, the champion must communicate with that office often. It is essential that a cordial (if not friendly) relationship be established, and that there be a common understanding both of key points guiding the champion's objectives, and of key linkages connecting the school's general mission and specific IB strategies. The champion can gain a lot from downplaying expectations, and by trading ample autonomy for full accountability.

Some deans have proven to be superb IB champions themselves while performing their other duties. This is not the most desirable approach, however, especially in schools experiencing frequent leadership changes, or intense rivalry for resources, or where there is unclear definition of priorities (such as hiring new faculty, upgrading the information technology base, or developing stronger recruitment and placement services). In such cases, it is more desirable for the dean to strongly support several initiatives, including the internationalization process, without necessarily being the IB champion. This approach maximizes the possible benefits for internationalization while minimizing possible conflicts that any initiatives may have with other goals. In addition, it gives a long-term continuity that goes beyond the dean's tenure.

The IB champion must also develop strong relations with the school's other internal and external constituents. This implies investing substantial time in meetings. Moreover, the champion must treat the input gathered professionally, insuring that confidentiality be maintained at all cost—otherwise mutual trust and collective commitment will not accrue. Successful strategies integrate and reflect the interests and concerns of *all* parties, no matter how powerful such an individual or group might seem at the time.

It is desirable to start the internal information-gathering process by conducting in-depth exploratory interviews with *each and every faculty member of the business school* with the following five purposes:

- to gain a clear understanding of their personal and professional backgrounds and goals

- to explore their willingness and interest in incorporating IB goals within their own professional development plans

- to help them formulate a professional development strategy customized to their expertise, motivations, potential, and other goals

- to make them aware of attractive activities, challenges, and rewards that might invigorate their respective careers

- to define how their own goals might fit into the broader goals and processes of both the IB team and the school

Either during the above one-on-one meetings, or afterward, it is very useful for the champion to administer a survey designed to systematically establish an inventory of IB resources and potential with respect to personnel, interests, resources, and availability. Following the one-on-one interviews and analysis of survey data, the champion needs to meet with *heads and faculty of other departments* throughout the university who have international interests (such as modern languages and political science, and the dean of international students). From such meetings it should be easy to ascertain their interest in international business education and to evaluate their likely contributions.

Focus-group meetings with representative samples of *students, alumni, and community leaders* are strongly recommended. Meetings with students and alumni can provide a sense of their satisfaction with the diversity and quality of the IB courses already offered, their most salient IB expectations, and a glimpse at their backgrounds (especially how their international travel experience might be factored into goals, such as forming an IB student association or promoting international internships).

Similarly, focus-group meetings with IB community leaders, including senior executives of corporations doing international business and support organizations (such as the state's economic development agency or the local chamber of commerce), should center on their needs, expectations, suggestions, and potential contributions. As a by-product, the champion can draft a list of alumni and community leaders (including others not present in the focus groups) who might eventually be invited to serve on the school's IB advisory board.

In addition, if there are any universities, colleges, or institutes which offer courses with an international component (whether it be business, language, or travel), the champion should investigate the possibilities of cooperation, even collaboration. Accredited course work for IB students is the most obvious productive outcome, but there could be other potential mutual advantages as well.

Finally, an IB audit would be incomplete without an inventory of potential *funding sources* (both internal and external, including individuals, corporations, private foundations, and government agencies). This inventory should include each source's requirements, administrative processes, deadlines, and conditions. A successful fund-raising effort is a common way of legitimizing and giving credibility to an IB program in development. External funding usually is well-received by administrators, while professors respond favorably to even marginal incentives, given that most schools are strapped for resources. Chapter 4, *Funding Your Initiatives*, provides a full discussion of this topic.

Prepare project proposals and an ongoing summary of your school's IB goals.

Information you gather needs to be processed in a systematic fashion to facilitate its analysis. Therefore, from the inception of the internationalization process, a *comprehensive database* needs to be created and maintained (updated regularly, and checked entirely at least once a year). All internal constituents willing to contribute to or help analyze its contents should have unlimited and easy access to this database so that information, analyses, and the proposals it contains can be discussed promptly and at ease by the team and school's entire faculty.

This transparent and open communication empowers all participants to actively prepare and *simultaneously* discuss several short-term project proposals and a comprehensive long-term IB strategy. The former will allow the school to start implementing some IB initiatives immediately, while the latter will integrate these projects into the long-term ongoing plan, which is an ongoing *living document* (that is, subject to change) which articulates the school's mission, goals, and strategies.

Members of the team should pay particular attention to *changes* in the following six components of this living document:

- trends and forces defining the IB strategy
- business education map
- strategic groups map
- IB-SWOT matrix
- short-term IB strategy
- long-term IB strategy

The *trends and forces* analysis should comprise the most crucial external factors affecting the global, national, and regional education industry in general, as well as those impacting your school's particular interests. By listing these factors and revising them periodically, team members can easily check their assumptions and recognize opportunities and challenges they should not ignore. Stale facts and old conclusions can lead to short-sighted blunders.

Some powerful forces that have had a significant impact upon business schools within the last decade include demographic changes, mergers and consolidations, outsourcing, the emergence of a more open and interdependent global economy, e-commerce, more efficient and less costly communication and transportation systems, significant fluctuations in emerging markets, the entry of new management-education competitors working with lower costs and different technologies (such as Internet-based, distance-learning education suppliers), and the increasing importance of knowledge-based management. These factors have lowered the cost of some IB tasks (such as managing student and faculty exchanges, and forming global education and research alliances), but have increased the cost of the institution's information-technology infrastructure.

The school's immediate business environment should also be addressed. For example, the decline of a given sector of the local economy, changes in leadership and in strategic thrust of competing local business schools, or worsening political and social conditions of a country where a leading local firm has a significant presence may affect the company's IB prospects and, therefore, what it expects from your school's program.

The *international business education map* identifies its main players, their functions, power, and interrelations (see Exhibit 2.4). This very simple but powerful graphic tool represents the diverse initiatives that must be implemented to maximize the school's benefits from working with each and every key player. Although this is a static picture, when critical changes in any of the defining characteristics of the map occur they should be updated on a new map. Contrasting consecutive maps gives a dynamic picture of historic trends. This contrast permits members of the team to visualize key strategic implications. This tool can also be used to illustrate how proposed strategies and tactics might affect the future balance of power and relationships in IB education. The greatest value of the map is its relative simplicity to facilitate the discussion of possible strategic changes among team members.

A *strategic group map* contrasts the perceived value (price/quality) and geographic market coverage (local, regional, national) of the services rendered by IB education competitors. Since this map is highly individualized to your school and the businesses you serve, there is no prototypical model—but one of your own invention will help you identify key players for different businesses and locations you serve, and define more precisely the nature of the programs you should consider providing.

The *international business-SWOT analysis matrix* (see Exhibit 2.5) summarizes the main strengths, weaknesses, opportunities, and threats to your internationalization efforts. To remain focused, list no more than five of each of these components. The lists of components are essentially a summary of the key conclusions which emerge from the data gathered in the strategic audit. While it is sometimes feasible to concentrate most of the school's efforts and resources on those aggressive strategies that leverage its greatest strengths and most attractive opportunities, often schools do not have any other option but to address severe forces threatening its weaknesses.

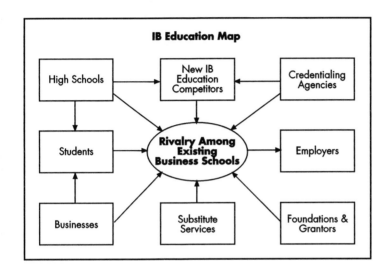

IB Education Map

High Schools

New IB Education Competitors

Credentialing Agencies

Students

Rivalry Among Existing Business Schools

Employers

Businesses

Substitute Services

Foundations & Grantors

Exhibit 2.4

The *short-term, mid-term, and long-term strategies* should be the result of discussion, and revision if deemed appropriate, of the maps and matrix. Cost, benefits, and risks will in most cases be primary considerations. The complete strategic plan should reflect shared values and compromise. Usually some short-term projects can be put into place immediately, long-term plans can be reflected in the school's mission statement, and mid-term plans can be revisited as the process of internationalization moves forward. If there are inconsistencies between the short-term and long-term plans, the IB team will have to decide on whether to (1) discontinue some ongoing projects, or (2) modify any of the previously agreed upon features of the long-term plan. Bringing evolutionary *long-term consistency* is one of the distinctive characteristics of the successful strategic plan.

Develop an assessment process that fosters learning and entrepreneurship.

The team, after choosing the short-term, mid-term, and long-term goals of its strategic plan, must focus on its implementation and continuous evolution and

Example of International Business SWOT Analysis

Exhibit 2.5

Strengths	Weaknesses
Internal	**Internal**
• University and college support from the administration	• Limited financial support from the dean
• Financial support	• Restrictive college policies
• Faculty with international business experience	• Faculty set in their ways
• Existing language and international classes	• Limited library resources
• Strong interest among students	
External	**External**
• Business community support	• Few international businesses in region
• Community cultural activities	• Restrictive state educational policies
• Small Business Development Center Activities	• Employers don't value international skills
• Strong employment market for students with specific international skills	• School located in a rural area
Opportunities	Threats
Internal	**Internal**
• Parents and students requesting more international classes	• Restrictive organizational structure
• Grants available to support internationalization	• Strong faculty resistance
• Up-to-date technology infrastructure	• Students can't absorb extra cost of overseas programs
• Language department is supportive of developing business language courses	• Limited opportunity for new courses
External	**External**
• Visiting international business executives	• Unsupportive economic environment
• Student internship opportunities (domestically and internationally)	• Less than enthusiastic company recruiters
• Strong institutional relationships overseas	• Study-abroad safety issues
• External funding sources	• Distance education
• International institutions interested in developing exchange programs	

Exhibit prepared by Kelly Jett Murphrey.

improvement. The latter will result from the lessons of past experiences and from promptly recognizing unexpected events and significant situations, whether internal or external to the school, which could affect the strategic plan. Therefore, IB teams should develop, at the outset, a process by which members regularly report and review initiatives underway *as well as* events and situations which might impact the overall plan.

Team members must select and adjust their assessment approaches to their changing personal and managerial styles, availability of time, and perceived importance of the matters at hand. It is during the initial development stages, however, that the team gains the most from meeting often and from being as informal as possible. Such an approach fosters the following four crucial attributes among members: (1) being broad-minded, (2) getting to know one another better, (3) cementing shared values (that is, enhancing the team's culture), and (4) broadening perspectives on internationalization.

With accumulated IB experience, however, meetings may become less frequent but more comprehensive, their reports more formalized and focused on key milestones (such as costs and benefits of new proposals, specific results from ongoing projects, results from tests measuring students' IB proficiency, reexamination of all IB syllabi, and review of strategic alliances). Moreover, the analytic and communication processes preceding their meeting may become more structured. Likewise, team members will be more prone to consider contingencies such as what to do if a professor participating in a crucial IB project falls ill or leaves, or how to strengthen the relationship in a floundering partnership.

Prepare a timetable outlining key activities, deadlines, and budgets.

After putting in place an internationalization strategic plan and a process to assess its ongoing effectiveness and efficiency, the IB team can concentrate on its actual implementation. To increase the probability of succeeding, team members should agree on an implementation timetable for each project, including each segment of the unfolding program. These timetables should not only be inserted into a comprehensive calendar, but should be specific about internal and external resources to be allocated such as personnel, budgeted hours, budgeted dollars, and any special materials or equipment. The systematic use of timetables will enhance the discipline and confidence of the IB team so that they may embark gradually onto more ambitious undertakings. Moreover, these control devices will facilitate the assessment process described in the previous section. Today's easy-to-use software can facilitate the preparation, integration, and follow-up of timetables and budgets.

Assess your performance regularly and take corrective actions as needed.

In devising its initial IB strategy the team must assure that its proposed performance indexes are consistent with the school's administrative processes for implementing, evaluating, and continuously improving other programs. The following preparatory work can assist the IB team in this regard:

- identify and assess potential sources of conflict (tight schedules, different expectations, weak communications systems) and resistance to change

- defuse or confront the more threatening sources, and ignore the less serious

- link, in very simple terms, the IB performance indexes to your school's reward systems in order to enhance motivation

- build upon elements of your school's culture that would support your intended internationalization strategy

- identify the most favorable elements of your school's fundamental functional strategies and integrate them with other elements of your IB strategy

- determine what activities will be economical, meaningful, useful, and timely in your school's future, and use these in projecting the team's future initiatives

- consider the dimensions of your school's policies associated with extreme scenarios and formulate contingency plans

- establish how your school's technological infrastructure can contribute to the future work of the IB team

Final Note

In this chapter, a strategic road map has been discussed that can help you identify your business school's most desirable internationalization strategy. You have been encouraged to follow eight pragmatic guidelines to articulate your short-term objectives and long-term destination. These guidelines are designed to create a favorable environment in which all members of your ever-expanding internationalization team can enthusiastically and significantly contribute to the process of reaching IB education objectives. The strategic planning discussion presented provides the means to drive your school's IB future. Your school is the vehicle. You and your team must provide the fuel.

CHAPTER THREE

Winning Collegial Support

Brian Toyne and Zaida L. Martínez

With your strategic plan in place, you have identified a specific set of goals and objectives. Yet without the financial, human, and physical resources necessary to implement the plan, the internationalization effort can fail.

How can your business school clear the often rocky road of as many obstacles as possible? How can your efforts to institutionalize international programming be sustained over time? These questions require that internationalization be more than an appendage to the business school's catalog of programs. It must be an effort to transform thinking, reallocate resources, and, most importantly, to gain support from colleagues. In this chapter we discuss the application of organizational development concepts to the problem of winning collegial support for the internationalization effort. We start by addressing the critical human resource factors.

Faculty and Administration: The Keys to Success

According to a study by Brenda J. Ellingboe, the internationalization effort must eventually have the explicit support of both faculty and administration to be successful. Vanderpool and Hamlin echo this finding, saying that the administration ". . . must set the tone for internationalization. Administrative proclamations, mission statements, and other documents must project that international thinking and activity are respected and expected." Because it is central to any planned cultural shift for reform, a university's administration is responsible for securing and allocating financial and logistical resources, providing a support system, monitoring, sanctioning, and rewarding departmental activities. It is not surprising that Vanderpool and Hamlin found that the single most important key to the successful implementation of an internationalization effort is a "rigorous faculty reward system that is flexible." Thus, a successful internationalization effort requires the explicit support of the business school's administration and faculty and an established but viable reward system.

While it may be obvious that the support of the faculty and administration is critical for the successful internationalization of business programs, we cannot assume that the faculty and administration will undertake such efforts enthusiastically. On the contrary, it is more likely that faculty members and administrators will be reluctant to make a commitment to the process. Below we (1) identify the types of resistance that may be encountered during internationalization, (2) present specific recommendations on how to overcome that resistance, and (3) discuss how to build the team and sustain the program it creates.

Resistance to Internationalization

As is common with most attempts to change an organization and its people, there is the potential (in fact, likelihood) for resistance. Fortunately, many of the sources of this resistance to internationalization have been identified and discussed in the literature (Ellingboe; Lim and Miller; and Toyne). An understanding of the reasons behind the resistance is an essential first step in developing a successful internationalization strategy.

As noted in Exhibit 3.1, administrative resistance primarily arises out of perceived conflicts for limited resources, the belief that the internationalization effort might detract from other worthwhile initiatives such as the introduction of other new programs or the upgrading of technology. Faculty resistance generally stems from a misunderstanding of what internationalization involves in terms of teaching responsibilities and research agendas, and from errors in judgment regarding both their own personal gains and losses and those on behalf of their students. In order to overcome these hurdles, we must understand and identify the forms of resistance.

Exhibit 3.1

**Resistance to the Internationalization Effort
and Ways to Overcome It**

Administration

Reasons for Resistance	Ways to Overcome Resistance
Failure to include the internationalization goals and objectives in the mission statement	Recognize that the internationalization effort involves planned change
Views the internationalization effort as imposing additional burdens on an already limited budget and resources	Undertake a critical examination of the school's culture, faculty, and capabilities
Failure to provide incentives in support of the internationalization effort	Gain the support of the institution's administration, including the dean and others who will be involved in the internationalization effort
Failure to recognize that institutional roadblocks may hamper the internationalization effort	Identify an IB champion and make it known he or she has administrative support and the authority to implement changes
Failure to recognize that the school's organizational structure and processes may be potential obstacles	Gain the support of a critical mass of motivated faculty
	Gain the support of key senior faculty by their early involvement in the internationalization effort
	Make clear the reasons for the internationalization effort, and assemble a faculty committee to develop and implement the internationalization goals and objectives

Faculty

Reasons for Resistance	Ways to Overcome Resistance
Views internationalization as adding to teaching and research burdens	Provide the faculty opportunities to enhance their international expertise
Failure to recognize the value of personal international experiences	Provide incentives for international research
Senior faculty view internationalization as upsetting the status quo	Provide incentives for international travel
	Provide incentives for the faculty to internationalize the courses they teach

Administrative Resistance

The administrative failure to recognize the far-reaching implications of the internationalization effort. The internationalization of a school ultimately affects the faculty, all the programs offered, and the administration at every level. Internationalization permeates all aspects of the institution. An understandable analogy is the far-reaching impact that technology has had on higher education over the last three decades. It is not just course content that has been impacted.

The attitudes and work habits of faculty, staff, and administration have also been affected. Similarly, the behavior of faculty, staff, and administration affects an institution's ability to make the changes needed for internationalization. Therefore, even when there *is* initial consensus for change, one of the first obstacles that usually needs to be overcome is the initial piecemeal, seemingly haphazard, approach that those in charge sometimes take.

The administrative failure to articulate internationalization goals and objectives. The challenge facing the U.S. business education community is to determine how best to respond pedagogically to fundamental changes in the world business environment. The ability to gain the support of the faculty most often centers around articulating a response to two critical questions. First, what does internationalization mean for the business school and faculty? Secondly, *exactly* to what extent should all business students and the faculty be internationalized? How individual business schools respond to these questions depends on many factors, but among the most important are the stated goals and objectives adopted by the school's administration (and pursued at every opportunity), the international experience and expertise of its faculty, and the availability of other resources, especially financial.

The failure to clearly articulate the goals of internationalization often results from the failure to include these goals in the school's mission statement, its strategic plan, and the faculty's incentive structure. These omissions, of course, provide the faculty with additional reasons for resisting the internationalization initiative. They also influence the dean when it is necessary to make decisions that require trade-offs such as budget allocations.

Budget allocations and resource limitations. Most business schools confront financial limitations that curtail their faculty members from teaching overseas at their own school's salary, undertaking research based outside U.S. borders, or partaking in other international faculty development opportunities—particularly when other faculty members are interested in obtaining those same limited resources to carry out equally worthwhile programs or projects of interest to them. Even schools that are well-endowed experience difficulties in financing newly-proposed programs because of major commitments in other areas.

Incentives. Many department chairs and deans do not give their faculty material incentives or even personal encouragement to internationalize their courses. For example, they do not encourage faculty to apply for travel grants or fellowships to teach overseas, participate in international faculty-development programs, or provide for faculty to formally share their international experiences with their colleagues upon returning to campus. More importantly, when faculty pursue these types of activities on their own initiative, their absence from campus is, unfortunately, just as likely to count against them as it is for them when it comes to tenure and promotion. In particular, senior faculty members may view such experiences as interfering with the development of junior faculty members.

Acquiring international knowledge and incorporating this knowledge into existing courses or designing new courses is a time-consuming task. Thus, an additional obstacle to internationalization is the administration's reluctance to provide release time as an incentive for faculty to develop classroom materials and course syllabi. Furthermore, administrators often fail to address the hardships experienced by family members of a professor who, for example, spends a semester teaching and studying in another country. Faculty simply cannot move forward in the internationalization process without workload incentives, financial assistance, and other forms of encouragement.

Organizational structure and processes. Another potential obstacle to the internationalization process is the school's organizational structure. A rigid, highly bureaucratic structure may make it difficult for faculty to become receptive to and engage in the internationalization process. A lack of open communication is a barrier. Some faculty may imagine "hidden agendas" and feel threatened by proposed changes.

Additionally, the administrative creation of a separate unit (such as an IB department) can work against the effort. It can cause faculty, who are not so involved or committed, to believe they have no responsibility toward the internationalization process.

Faculty Resistance

The teaching and research burden. The international dimension is often viewed by faculty members as not adding educational or training value. Indeed, it is often viewed simply as additional work. Since more than eighty percent of the typical business school's students are not interested in international careers (Arpan et al.) internationalization may be seen as placing an unnecessary burden on the faculty to add international content to their courses, and as detracting from their main teaching objectives. International travel and research, for example, is not always viewed by faculty as an opportunity to increase their mobility and knowledge base, but rather as a largely unwanted vacation from their responsibility to write and publish in mainstream journals.

Faculty frequently cite the existing lack of IB expertise as an excuse to not internationalize their teaching and research. Moreover, they believe the time and effort spent developing international skills and expertise is better spent in keeping abreast of developments in their functional areas of teaching and research. The lack of expertise can be aggravated by many forms of apprehension. For example, some faculty members may not be willing to participate in an international research project for fear of traveling to unfamiliar countries.

Cognitive component. According to Ellingboe, some faculty who have experienced living abroad still do not make the cognitive shift to internationalize their courses. They do not connect their experiences with their teaching. Some become aware of internationalization opportunities but are unsure how to implement them; still others are aware but remain focused on their disciplines as traditionally defined (which is almost always the "U.S. standard"). This cognitive block can be aggravated by the false belief held by some faculty and administrators that business practices, products, and services are universal or are becoming standardized according to the U.S. norm. Because they believe that there is only one best way of doing business, the U.S. way, some faculty see no reason to internationalize business programs and further harbor the illusion that internationalization dilutes *best business practices.*

Senior faculty resistance. While any faculty member may be reluctant to change, some senior faculty in particular may reject the idea of internationaliza-tion simply because change upsets the status quo. Senior faculty may also be concerned about the impact that internationalization may have on their own power positions within the school. Additionally, a junior faculty member may be hesitant to support certain types of initiatives that may be unattractive to senior faculty, simply because of fear of recrimination in tenure and promotion decisions.

Overcoming Resistance and Winning Support

As noted in Exhibit 3.1, overcoming resistance and building capacity for any multilevel organizational change, such as the internationalization of a business school, involves a basic change in a school's culture and a refocusing and enhancing of its resources and capabilities. Thus, achieving such a goal involves a good deal of critical examination and a planned effort to define new values. Ultimately, it involves planned change and the effective implementation of change in such areas as curricula, resource allocation, and individual behavior (often modified through the faculty evaluation and reward systems). This requires persistence, commitment, and compromise.

Prior organizational change research, related to the IB educational process, provides the basis for a schematic representation of the change process (see Exhibit 3.2). This model suggests a series of recommendations for overcoming the obstacles which typically accompany the internationalization effort. The various recommendations are grouped according to their primary audience: either administrative or faculty. However, one must remember that a school's internationalization process should be viewed as holistic. This involves changing the behavior of all those affected by the process. Furthermore, and for obvious reasons, the internationalization efforts must be tailored to the particular mission, goals, and objectives of the school.

Exhibit 3.2

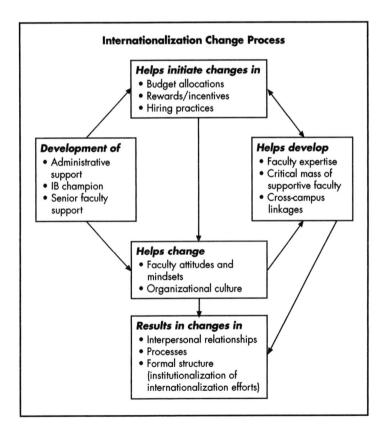

Seek support from the administration. For the internationalization effort to have a meaningful impact, the faculty must be aware that the administration at all levels is supportive of the initiative. This, of course, means that the dean and associate and assistant deans are openly committed to the effort. Moreover, because truly internationalized business programs require the collaboration of units outside the business school (such as language and area studies departments), commitment at even higher levels (such as the president and vice president for academic affairs) are equally important.

The role of the administration in the process cannot be overemphasized. Because the administration is usually the dominant coalition with respect to fiscal issues, political (power and control) issues, and for handling disenchanted faculty. The administration's support is critical for creating a new organizational culture that values the international dimension of business education.

Identify an IB champion. A successful internationalization plan is usually initiated by an IB champion, a particularly strong proponent or advocate, often called a "champion," as discussed also in Chapter 2, *Charting Your Course.* The IB champion often manages the change process. Sometimes the champion emerges out of interested faculty. Sometimes there is more than one champion. But often enough the champion is assigned the role—by the school, the college, even the university, which has recognized the need for change. One of the initial decisions that needs to be made early on is whether the IB champion should be someone from inside or outside the institution.

Both possibilities have their pros and cons. An insider is typically knowledgeable of the political atmosphere within the school and understands its history and cultural environment. This knowledge can be useful in interpreting data and galvanizing support. However, an insider may be too close to the school's environment to view it objectively. An outsider has the advantage of not being tied to any preexisting coalition or political block within the school, and will likely have a better chance of being accepted as a valid change agent. Regardless of approach, the IB champion must be someone who is respected and enjoys a high degree of legitimacy within the business school. This person must also possess a broad charter to initiate and guide the internationalization effort, and the authority to implement changes.

Move from a champion to critical mass. An IB champion alone, or even with a cohort or two, will not be able to institutionalize the internationalization process. This individual must seek ways of motivating and gaining the support of a critical mass of faculty (as well as the support of the administration if it is not already there). This critical mass is essential for providing the breadth of scope and depth of commitment needed for the effort to succeed. Developing this critical mass helps reduce problems related to resistance, control and power, and facilitates the development of a new culture at the school.

Articulate an internationalization vision and develop goals and objectives. The faculty needs to embrace the need for international business education. One possible approach is for either the dean or the IB champion to assemble a representative faculty committee to review and evaluate programs at other well-respected universities and then develop a vision statement for final approval by the faculty. This statement would then be made part of a revised mission statement tailored to the school's existing long-term goals and objectives. Faculty involvement is critical if the internationalization effort is to be successful. Open communication is essential for this process to work effectively.

Gain faculty support. Similar to the development of a vision statement, a school's internationalization goals and objectives should be faculty-driven. The role of the IB champion is to initiate and guide the development of these objectives and goals, but an internationalization committee can play an important role in moving the task forward. The committee is in the best position to engage other faculty in healthy, open discussion which can address their interests and lower their resistance to change. It can also simplify approval of changes in a faculty vote.

Senior faculty understanding and support is especially important to the success of any internationalization effort (critical when we remember they sit on promotion and tenure committees) and, unfortunately, senior faculty members are also the most likely to view the effort as a threat to their power and influence. Therefore, it is important to determine ways to motivate senior faculty and find ways to include them, whenever and however possible, on the internationalization team. When possible, it is advantageous to include senior faculty from the very start of the internationalization process, thus giving them the satisfaction (and power) of early investors and initiators of change.

Develop the faculty's IB expertise through exposure and research. Because the majority of business doctoral programs in the United States do not include an international dimension, most business faculty lack the expertise and skills needed to internationalize their teaching and research. Thus, the internationalization effort depends heavily on faculty development efforts. Numerous venues for this development exist. For example, faculty can participate in faculty development programs offered by the CIBERs, or a school can have recognized experts hold seminars and workshops on campus. Faculty can also be provided with opportunities to participate in second-language training, and attend international business conferences or conferences which focus on the international dimension of the functional teaching and practicing areas of business.

All these faculty activities require financial support, release time, and other types of incentives. If the internationalization process gains the support of the administration, faculty development activities will receive priority. Failure to provide support will most likely jeopardize the internationalization efforts of the school.

Encourage travel abroad. One effective method of enhancing faculty support of the school's internationalization goals is to provide opportunities for international travel, study, and research. Faculty exchange programs with universities in other countries can make all the difference in internationalizing faculty. However, as with other faculty development activities, the administration must provide financial support and encouragement. Furthermore, since these types of assignments usually cover an extensive period of time, the faculty member's family is affected, as is the faculty member's disposition toward such a proposition. The faculty member's family must be included in the international experience early in the planning process. Such issues as adequate school arrangements for children must be addressed and satisfactorily resolved in advance.

Encourage individual course modification. As the faculty gain international expertise in their specific areas, they should be encouraged (expected really) to internationalize their courses. This can best be facilitated by expanding the incentives, by offering course release time, or by offering summer stipends. The value of travel, international research, and other activities that internationalize the faculty become most apparent when faculty teach their new or recently revised courses. There is no substitute for a professor's ability to discuss events occurring in a specific part of the world from first-hand experience and knowledge.

The Importance of Sustainability

The internationalization of a business school is a long-term commitment requiring ongoing efforts to sustain changes in a school's structure, culture, policies, and reward systems. External pressures on the faculty are such that continual reinforcement of the internationalization effort is a must. Several of the approaches that facilitate the changes necessary for an internationalized business school are discussed below.

The budgetary implication of reinforcement. Any effort at establishing an internationalization process requires more than passive administrative vocal support. The administration must also be persuaded to undertake budgetary reforms that are supportive of such a process. Needless to say, travel funds to support the international faculty-development efforts should be made a priority. Faculty members without international travel experience have little credibility in the classroom. Furthermore, faculty who are attempting to engage in international research need to be exposed to the environments of other countries.

The IB champion and the internationalization committee can pressure the administration for budgetary changes by demonstrating the connection between the ever-changing world marketplace and business practices, the ongoing internationalization effort, and hence the need for faculty travel. In this way, they can also demonstrate that the internationalization effort has received faculty support through the approval of an internationalization mission statement and the development of clear goals and objectives.

Gradual modification of the incentive structure to support the internationalization initiative. As an ongoing part of the internationalization effort, the faculty's evaluation and reward system should be gradually modified to include the goals and objectives of the internationalization effort. Faculty will not become committed to internationalizing their teaching and research if those efforts are not considered in tenure and promotion decisions. If managed skillfully, however, each change to the evaluation and performance process need not be seen as threatening to other faculty who are less involved and committed to the change.

Modification of faculty hiring practices. Another way the administration can strengthen its commitment to internationalization is to hire new faculty who have demonstrated some dimension of internationalism in their area of expertise, either through their doctoral study or through direct business experience abroad. One step that the IB champion can take is to request that the search committee include a faculty member who is a strong proponent of the internationalization process.

Cross-campus linkages. Because of rapid changes in technology, political boundaries, and economic regionalization, the future of business and its practices is increasingly ambiguous. This ambiguity has been interpreted by accrediting organizations (such as the AACSB) and by business scholars (Cavusgil; Oblinger and Verville; Toyne and Nigh) as requiring greater emphasis on the humanities and social sciences. One implication is that linkages need to be forged between faculty and administrators from these areas so that constructive dialogue can take place. The development of relationships among departments such as anthropology, modern languages, history, and political science is critical for implementing truly internationalized programs.

Institutionalization of the internationalization initiative. What happens if the IB champion or a supporting administrator steps down or leaves? The answer to this question emphasizes the importance of involving a critical mass of faculty members in the internationalization process. It also emphasizes the need for this process to be embedded in the overall structure of the institution.

The internationalization process must become a core part of the institution's mission statement, planning activities, and day-to-day operations. This can be done in a number of ways. As noted earlier, key administrative staff and faculty who are supportive of the internationalization process need to be identified and placed in strategic positions, such as on critical administrative and faculty councils and committees. Moreover, the school's procedures for evaluating and rewarding administrators and faculty need to be modified, possibly incrementally over time, to reflect the growing importance of the internationalization process. Finally, the school's budget needs to be revised to include allocations for the international development of the faculty and the courses they teach.

Final Note

Even before 1990 the Graduate Management Admissions Council (GMAC) and the AACSB were contending that business schools need to place increased attention on the educational process (without reducing the attention placed on educational outcomes) because of the rapid change in skills and training needs arising from technological, global, and other environmental transformations. The approach described in this chapter places considerable emphasis on achieving permanent change by seeking fundamental shifts in the administration's and the faculty's attitudes and behaviors.

While it is not essential to have *all* administrators and faculty support the internationalization effort, it is important to achieve critical mass early on. The involvement of top administrators and respected faculty, along with enthusiastic collaboration with departments outside the business school, is the only sure route to meaningful long-term programmatic change. Finally, the role of incentives and rewards has been emphasized. To create an environment where the transition to internationalization can be sustained, faculty members in particular must enjoy both intellectual and material recognition and satisfaction for their efforts.

CHAPTER FOUR

Funding Your Initiatives

Claire D. Cornell

Your university, college, department, program, or center has decided to internationalize its business curriculum. The strategic plan has been approved. Good! But new course content involves research and time-consuming preparation on the part of faculty, some of which is best conducted in the business and educational environment outside the U.S. Students in such a program need to undergo language immersion and intense area study, and be encouraged, perhaps required, to study and consider an internship abroad. These are exciting prospects (and many would say a matter of survival in today's world economy). The provost and dean are delighted! Or not. In any case, it always seems there is little (or *no*) money available from the administration's already limited budget to fund even the most modest internationalization initiatives that involve real change.

Fortunately, there are external organizations *with* money, a good deal of money; entities that are in the *business* of funding organizations with ideas like yours. This chapter is about the world of grants: how to locate them, how to apply for them, and how to *get* them.

"Grants development" is a catchall phrase that refers to identifying internal and external possibilities of funding, and the means of developing strong grant proposals. The end result of "grantsmanship" will be an application to a funding entity (whether government agency, nonprofit foundation, corporation, or the university itself) that will likely support all or part of the internationalization of your business program; but as seasoned grant writers will assert, it is just that, an end product of the all-important preliminary effort: *the fundamental groundwork.* In addition, the entire process relies on common sense and effective business practice.

At all times, the applicant must keep in mind that the process has target results for all concerned. Your successful grant application must eventually yield financial gain and lend prestige to the business program, college, and university. Meanwhile, the grantor expects the grant proposal to demonstrate institutional commitment, including cash or in-kind contributions which indicates that the institution will sustain a project after grant-funding expires. With the knowledge that this factor can make or break a submission, the IB champion or committee should secure support from the school's administration (and, if at all possible, from external groups like a local chamber of commerce or Rotary Club chapters) early in the project development cycle. Support from the school and its "partners" can come as cash allocations, human resources, or equipment and space allocation. However, in order to cultivate these relationships of cooperation and mutual advantage, it is best to have already investigated and identified granting programs and funding agencies that can assist you in your internationalization plan.

Researching Funding Sources

In order to sustain (or in some cases to attract) the administration's interest in internationalization, the IB team must initially research potential granting agencies and their programs. Both public and private funding are quite widely advertised. Faculty, staff, or graduate student assistants can find federal-funding sources with a fair degree of ease. The World Wide Web, the institution's library, or its office of sponsored programs are all helpful. Reference librarians usually assist faculty members who are not experienced in Internet searching. Along with books, periodicals, and newsletters, the task of researching and then compiling a list of funding leads applicable to your own situation *may* seem daunting, but can in fact be relatively painless, even if time-consuming.

Public Funding

It is easiest to begin with an investigation of public funding. Federal agencies must announce their competitions in the *Federal Register* and the *Catalog of Federal and Domestic Assistance*, which emanate from congress, and can also be found in the *Commerce and Business Daily.* Federal funding competitions are also generally easy to find on federal, state, and local government websites, and on websites established by specific grant newsletters. Private corporations like the Foundation Center, and university and college offices of sponsored programs collect and provide federal grant bulletins (for instance, the *Community of Science Bulletin* provides listings).

Faculty or research assistants can begin by focusing on specific federal departments that fund businesses (the U.S. Department of Commerce), departments that fund education (the U.S. Department of Education), and departments that fund international endeavors (the U.S. Department of State and the U.S. Department of Defense). All their respective websites are easy to locate, and include a section that in turn clearly indicates "funding opportunities" or "grant programs." Preliminary research will yield *basic* information on federal grant programs and requests for proposals (RFP) in the form of "guidelines."

Government RFPs and RFQs (requests for quotations) will state why the agency is offering funds (the program purpose, goals, and objectives), and how to apply (the rules and regulations, evaluation criteria, and required narrative and budget parameters). Most importantly, perhaps, it will indicate the opening and closing dates for application. This is vital information because you need adequate time to prepare an effective application. A *late* application is a *dead* application.

The next important and informative step is to determine what the RFP *really* calls for, what is really in contention, and who are the contenders. The individual program officers and managers have these answers. These individuals design and oversee the grant competitions. They know what the agency is looking for, what kind of application will work and what won't. They also know the common misinterpretations of the guidelines that will undermine an application. Therefore, before preparing an actual written application, applicants should undertake a more interpersonal form of research. It is easy to discuss guidelines with a program officer because it really *is* part of their job. Program officers can also tell you about previous grantees, as matters of public record, whom you might in turn contact for clarification or assistance in preparing your proposal.

Learning, for instance, that second-language acquisition is an element in 99% of all funded proposals will help to explain an evaluation criteria that reads "special consideration will be given to project initiatives which stress utilization of second-language and area studies faculty in its endeavor." The program officer can emphasize that second-language involvement is really a necessity, not an option. Speaking with previous grantees can help you better understand how they incorporated that particular component into their successful application.

Ideally, your dean or chair will encourage and accommodate you in this necessary research by releasing you from some of your teaching and service duties. Too often this is not the case, at least initially, and faculty and professional staff may only be able to develop one grant proposal while they fulfill their full complement of teaching, research, and service responsibilities. Even without proper support, however, the enterprising faculty member can develop a viable grant proposal, provided there is a strong foundation based on careful preparation and thorough research.

Private Funding

When searching for private funding sources such as foundations, corporations, or nongovernmental organizations (NGOs), the IB champion or team should reference the *Annual Register of Grant Support* or the *Foundation Grants Index* (both on line and in print). Any grant research effort will have a number of starts and stops, but within a short time, you can compile an additional short list of grant programs offered through NGOs such as International Research Exchange Scholars (IREX) or the Social Science Research Council, and programs in foundations and corporations or private concerns such as the World Bank (WB).

The next phase of research is essential. Applicants should carefully review program guidelines, but also pay close attention to descriptions of "eligibility criteria" and "allowable costs." If essential expenses do not seem compatible with a program's "allowable costs," the program will not address your needs and you will waste your time applying. Furthermore, if your institution is not described under "eligible applicants," there is really no point in continuing. Your primary concern must be to match your institution and your needs to a program that provides grants.

In the private sector, some NGOs and foundations do not use deadlines and will accept "proposals" at any time—though these are rare. Another extremely useful piece of information that usually does *not* appear anywhere in the announcement or guidelines is how much money the grantor has to disperse, and how *many* applicants will be successful (or have been in the past). The answer again is usually obtainable (by phone) from a grants officer.

Foundations and corporations frequently display abstracts of previously funded grants on their websites. As your list gets shorter, studying these abstracts can be extremely useful. They reveal the *who, what, where, when,* and *why* of funded proposals.

However, abstracts are but summaries, and full proposals are virtual blueprints of project design. You can refine your search and read the full proposal by contacting the grantee (identified in the abstract) or by asking the program officer to identify several relevant proposals. Do not shy away from calling or e-mailing the program officer to inquire about last year's grantees. Focus on proposals from those applicants who work for institutions similar to your own, and that address needs similar to yours.

Contrasts between Public and Private Funding

The most profound difference between public and private funding is the extent to which the public is provided with information. Federal support is your tax dollar at work. Federal agencies are subject to the provisions of the "Freedom of Information Act," and as such, you are entitled to explanations of funding mechanisms and you are entitled to learn about the agency's previous awards.

By contrast, private support reflects the benevolence of an individual, a corporation, or a foundation. In NGOs, a nonprofit corporation forms to support a specific endeavor. It pursues funding itself, then redistributes those funds for its specific purpose. For example, the Council of Graduate Schools has secured federal and foundation funding to promote "Preparing Future Faculty" initiatives. There are also foundations that focus just on business education, such as the Kauffman Foundation in St. Louis, and there are NGOs that focus on internationalization more generally like the Social Science Research Council in New York City.

Although in most cases, the private entities *are* very informative, this is a bonus, not a given. In many cases, foundations provide assistance or access that is comparable to the service provided by federal agencies. They host technical-assistance workshops, and post abstracts of last year's grants on a website. They give the potential applicant extensive guidance (for example, the World Bank Innovation Solicitation website contains guidelines, contact names, telephone numbers and e-mail addresses, abstracts of funded grants, and frequently asked questions). However, some foundations, corporations, and NGOs provide little or no information.

Regardless of their stated mission, only their previous actions can indicate whether you might be a viable applicant. For instance, if the foundation has historically selected only the most elite, private eastern universities, a small, public midwestern college might not be competitive.

But how do we gain information regarding a foundation's grant selection history? What if the foundation does not have a website, or does not readily provide information on its previous awards? The foundation's, corporation's, or

NGO's annual report should be available in print or in electronic format. Moreover, all nonprofit corporations must file a form 990 tax return which *is* open to public inspection. This document will reveal the entity's gifts, grants, and donations (if it has nonprofit status, it must be philanthropic or public-serving) during the year. The 990 form will also list the entity's officers, its legal council, and other valuable information.

Every state provides a repository (usually in a public library) of the 990s from the preceding year. Moreover, the Foundation Center is a private corporation that compiles all of the information, and leaves copies in major libraries across the country (at least one in every state). This is very useful and you can locate profiles of foundations in the various reference books published by the Foundation Center. However, be aware that by the time the Foundation Center compilation goes to print, the information can be one, sometimes two, and even three years old. If you need up-to-date information on a particular foundation, identify the state in which the foundation resides, then call the largest public library in that state's capital city. If the most recent 990 document is not housed there, the reference librarian should know its location.

If you cannot determine the genesis of a particular program, there are a number of further research efforts that can augment available information. In the case of an NGO this usually means developing a good working relationship with a grants officer. This may provide the best possible historical perspective on the program and its original aims.

When federal funding is at stake, a program officer or a congressional staff person can provide the name and number of the specific legislation (the bill) from which the program emerged. When a bill is passed, the U.S. Congress produces a written record that must be readily available to the public. In many cases, this bill is summarized in the program's guidelines. However, the very best way to prepare a successful application is to fully familiarize yourself with the actual underlying legislation.

Whether public or private, your final research effort should proceed after you have seen how others have interpreted guidelines. Be cautious, and do not assume that the previous year's grant competition is identical to the current competition. In a year's time, guidelines and regulations may have changed, and the grantor may have more or less money available. There is only one way to learn this information. If necessary, speak again with the program officer and contact previous grantees.

Attend any technical workshops and training seminars presented by agencies and foundations. At these valuable sessions, officers explain their programs in detail and answer questions. The sessions also provide the IB champion or representative with the opportunity to become personally acquainted with the officers, previous grantees, and other current applicants. The two themes of grant research and writing are thoroughness and personal contact with informed people.

Should You Use a Professional Grant Writer?

The research described thus far surely sounds like a great deal of time-consuming work. You feel inexperienced and anxious about the process. You know there are professionals out there who specialize in this sort of thing. Should you make that call?

A grant writer can help an institution to secure funding, but it is essential that you be involved in the proposal development. For instance, if an external consultant develops a proposal that the institution cannot support, the project can be very difficult to implement, and you will have a difficult time securing future funding as a result. However, you might be well-served by a writer, or even better, by a knowledgeable, experienced editor who can help you to produce a proposal that conforms to program requirements. If you hire any consultant, take notes and learn from the experience so that you are better prepared for your next application. In all cases, the IB team must be involved in the design of a proposal, even if they do not have a hand in producing the final product. As the IB champion, you must fully understand how you are representing your project in order to conduct it effectively.

Developing the Proposal and Writing the Grant

Link the Institution's Needs to the Funder's Priorities

Once the champion or IB team has targeted a specific grant, the development of a proposal can begin. In order to be successful, this proposal must respond to evaluation criteria that appear in the guidelines. This point should be underscored: the proposal must address *all* evaluation criteria, including the program's priorities and legislative mandates.

Examples of Specific Grant Programs

Example #1 (a federal agency): The U.S. Department of Education, Business and International Education Program. Let's assume you have determined that the U.S. Department of Education's Business and International Education (BIE) Program is suited for your needs and circumstances. BIE funding can underwrite faculty release time, graduate assistants, library acquisitions, research travel, other efforts, and a modest indirect cost rate (eight percent)—all of which can help develop and establish an international business program.

Among other concerns, the guidelines require that applicants collaborate with business organizations or business associations. This factor distinguishes the program from many other competitions in the office of International Education and Graduate Programs, ensuring that BIE-funded internationalization efforts extend beyond the college campus, and obligating applicants to influence business practitioners and businesses. Ultimately, a BIE-funded grant obligates applicants to promote international trade.

Potential applicants can learn this and more from examining the guidelines. Abstracts of successful projects appear on the World Wide Web. Funded proposals are available for review in the BIE's Washington, DC office. More importantly, the program officers are pleased to answer questions and clarify program requirements. Every year, the BIE program holds a project director's meeting at which faculty and staff describe project accomplishments, obstacles to success, project twists and turns, and other program elements. Frequently, in order to prepare themselves for the coming year's competition, prospective applicants attend this conference and the following Academy of International Business meeting. These conferences can provide insights that greatly benefit the new applicant.

Example #2 (a nongovernmental organization): The World Bank Group Development Marketplace Innovation Competition.

Let's assume that you have determined that the World Bank's Development Marketplace Innovation Competition Program can help to further internationalize your business program. This innovation program can underwrite faculty release time, student assistants, library acquisitions, and research travel, among other things. Its specific mission is to nourish small or large business development in an economically-disadvantaged nation or community by providing funding for reducing poverty, bringing people and institutions together, and encouraging the dissemination of globalization benefits.

The program places no limitations on an institution's request for indirect cost allocation, but does require that applicants collaborate with a multilateral development bank, a UN agency, or a bilateral development agency (such as USAID). This factor distinguishes the program from many other privately funded competitions. It ensures that internationalization efforts have the approval and collaboration of major players on the world development scene. Moreover, collaboration obligates applicants to integrate their efforts with ongoing work from development agencies and entities, and ultimately, it obligates applicants to promote business in less-developed nations of the world.

Don't Let the Guidelines Stifle Your Ability to Be Innovative

Although proposals must address all elements in the published guidelines and regulations, they should not simply replicate or emulate efforts that have previously succeeded. In reviewing previously-funded proposals, the applicant should devise strategies and activities that differentiate the project from those that are already up and running. Many funding awards require some aspect of "uniqueness"—some do not. Regardless of whether uniqueness is required, it may well benefit the applicant to propose something innovative. In the case of a federal agency grant, for instance, this might mean an aspect of your proposal which helps internationalize new communities and new environments.

Secure and Show Institutional Commitment to the Proposal

A thorough grant research effort will reveal the need for institutional preapplication commitment to your proposed project. If your administration supports the idea of international business education, it should be predisposed to leveraging its resources (regardless of how limited the budget) to attract federal, state, or private funding. Administrators are often more readily inclined to help if they participate in the proposal development effort. Therefore, it is wise to convene project development meetings to which the dean, provost, vice president(s), and the president are invited and personally encouraged to attend.

In your search for external support, enlist the support of anyone who both has ties with your administration and who also does business, knows business, reads national and international newspapers, or invests in the stock market. Carefully canvas the local business community and invite into the process any players whom you think can make a real contribution, either in terms of matching funds or resources, or simply providing insight. The earlier they are involved, the more committed they will be, and this is especially valuable in the grant application process.

Be Prepared to Realign the Project for Feasibility

If the champion or IB team becomes frustrated with the dearth of institutional resources, it may be necessary to shrink the project scope. This will enable you to proceed without delay and submit at least one grant proposal to support the core of the internationalization effort while you search for additional funds that can support those elements you have set aside for the moment. After the first submitted (and hopefully successful) application, the second will be far less difficult.

Exhibit 4.1

Draft Budget for a Typical Federal Grant Program

Research Personnel
- Department A faculty
  Release @ 12.5% @ $60,000 x two (2) faculty members — $15,000
- Department B faculty—in subcontractor college
  Release @ 12.5% @ $ 88,000 x two (2) faculty members — $22,000
- Graduate assistant (to be shared by Depts. A and B faculty)
  1 half-time equivalent @ $16,000 — $16,000
- Small Business Development Center (SBDC) counselors — $15,000

Fringe Benefits
@ 25% of salaries — $17,000

Total Personnel Cost	$85,000

Travel
- 4 trips @ $2,000 per trip — $8,000
- Roundtrips to South Carolina from Cali, Colombia — $4,000
  In-state travel (mileage) — $750

Lodging
- Hotels faculty and
  SBDC project personnel in Colombia — $4,000
- Hotels for student interns — $1,000

Total Travel and Lodging	$17,750

Instructional and General Office Supplies
- Videotapes, manuals, books, periodicals — $3,000
- General supplies — $500
- Postage and shipping — $250

Total Supplies	$3,750

Contractual Services
Project administration—in-country implementation
- Contractual — $35,000
  — Only $25,000 in funds from subcontract are eligible for indirect

Total Direct Costs	$141,500

Indirect Cost
@ 44.5% of total costs (indirect taken on first $25,000 of contractual — $11,125
  agreement)
@ 40% direct costs—for subcontractor college — $11,000

Total Indirect Costs	$22,125
Total All Costs	**$163,625**

Write the Narrative Part of the Proposal Carefully

Proposals that express ideas clearly, simply, and concisely are more likely to be successful. This is a simple notion, but one that eludes many applicants. The applicant should review basic writing manuals, and read both popular and professional journals to find models for clear prose. Again, the most important element in a successful grant proposal will be the applicant's ability to respond to all of the grant selection criteria, and to ensure that the application narrative addresses the program purposes.

Prepare the Budget with Thoroughness

Budgets should contain estimates that reflect projected costs. Remember that all project efforts will begin at least nine months from the day on which you submit a proposal. A travel agent can help applicants to project future costs. Be sure to factor in estimated and reasonable salary increases. Also be sure that you include fringe benefits, students' stipends, and the cost of library acquisitions. Use a computer spreadsheet program to make sure that your calculations are correct. Ask someone in your sponsored programs office to double-check your figures. Although the budget person should understand the project costs, they need not be an accountant. Grant budgets are fairly straightforward. In Exhibit 4.1 you will find a sample budget that you can use as a template.

Final Note

Preparing a grant proposal can be compared to preparing a business proposal. You must review the competition, compare your ideas with other *successful* proposals, and enlist institutional support. And, as in business, your first effort may not be accepted by your potential "investors." It is very common for grant applicants to make repeated attempts before they secure awards.

You must be persistent, and you should not be overly selective. Do not apply for every program to which you are attracted. Apply for those programs that are right for your IB program initiative and your institution, and for which you have time to do a good, thorough job. And remember, this is a *business* you are engaged in, not a trip to Las Vegas. Yes, it is important to play your cards right, but *winning* has far more to do with investigation and diligence than it has to do with luck.

CHAPTER FIVE

Crafting
the
Undergraduate
Curriculum

Kelly Jett Murphrey

Congratulations! Your school just received its first grant to fund undergraduate curriculum development. But how do you get started? To assist your IB team in its development of a program, this chapter provides a practical and interdisciplinary approach. While there is much literature in the field, what seems to be lacking is a systematic approach to curriculum development. Most business schools have many more international resources (faculty, visiting executives, Internet resources, international Small Business Development Center (SBDC) staff, international students, language courses, cultural courses) than they realize—what they commonly lack is a strategy of discovering and incorporating those resources into their business curriculum. Presented and described below is a seven-step process to identify and integrate resources for crafting the undergraduate curriculum:

Step 1   Form an interdisciplinary undergraduate IB curriculum team.

Step 2   Apply the business, culture, and language skills framework.

Step 3   Establish the goals of internationalization.

Step 4   Execute a SWOT analysis.

Step 5   Conduct a needs assessment.

Step 6   Select curriculum internationalization methods.

Step 7   Determine international education objectives.

Step 1. Form an Interdisciplinary Undergraduate IB Curriculum Team

As discussed in Chapter 2: *Charting Your Course*, the first step in designing an undergraduate curriculum is to form an interdisciplinary undergraduate international business curriculum team (IB team) of faculty members to serve as the focal point for planning and facilitating the other six steps identified above. Internationalization is an interdisciplinary process. Therefore, this team should include representatives from each business discipline, as well as representatives from regional studies, the modern language departments, study abroad programs, and other relevant academic and support areas. In addition, it is usually beneficial to include a representative from the dean's office to demonstrate support for internationalizing the business curriculum and to provide a direct link for getting questions addressed in a timely fashion. You should strive to develop broad representation and a spirit of collaboration within your team. Remember that team members are from different disciplines, organizational structures, and environments. Your efforts will accrue and you will profit by the many different ideas and perspectives that will arise.

Why should the international business curriculum development team be interdisciplinary? The skills and knowledge needed to practice international business are interdisciplinary in nature. Therefore, it makes sense to include representatives from disciplines other than business that will be actively involved in the education of those seeking an international business focus. This is not the time to become territorial; cross-disciplinary cooperation is needed to successfully internationalize a program. These "outsiders" (those from the disciplines other than business) should be included in the curriculum planning from the very beginning, so they can share their knowledge and expertise as true contributing members of the team in the planning of the business curriculum. Do not make the common mistake of thinking you can bring in the faculty and staff from other disciplines at a later time and receive full cooperation from them. Think *interdisciplinarily*, from the very start.

Who should be selected for the curriculum team? Select faculty members who are supportive of internationalizing the curriculum, respected by fellow colleagues, and flexible in their approach to internationalizing. Although these characteristics may seem obvious, they are often overlooked under the pressure to move forward rapidly. Invest time early on carefully selecting select team members; it will pay off in the long run.

In some institutions, it may be helpful to include an international business professional from the private sector. They can provide a practical international business perspective, often lacking in a strictly academic group, which may prove beneficial in planning the international curriculum and activities. However, on the negative side, the individual may not fully understand or appreciate the rules and culture of academic institutions. The environment of your institution will usually dictate whether it would be useful to include someone from the private sector on the IB team. Most often it is.

The team will be responsible for executing a SWOT analysis, conducting a needs assessment, developing educational objectives, and a broad array of other activities to support the design of an international business curriculum that will meet the needs of your business school and its stakeholders.

Step 2. Apply the Business, Culture, and Language Skills Framework

The next step is for the curriculum development team to become familiar with the three interrelated skills necessary to accomplish internationalization.

It has been said that the only common characteristic one can find among international business professionals is the fact that each seems to have followed a different path to their profession. It seems fairly simple to advise a student on how to become an accountant or a manager, but the task becomes much more difficult when it comes to giving sound advice on how to become an *international* accountant, *international* broker, *international* salesperson or sales manager. The world is full of people with ideas and advice on how to become "international," but in truth no definitive standards exist for becoming an international professional. This explains why it is not always clear what the IB curriculum should include or which educational path one should take to prepare for an international business career. Although specific standards are not well-established, and may never be, three components of internationalization—international business skills, fluency in a second modern language, and an understanding of another culture—are generally accepted as forming the building blocks for an international business career.

The skills framework should be used at every stage of the planning, development, implementation, and evaluation of the international curriculum-building process. It will become increasingly clear how to apply this framework as you read through the next steps involved in developing the undergraduate IB curriculum. Without this framework, the team would find it difficult to stay focused while planning and implementing the internationalization process. The framework can also serve as a tool to help you explain to faculty, administration, and to the business community what the team is trying to accomplish with the IB curriculum.

All three skills areas should be well-represented on your IB team. If any areas of the framework are not represented with faculty, staff, or business practitioner expertise, then additional team members should be added.

Step 3. Establish the Goals of Internationalization

Once the IB team has been formed and the members have embraced the business, culture, and language-skills concept of internationalization, the next step (and a very critical one) is to establish specific goals for the undergraduate international business curriculum. Without such goals it will be difficult for the team to come to any consensus on the many issues which will arise. How might you go about establishing these goals? One place to start is with a set of goal-related concepts such as those discussed by Jeffrey Arpan in *Internationalizing Business Education–Meeting the Challenge* (Cavusgil). Arpan notes three primary internationalization goals as they apply to both faculty and students—*awareness*, *understanding*, and *competency*. The three goals are not mutually exclusive and are generally hierarchical in nature.

Awareness is the first goal of internationalization and often the most difficult to achieve. Students and faculty who develop an international awareness respect the increasing connectivity and interdependency of the world. An overseas experience is one of the best ways to provide students and faculty a sense of the global village in which they live and work. However, many students will not be able to travel abroad, so one of the major challenges in developing an IB curriculum is to be sure your students are truly gaining an international awareness in their native classroom. An example of students demonstrating international awareness would be participating in a class discussion about the cultural differences of Germans and Americans and how those differences affect business practices in some specific area (such as selling, technology, or medicine).

Understanding is the second goal of internationalization. It should be emphasized that a student cannot move from a level of *awareness* to a level of *understanding*, which is a significantly higher level of learning, without first internalizing a familiarity with the larger world in such a way that it becomes a functional part of their daily perspective. At a level of *understanding* a student not only becomes aware of cultural differences and facts, but can also demonstrate comprehension. For example, it is one thing for a student to be *aware* that the North American Free Trade Agreement (NAFTA) exists, but it requires a much higher level of learning for that same student to *understand* the impact NAFTA is having on its partner nations, on world trade organizations, on the global marketplace, and on the world economy.

Competency is the highest goal. At this level a student not only possesses international *awareness* and *understanding* but is also able to demonstrate *competency* by being able to *analyze* international concepts, which is a matter of synthesizing various aspects of the subject area. For example, to be able to successfully compare and contrast the political, economic, and cultural environments of Argentina and Egypt would demonstrate a level of *competency*. At the highest level of competency, a student is able to *synthesize* new concepts by putting together information and concepts from a variety of subject areas and disciplines in order to create new ideas.

Selecting the appropriate internationalization goal level (awareness, understanding, competency) can help your IB team determine which classes, programs, and activities are appropriate for your curriculum. The team should continuously ask these questions: "What is the goal for this activity?" and "Are we trying to achieve awareness, understanding, or competency?"

Step 4. Execute a SWOT Analysis

A SWOT analysis is a review of the strengths, weaknesses, opportunities, and threats, as they relate to the current status of your educational institution. It is vitally important to gain a strong understanding of the present condition of your school which will highlight many of the critical issues facing the curriculum development team. The SWOT analysis should consist of an evaluation of both the internal and external environments as they relate to your overall international-ization and curriculum development goals. Consider the strengths, weaknesses, opportunities, and threats from your point of view and from the point of view of other stakeholders that will be watching your activities. Ideally, the SWOT analysis should be prepared before venturing into curriculum planning, and reviewed at regular intervals thereafter as a part of overall IB curriculum planning. See Chapter 2: *Charting Your Course,* for a complete review of the strategic planning process and the SWOT model.

The IB team should review closely the information collected during the SWOT analysis to determine the current status. This information will be very helpful as the IB team develops a plan for the curriculum.

Step 5.   Conduct a Needs Assessment

The SWOT analysis should have provided you with a clear snapshot of the current international status of your institution. The *needs assessment* will help to identify those factors that need to change. Well-meaning efforts by those working to internationalize the business curriculum may fail if the international needs are not accurately identified and fully assessed for your specific institution. It is absolutely essential that the interests of *all* stakeholders be considered.

The concept of an IB curriculum needs assessment connotes a process by which (1) information is collected to determine the perceived needs, (2) identified needs are evaluated and ranked according to priority, and (3) a plan is developed to meet those needs of highest priority. The needs assessment should ask what types of *international business* knowledge, *cultural* understanding skills, and *second-language* proficiency will be necessary for future international business professionals.

It is useful to review the needs assessments conducted by others, but do not let those reports substitute for completing your own assessment in order to determine the specific requirements of your stakeholders. A number of approaches exist to gather information on needs. The survey method, the Delphi technique, interviews, and focus groups are a few. Any or all of these may be used and be helpful (and there is certainly no reason for the champion or team to be limited in approach), but since the terms *international, internationalization, global,* and *globalization* seem to have different meanings to everyone, face-to-face meetings and interviews can often render the most useful information in the shortest amount of time. Also, the interview process allows for a rapport to develop that can allow the curriculum developers to get closer and probe deeper into specific needs and, of course, that rapport can be invaluable in the future.

Whom should you interview? It makes sense to start close to home: business college faculty, administration, and students; then colleagues in modern languages and regional studies; and then more university administration. Outside the university there are business leaders to speak with, as well as business association representatives, and representatives of government agencies. All of these people should have a vested interest in your proposed internationalization program.

The needs assessment will usually produce more needs than can be addressed with existing resources. When this happens, the IB team will need to take into consideration a number of factors, including the existing business, culture, and language framework (Step 2), the goals of internationalization (Step 3), and the findings of the SWOT analysis (Step 4), to select criteria that will be used to rank the identified needs according to priority. Priority setting provides a rationale for resource allocation.

Once the needs are specified, each should be presented in a format that makes both the current status and identified need as explicit as possible. The following are examples of current status and identified need statements:

Example #1

Current Status:	Very little of the undergraduate curriculum provides content that will help students achieve a goal of international awareness.
Identified Need:	To ensure that 100% of undergraduate business students achieve international awareness by graduation.

Example #2

Current Status:	Local companies are interested in hiring more business students with international business skills and knowledge, but few of the current graduates have these skills.
Identified Need:	To increase the number of IB and cultural courses offered for undergraduate business students.

Example #3

Current Status:	No formal international business program exists for those interested in pursuing higher goals of international understanding and competency.
Identified Need:	To develop a minor or certificate in international business to enable students to achieve international understanding and competency by graduation.

The current status and identified-need statements will assist the IB team in determining and developing their international education objectives in Step 7.

Step 6.   Select Curriculum Internationalization Methods

Internationalization of the business curriculum is a multifaceted process that can be achieved in a variety of ways, but there are two common methods: course *infusion* and *new international courses*. Each method has its advantages and disadvantages, and for this reason most business programs apply both methods in their quest to internationalize the curriculum and to involve as many students as possible.

The *infusion method* supports the integration of international content into already existing courses, which can be very appealing to those programs and colleges with budget constraints or institutions interested in implementing less radical curricular changes. In the early stages of infusion, a single international lecture, chapter, or guest speaker may be added to a domestically focused course, although, over time, the goal of infusion should be to integrate international content and perspectives throughout the course by including internationally inclusive readings, lecture examples, video tapes, group projects, or discussion of current events. One of the major advantages of infusion is the ease and speed with which it can be applied to a broad array of business courses, therefore greatly increasing the number of undergraduate students being exposed to the rudimentary aspects of international business and achieving international *awareness*. Also, most faculty seem to like the infusion method because it allows them to carefully introduce international issues relevant to their discipline and also provides the flexibility to add as much or as little international content as they deem appropriate.

The development of new courses is the other widely used method for internationalizing the business curriculum. Discipline-focused international courses can be developed, such as international marketing, or international finance, which have the advantage of covering and exploring in more depth the international aspects of a particular functional area—supporting the goal of developing international *understanding*. In addition, special-focus international courses (such as "The Impact of NAFTA" or "The Changing Environment in Europe") can be offered by faculty and visiting faculty to help students gain an understanding of timely international topics of interest. The major reasons often stated for not developing new courses are a lack of faculty with international expertise, insufficient funds, insufficient time, and a lack of space in the curriculum. Do not overlook the fact that many international courses offered outside the business school (modern language, history, sociology, geography, anthropology) are appropriate for business students and may even be cross-listed to add a new dimension to the international business curriculum. A list of the courses offered in other schools and colleges that the business school will accept for credit should be developed to assist students with their course planning.

Exhibit 5.1 illustrates some of the various advantages and disadvantages of both the course infusion method and the new international course method.

Exhibit 5.1

**Advantages of Course Infusion
and New International Course Methods**

Course Infusion Method

Advantages	Disadvantages
• no new faculty or courses needed	• may achieve only limited goal of internationalization
• achieve international "awareness" goal for many students	• hard to monitor level of internationalization in classes
• may involve a number of faculty in the internationalization process	• students, parents, and others may not perceive courses as international
• limited change to curriculum	

New International Course Method

Advantages	Disadvantages
• provide more international depth in courses	• may need to hire new faculty
• higher goals of *understanding* and *competency* addressed	• usually requires extra financial support and faculty time
• able to offer courses on timely topics	• may have limited enrollment
• may be able to add international minor and certificates	• may inhibit infusion of international topics in other classes

Regardless of the methodology initially adopted, it should be noted that many IB academicians and practitioners support the idea that *infusion* should be the ultimate goal, rather than simply adding the word *"international"* into the title, which may imply to students and faculty that courses without the word in the title *do not* or *should not* contain international content.

Step 7.   Determine International Education Objectives

In Step 7, the IB team needs to put together all that they have learned from the previous six steps to determine what their specific international education objectives should be. Stated as questions, should the objective be to

- add a new international business class?

- try a pilot program of infusing international content into the survey of management and survey of marketing courses?

- develop a certificate in international business?

- create a minor in international business?

- create an international degree?

- expand study abroad and internship offerings?

- allow students to take courses outside the college of business?

- promote competency in a second modern language?

- develop a certificate of Latin American business studies?

The choices can be limitless. The team will need to determine the educational objectives that will best match their institution by considering a variety of factors: the business, culture, and modern language framework (Step 2), the goals of internationalization (Step 3), the results of the SWOT analysis (Step 4), the identified needs (Step 5) ranked according to priority, and the use of infused and new courses (Step 6).

The education objectives, statements of anticipated results, should flow from the "current status" and "identified needs," which were determined earlier in Step 5. Each educational objective should be presented in a format that clearly describes the *current status*, *identified need*, and, now, the *educational objective* being suggested to meet that need. This process will put you on the road to developing an IB curriculum that will meet the specific needs of your institution with the resources that are available. Below are three examples using this process and format:

Example #1 Course Infusion Method

Current Status: Very little of the undergraduate curriculum provides content that will help students achieve a goal of international awareness.

Identified Need: To ensure that 100% of undergraduate business students achieve international awareness by graduation.

Educational Objective: Each business discipline will select two courses to target for infusion of international content.

Business, Culture, and Modern Language Framework:

	Business	**Culture**	**Language**
A. Infusion Courses	✔	✔	

Goals of Internationalization:

	Awareness	**Understanding**	**Competency**
A. Infusion Courses	✔		

Example #2   **New IB Courses Method**

Current Status: Local companies are interested in hiring more business students with international business skills and knowledge, but few of the current graduates have these skills.

Identified Need: To increase the number of IB and cultural courses offered for undergraduate business students.

Educational Objectives: A) All business majors will be required to take the "Introduction to International Business" class.

B) All students will be required to take the IB course associated with their major and one cultural class.

Business, Culture and Modern Language Framework:

	Business	**Culture**	**Language**
A. New IB Course	✔	✔	
B. Culture Courses		✔	

Goals of Internationalization:

	Awareness	**Understanding**	**Competency**
A. New IB Course	✔	✔	
B. Culture Courses	✔	✔	

International Business Requirements:

International Business (one course)
All students are required to take *"Introduction to International Business."*

Culture (one course)
All business students are required to take one course from the culture course selections.

Core International Business Course
"Introduction to International Business"

Culture Courses
"Cross-cultural Communication in the Global Village"
"Doing Business in Latin America"
"Doing Business in Europe"
"International Negotiations"
"History of Latin America"
"History of Europe"

Example #3   Certificate in International Business

Current Status: No formal international business program exists for those interested in pursuing higher goals of international understanding and competency.

Identified Need: Need to develop a certificate in international business to enable students to achieve international understanding and competency by graduation.

Educational Objective: A Certificate in International Business will be developed that will require (a) three international business classes, (b) two culture classes, (c) three modern language classes, and (d) an optional overseas experience.

Business, Culture, and Modern Language Framework:

	Business	**Culture**	**Language**
A. New IB Course	✔		
B. Culture Courses		✔	
C. Language Courses			✔
D. Study Abroad	✔	✔	✔

Goals of Internationalization.

	Awareness	**Understanding**	**Competency**
A. New IB Course		✔	
B. Culture Courses		✔	
C. Language Courses			✔
D. Study Abroad		✔	✔

Certificate in IB Requirements:

International Business (three courses)

All students are required to take (a) "Introduction to International Business," (b) the international business core course associated with their major, and (c) one other international business course from either the core IB courses or electives.

Culture (two courses)

Students must take two courses from the culture course selections, which complement their modern language studies.

Modern Languages (three courses)

Students are required to take three modern language courses in the same language.

Core International Business Courses

"Introduction to International Business"
"International Marketing"
"International Finance"
"International Accounting"
"International HRM"
"International Information Technology Management"

Culture Courses

"Communication in the Global Village"
"Doing Business in Latin America"
"Doing Business in Europe"
"International Negotiations"
"History of Latin America"
"History of Europe"

International Business Electives

"The European Business Environment"
"Implications of NAFTA"
"Fundamentals of Exporting & Importing"
"Fundamentals of E-Commerce"

Modern Languages Courses

"Spanish I"

"Spanish II"
"Business Spanish"
"French I"
"French II"
"Business French"
"German I"
"German II"
"Business German"

Study Abroad

Although a study abroad experience is not required, students are encouraged to fulfill some of their IB requirements while participating in one of the many study abroad programs offered by the university.

Final Note

Developing an international business curriculum does not have to be a complicated and overwhelming task. The systematic, seven-step, practical approach described in this chapter offers a method for building upon your resources to develop the undergraduate curriculum that will be most appropriate for your business school and those you serve. It is important to involve representatives from disciplines both within and outside your business school, and from outside the university itself, as you develop the curriculum so that you can include all three components of the internationalization framework (international business skills, communication capability in a second modern language, and understanding of other cultures). It is important to remember that the curriculum you establish today will have far-reaching impact on the students who participate in your programs tomorrow.

CHAPTER SIX

Crafting the Graduate Program

William R. Folks, Jr.

Undergraduate business programs can go a long way toward preparing students to better understand the new perspectives of world trade. Graduate programs, solidly built and with good navigation, can take the school, along with its student and business constituency, even farther. You have your grant in hand, or can see it on the horizon (and you have wind in your sails) but there is still much to be done.

This chapter is structured from the strategic perspective, and is broken into discussions of eight major components, all of which call for considerable thought, calculation, and planning:

Component 1   Identify the constituency you intend to serve.

Component 2   Redesign the existing graduate program or develop a new program, as appropriate, to incorporate international concepts.

Component 3   Determine what faculty-development activities the curriculum revision or new educational program requires.

Component 4 Determine any organizational changes necessary to implement strategic changes, including creation of necessary cross-campus links.

Component 5 Develop assessment activities to determine whether program goals are being met.

Component 6 Determine how to market the program to the identified constituency.

Component 7 Develop linkages with external constituencies to implement the program.

Component 8 Acquire the financial resources necessary for the program activities.

For many business schools the masters program, with its M.B.A., is its major offering, the one upon which the school's reputation (both graduate and undergraduate) for excellence is built. How it is internationalized will go a long way in determining how competitive the school will be in the future.

A preliminary consideration in identifying the appropriate approach to internationalization of a graduate program is to consider the mission of the school and the global dimension of that school's mission. Different schools have different missions. The current accreditation standards of the AACSB recognize variety, but insist that ". . . the mission must be appropriate to higher education for business and management and consonant with the mission of the institution of which it is a part" (AACSB, Accreditation Standard M.2).

Public-funded state institutions may have their mission in part mandated for them. Private institutions may have greater flexibility in determining their mission, but must respond to the exigencies of the marketplace. Institutions with a religious mission must consider yet a third set of priorities.

How to internationalize the graduate curriculum ultimately depends on the purpose of the masters degree, which typically is driven by the perceived needs of those firms who are apt to hire graduates. Additionally, the school's own self-identity plays a role. How a "top twenty" business school chooses to internationalize its core M.B.A. curriculum is likely to differ significantly from the approach adopted by a large urban evening M.B.A. A nationally prominent Executive M.B.A. program will undoubtedly take an approach different from that in a specialty masters program in human resources, or taxation, or information technology. Although there are fundamental international business concepts that ought to be taught in nearly all masters programs, there are special issues, such as trade finance, that merit detailed inclusion in certain types of programs, but only need to be introduced briefly in others. These are the preliminary planning issues which must be addressed.

Component 1. Identify the constituency you intend to serve.

The three elements to consider in internationalizing a business school are the mix of existing graduate programs (the *product mix*), the existing group of corporations and other institutions that hire the graduates of the programs (the *customer base*), and the existing characteristics of the students that enroll in each program (the *participant base*). One can change, and change radically, any of these elements through the process one selects. Indeed, one can define a strategy as an effort to determine (1) what kind of program or programs to offer, (2) which students will participate in each program, and (3) potential employment with what customer firms.

Analyzing the Product Mix of Graduate Programs

The mission of the business school generally defines the product mix of graduate programs as differentiated primarily by the type of individual who might most benefit, and are most easily identified by (1) the degree of prior academic preparation typical of the student admitted to the program, (2) the extent of prior business experience typical of the student admitted to the program, and (3) the geographical area from which prospective students are typically drawn.

A key early decision in the program development process is to determine whether to adapt existing products to the realities of the international business environment, or to develop and introduce a new academic product. Business schools with excellent programs generally tend to favor the adaptation strategy. Typically, adaptation of content curriculum can be implemented through one of three approaches:

- Infusion, in which the existing content of academic courses is "internationalized" through the use of international examples to illustrate particular teaching points, and the insertion of specifically international content into core courses and electives.

- The requirement of one international survey course designed to cover the international dimension of business.

- The requirement of at least one (if not more) course from a menu of new international courses, either in functional fields or more broad-based courses.

The inclusion of second-language, area studies, and experiential components in the curriculum, such as overseas studies components, internships (domestic or abroad), international speaker series, inclusion of non-U.S. nationals into the student group, use of local area groups with overseas links, are a few of the more common activities implemented.

The alternative to product adaptation is the creation of a new masters level program that has an explicit international structure or emphasis. In these programs international content is clearly identified and taught, usually in courses or modules specifically labeled "international." Examples of such international programs that coexist with other business graduate programs are the Masters of International Business Studies (MIBS) program at the University of South Carolina, the International M.B.A. at the University of Memphis, and the MIBS program at the University of Miami. Other schools, such as Thunderbird, offer internationally-designated degrees without offering an M.B.A. in parallel.

Most universities have substantial investment in their M.B.A. programs, and the deliberate creation of a significantly different kind of business program may be viewed as potentially damaging to the reputation of the M.B.A. Some schools fear that businesses will find "international" graduates too specialized for positions in their firms, that they are insufficiently trained for functional positions, or that these graduates' expectations for overseas assignments will be unrealistic.

Even more challenging for the college is the necessity of attracting students to the "new" international program, usually by stressing its advantages and "uniqueness," yet without detracting from the solid utility of the existing program. Thus, the marketing effort for potential students must be carefully crafted.

Analyzing the Customer Base for Academic Programs

The driving force behind the internationalization of masters programs is the need of U.S. and international businesses for potential employees (and, in turn, potential managers) with relevant skills. Businesses (usually corporations) comprise the customer base for the college, and the college's graduates are its product. One might broadly characterize the customer base of IB education into three categories:

- Global firms—international businesses whose activities incorporate substantial involvement in marketing and manufacturing outside the United

States, including non-U.S. firms with subsidiaries in the United States.

- National and regional firms—businesses whose activities are substantial in scope, who may or may not export, that have not yet established major offshore markets or manufacturing facilities.

- Local firms—businesses whose operations are confined to the locale in which the school operates but, in this world economy, utilize overseas parts, components, or wholly-made products in the course of doing their business.

The customer base of the business school is certainly far more complex than this simple model would suggest. Importantly, it implies overall graduate learning requirements and the type of IB activities that must be developed. For example, nearby firms will be the normal customer base of an evening M.B.A. program. Thus, if the school is located in an international financial center, there will be a natural demand for coverage of international capital markets in the curriculum. If the school is in a port city, greater emphasis might be placed on trade finance.

Business schools (whether commuter or residential), whose client base is already internationally inclined, have both the easiest and most difficult tasks. The necessity for some sort of internationalization of curriculum and activities is evident, but there can be fierce demand for successful IB content from the customer base and from students. Schools whose graduate programs serve a regional or local need are less likely to feel the competition, unless the market they currently serve has a high proportion of international firms.

The post-graduate employment record of the business school is perhaps the most useful indicator of the client base of a particular business school, and it should be assessed continuously. Any lack of continuity between the desired and actual placement of graduates merits attention, and one issue to be addressed is the need for further internationalization of curriculum and activities. If at all possible, the early career patterns, not just placement records, of recent graduates should be studied to determine what specific curriculum needs might be addressed.

Graduate programs that adopt a specific "international" label must address any concerns and possible misperceptions businesses might have about the expertise and expectations these "new graduates" might bring into the job market. Even within international firms, the majority of day-to-day business decisions have only a global *context*, rather than substantial global *content*. The manager of a plant in Cleveland may work for a global conglomerate, but the primary set of problems to be faced is still not international in nature, and those in charge of hiring must know that international programs are fully aware of this. Curriculum design must not focus so exclusively on the international components of business education that the ability to function as a manager within a wide range of environments is compromised.

Yet in top executive positions, the international nature of business becomes an almost routine component of managerial decisions and internationally-labeled programs must also respond to customer perceptions that "all business is international." In response, colleges can point to the specific areas of the value-added education offered by its international program. There is the body of academic research that focuses on the specific issues originating from cross-border and cross-cultural operations, and the implications of this knowledge are incorporated in the coursework undertaken by the international business student. Additionally, many of these life experiences useful to business managers can be incorporated into an academic context. Internships, second-language acquisition, and cross-border living provide managers with the skills and experience necessary for building an international business career.

Analyzing the Participant Base

In designing an internationalization strategy for graduate programs, the first objective for the program must be to identify the kind of students it seeks to attract. Although all schools ought to practice equity in admissions, the type of international courses and activities provided will be affected by the geographic mix of students who enter its program. In turn, enrollment promotional activities need to be congruent with institutional and program goals. Also, viewing the purpose of graduate business education as meeting the needs of the multinational corporate customer base for well-trained managers, one must recognize that U.S. academic institutions have a market opportunity to provide degree programs for non-U.S. nationals, either on campus or at non-U.S. locations. Indeed, while U.S. universities have always attracted international business students, in the nineties the competition in that market increased and so has international recruitment and promotion.

Masters programs can be located offshore to appeal to a specific student market, either as a joint-venture or on a stand-alone basis. Whether an extension of an existing M.B.A. program or of a newly designed IB program, the primary purpose for such a venture ought to be enhancement of the resources of the institution. Offshore teaching assignments, for example, are a powerful method for developing the international experience and skills of existing and new faculty. The alternative to a location abroad is to promote existing programs on an international basis, or promote to a specific region of the world. In fact, the very design of the on-campus M.B.A. program may provide a natural recruitment tool.

Component 2. Redesign the existing graduate program or develop a new program, as appropriate, to incorporate international concepts.

Most business schools have confronted the need to redesign their current programs, and in many cases have adapted an approach to internationalizing current programs. Unfortunately it is not yet evident that the results have yielded truly effective curricula. But if schools are still in the early stages of internationalization, remember that there is still time to review and revise the curriculum and to make changes in the approach. Two key components to redesign are inclusion of second-language acquisition and experiential learning.

Second Language Acquisition and Graduate Business Education

In creating a graduate business curriculum for the global manager of the new century, one important issue is the role that second-language education should play. Very few conventional M.B.A. programs require second-language coursework, much less fluency, and unfortunately only some IB programs require significant coursework or fluency. Other programs, such as the International M.B.A. at the University of Chicago, the programs of the Lauder Institute at Wharton, and the International Fellows program at UCLA, require substantial expertise in a second language to gain admission to certain experiential activities associated with the program. Once admitted, students are expected to build on their expertise with advanced foreign language courses. Most graduate business students begin study when they are in their mid-to-late twenties; Executive M.B.A. programs typically have even older entrants. Most of these students are at an age where the ability to acquire new languages is both a function of their past experience of learning other languages and whatever natural talent for language learning they might possess. Learning a language *de novo* is a challenging endeavor, and one that consumes significant hours, hours that might be profitably employed in other activities. Programs with language requirements either must restrict admissions or develop highly intensive and effective language-acquisition experiences. Since graduate business students are paying a cost in time and lost opportunities for the time they are enrolled in language study, there must be a substantial payoff.

Therefore, language learning may be best incorporated into the graduate business curriculum only if there is some specific need for it to meet other requirements of the program. For example, in programs that have an overseas living experience, such as internships, at least basic survival language skills should be required. Also, if academic study at non-U.S. institutions is provided through exchange programs, participants' language needs must be addressed.

If one decides to introduce one or more languages into the curriculum, what languages should they be? Ideally, they should be languages whose acquisition enhances the business value of the individual substantially, and languages that are widely used in substantial international business activity. Regrettably, language learning must meet a market test that is a combination of scarcity in value (number of other business graduates who have the language) and utility in business (number of potential customers who have need of the language). Chinese, Japanese, French, German, Italian, Portuguese, and Spanish certainly meet the utility test.

Inclusion of second-language components requires sourcing of instruction. While in comprehensive universities the modern languages departments are the conventional source for such instruction, teaching business students requires substantial adjustment in traditional approaches to language instruction geared primarily for the more classical study of language and literature. Outsourcing language instruction is always a possibility, depending on program design.

Experiential Learning: Study Abroad

Study abroad as a part of an integrated internationalized graduate business program can be extremely valuable. Participants live and study in a culture substantially different from their own, are exposed to alternative views with regard to the various functions of business, and may have the opportunity to gain access to expertise not readily present on the home campus.

The simplest of all study abroad programs is for the participant to spend a semester at a cooperating non-U.S. institution. Creating even this alternative within the tightly-packed graduate business curriculum is difficult. Effective curriculum design would be structured so that one semester, typically the fall semester of the second year, has a limited number of required courses and has sufficient flexibility such that a student studying abroad might possibly find an analogous experience at the host institution. Potential host institutions should be consulted for availability of courses that would meet requirements of the academic program. Nonetheless, choice of the fall semester of the second year means that the participant misses a substantial portion of on-campus placement activities, and this factor is always a deterrent. Further, unless the student already has acquired second-language skills, the choice of institutions is limited to those where English is the primary language of instruction.

An alternate solution is a summer program at a non-U.S. university or college. The business school can utilize existing summer programs offered by local or U.S. institutions, or develop their own program in conjunction with a partner institution. These programs might run anywhere from three to ten weeks. They may offer a particular regional focus, or a specific functional area, or some combination of courses, such as advertising in South America. Business schools may form consortia to offer these programs or choose to market their program to other schools.

Summer programs are least disruptive of the academic design of the graduate business program, but they do reduce the possibility of summer internships. A consortium of CIBER business schools is developing three-week international programs for late May, with the idea that the programs could be completed prior to the beginning of an internship.

For executive or other part-time M.B.A. programs, the primary in-country experience is a class trip, in which participants visit a particular region for a combination of academic activities, meetings with managers and government officials, site visits, and cultural activities. The experience may include a predeparture briefing. The country visited may be rotated with each class, or may remain the same. This methodology is a cost-effective mechanism for time-constrained managers to obtain an introduction to another culture. To enhance effectiveness, some post-trip analysis with regional experts can be useful.

Another vehicle for providing a more substantial living and learning experience abroad is the joint-venture M.B.A. In this form, two schools host substantial portions of the M.B.A. Prototypes are the joint M.B.A. of the University of Texas at Austin, with ITESM in Monterrey, Mexico. Another is the International M.B.A. of the University of South Carolina with the Wirtschaftsuniversitat Wien in Vienna, Austria. Participants in the latter spend July-December at the campus in Vienna and January-August at the South Carolina campus in Columbia.

The key success factor in all of these ventures is to balance the value provided by the international educational experience against the cost of the program. Costs are of three kinds: the actual out-of-pocket cost to the student of the international experience, the possible loss of efficiency in business education arising from the necessity of moving from one location to another, and the lost opportunities from not being available for other value-enhancing activities such as corporate recruiting. Clever program design can reduce all these costs.

Any sort of exchange arrangement, overseas academic offerings, travel-abroad program, or joint-venture degree, has substantial strategic implications beyond graduate business education. In particular, by making the name of the business school better known in a specific region of the world these arrangements can serve as strategic points of entry for more lucrative executive education programs. Faculty linkages can lead to significant research opportunities. It is best to approach the use of these relationships by assessing the total value that each relationship brings to the total business school or university. The graduate education component is only one portion.

Experiential Learning: Internships

One of the most important elements in the design of graduate business programs is a module that offers participants the opportunity to experience living in another culture while simultaneously learning and increasing business skills. The classical vehicle for such an experience is the opportunity to study at a business school abroad, either in a second language or in English. But recently, schools have begun formalizing the use of internships abroad as part of the educational mix. The practice of many schools is simply to use the summer between the first and second year for an informal, noncredit internship.

At least five major benefits of the internship experience have been identified:

- Internships provide the opportunity to live in a second culture and to improve one's ability to communicate in its language.

- Internships provide the opportunity to work in a non-native business environment and to learn alternative approaches to resolution of managerial problems.

- Internships provide the opportunity for interns to affirm their job interests.

- Internships ease the transition from school to work environments.

- Internships enhance opportunities for full-time employment, either with firms that give the internship, or with firms with which the interns interact during the internship.

In developing an international internship program, the business school needs to resolve a number of issues related to student and program concerns, and some issues that are site-specific. Chapter 10, *Developing International Relationships*, addresses a number of these issues.

The following presents an overview of the issues related to internships:

- Should the intern be required to have or acquire proficiency in the language of the internship country?

- How long should the internship be? Most internships attempt to fit into the U.S. summertime period, and thus last a little less than three months.

- Should the internship carry academic credit?

- Should the internship be compensated?

- Who bears the responsibility for arranging the internship?

- How are companies assigned to students, and students to companies?

- How are internships evaluated?

- Who manages the internship process?

The decision to add an internship as a major part of graduate business education is an expensive one. It requires staff and travel funding. It takes students away from classroom learning. Yet the internship has enormous payoffs for participants, particularly if the academic program points *to* the internship (through business courses, language, and area studies) and then *through* the internship (advanced courses and placement). The internship can cause a visible change in personal and professional maturity of returning students, based on the confidence that they have obtained from functioning in a foreign business environment.

Component 3. Determine what faculty development activities the curriculum revision or new educational program requires.

The particular skills and experience of existing faculty play a major role in defining the business school's strategy, but it does not need to be the determining factor. Creativity, faculty development, and long-term faculty recruitment all become important factors.

Such faculty considerations are likely to include:

- Participation by current faculty members in faculty-development content seminars, in which they are trained in how to teach a course in the international dimension of a particular subject, or in how to infuse international content into a given core course.

- Participation by current faculty members in international faculty-development experience seminars, in which they are introduced to the business practices of certain regions through a study-tour mechanism.

- Provision of support for international research projects by current faculty members. Most nontenured faculty members have a specific research agenda designed to secure tenure, and it is difficult to involve them in international projects that divert attention from this agenda.

- International teaching assignments, including executive education activities, can provide an introduction to international business and to managers from other countries and cultures. Even short-term assignments, properly structured, have a substantial impact on the faculty members' point-of-view.

- Changed hiring policies for new entry-level faculty, stressing international content in doctoral training or international living and working experience, can be very useful.

- Hiring of scholars in international business or in the international dimension of a specific functional area is particularly useful. New faculty and current faculty adjusting their teaching program and research agenda, need support from senior faculty that can guide research and teaching, and stimulate thinking about international activities.

Component 4. Determine any organizational changes necessary to implement strategic changes, including creation of necessary cross-campus links.

There are two dimensions to the organizational issues: organization within the business school and the structure of relationships within the university, and the structure of relationships external to the business school. The second only applies to those schools that incorporate significant experiential and internship work in their graduate business degree.

Within the business school the issues are as follows:

- How does one position the organizational location of faculty members who conduct international research or provide international instruction? Numerous models have been developed. One approach is simply direct assignment of international faculty to existing business departments, possibly with some sort of designation that the individual has "international" responsibilities. A second concentrates these faculty in the management, or more rarely, the marketing department. More creative approaches involve the creation of some sort of international group to oversee international research and programmatic efforts, although the organizational motif remains one of department. Rarely, schools have formed separate international business departments. Schools that adopt the infusion technology of internationalization or the offering of functional field courses in international business can utilize the departmental assignment mode. Schools that have substantial separate programmatic international content may need a more concentrated grouping of their international talent.

- How does one position the organizational location of those who manage the international components of the international graduate program? If the program is separate from the traditional M.B.A. curriculum, are the two managed together or separately? Pure international programs typically are promoted to a different group of potential students and may in part be executed abroad. If there is a significant divergence between the two programs along the dimensions of location and participant base, the perceived increased cost of duplication of functions (e.g., admissions) may be illusory.

To the extent that the international business program incorporates instruction by nonbusiness faculty, business school administrators must establish systems to incorporate this activity into the management of the graduate business program. There are cultural distinctions between the departments on campus, and a number of differences between business and other faculty which can make smooth functioning difficult.

In arranging these *cross-campus linkages*, numerous issues, both academic and financial must be resolved:

- Where does the ultimate managerial responsibility for the program reside? The culture of responding to market opportunities by adding market value to the student that permeates thinking at many business schools is not necessarily the culture of departments in the remainder of the university. While a team approach might appeal to the post-modern manager, this philosophical conflict makes teamwork difficult. Active participation in decision-making by nonbusiness faculty is imperative, but in the era of borderless competition, focus must be maintained on delivering a program of both academic rigor and market value. It is best to sort these issues out in advance.

- What are the appropriate areas where nonbusiness departments should have reasonable autonomy? Area studies may view their participation on a nonprogrammatic course-by-course basis, but language proficiency will undoubtedly be in the dual domain of both language and business. In all instances, cooperation must rule.

- How is the flow of program funds managed? In particular, how are transfers to cooperating departments outside the business school determined? Probably the most fiscally sound, most practical, and most efficient approach is to have a unified program budget. While it may not be necessary to treat the program as a for-profit business, a complete understanding of the costs and revenues associated with the total program is essential for sound management.

In a sense, the business school is the educational customer of the modern languages and other departments that participate in these programs. While historically it is clear that this customer is not always right, it is also clear that the business school typically has the vision of what it wants the academic program to accomplish. That vision needs to be transmitted to other departments in such a manner that participation is fair and all parties can share equally in the program's success. Further discussions of these issues can be found in Chapter 7, *Building a Bridge to Liberal Arts*.

Component 5. Develop assessment activities to determine whether program goals are being met.

Conducting an assessment of outcomes is essential for the graduate business program. Part of the assessment activity is customer-driven. If initial placement and career paths of graduates are congruent with program goals, there is at least the presumption of effectiveness in the educational process in meeting the needs of the corporate customer base. For international programs it is especially important to track the type of corporate assignments graduates receive. Since, for some graduates, a good working knowledge of the chosen industry needs time to develop, it is preferable to study the career paths of graduates. Overseas assignments, assignments with international responsibility, assignments in which regional expertise or language skills are used, are all important to track. Starting salary distributions and rates of salary increase are important to track, as well, although graduates may be reluctant to provide such information.

Market tests can also determine if the goals of the participant base are being met. Growth in requests for information, growth in the quantity and quality of applications, higher acceptance rates (and of those, higher actual enrollment rates) are all strong indicators that the program is meeting real needs. Depending on programmatic goals, the geographic distribution of inquiries, applications, acceptances, and enrollments are also important to monitor.

It may also be possible and useful to evaluate the success of certain program components. When programs incorporate the development of second-language competencies, assessment of the level of student language skills is essential. Such evaluation is necessary for placement at the proper level of instruction, for assignment to internships or field study teams, and as indicators of readiness for academic course work conducted entirely in the nonnative language.

The key in assessment is sorting out the longer-term and shorter-term issues of program effectiveness and student satisfaction. Ultimately, one might assume that satisfied participant students are those for whom the program has provided efficient and sufficient training for those desired positions they will assume later in their career. However, satisfaction is measured in the past and present tense, and students, like all of us, can hardly see into the future. As graduates are followed into their futures, they can be asked periodically to reflect on and measure the program in a great many useful ways—indeed, in as many categorical ways as the program itself can devise to assess.

Chapter 12, *Evaluating Your Program*, provides additional information on this important component.

Component 6. Determine how to market the program to the identified constituency.

In designing graduate IB education, the needs of both student participants and business customers must be analyzed. Nowhere is this analysis more valuable than in the marketing of the program to these same important stakeholders.

In the early stage of internationalization of graduate business education, early movers such as Thunderbird and the University of South Carolina had a relative advantage in that their programs were designed specifically to produce international managers and were clearly and unambiguously designated as "international" programs. Both were able to rely on "name" recognition for student recruitment, and marketing could be based on selling the distinct experiences the programs provided in whole or part (language acquisition, geographically-directed business courses, and overseas internships). These degrees were marketed as an alternative, possibly a superior alternative, to a traditional M.B.A.

Schools that have chosen to internationalize an existing graduate business degree face the alternative task of convincing prospective students that the curriculum provides adequate IB managerial skills for the participant to become an effective international manager. Strategies for doing so include emphasis of the international content and international experiential aspects of the program. The particular method chosen depends on whether the school has heavily internationalized the core or whether specific international courses are now required in the curriculum. The former group tends to stress the overall commitment of the school to IB education; the latter, the availability of a wide range of international courses. Both can market any international educational components and highlight any summer internships done abroad by students. The necessary effect is the creation of an image of the school as an international player.

Potential IB students must be careful in evaluating how *international* any given program actually is. The most reliable indicators would seem to be the same indicators used by the school in tracking and assessing their graduates; unfortunately, such information is not readily accessible to applicants, except in the form of vignettes in promotional materials. Schools that have a comparative edge in inclusion of "international" in their curricula must still make a persuasive case in their published materials, and the careful applicant will look for programs where the international content is substantive and preferably tied to international experiential learning, such as internships or study abroad.

Component 7. Develop linkages with external constituencies to implement the program.

Most major internationalization activities require the development of both academic and corporate linkage for support. Business schools can enter exchange agreements with specific non-U.S. business schools, or become participants in global networks of academic institutions. Further, internship programs require the development of relationships with major corporations that do business abroad, and must be able to manage and maintain those corporate relationships.

On the academic side, student exchange or academic-service agreements should be developed only if they serve a strategic purpose. By student exchange agreement we mean an agreement that contemplates a two-way flow of students between academic institutions, or, in the case of multilateral exchange, among a number of institutions, with the obligation of each institution to receive and to send participants. An academic service agreement is one in which one institution provides academic services on behalf of another institution.

Once you have identified the activity you want or need to have conducted by another institution, you must identify potential partners and determine those that have the capacity to deliver and their willingness to work with you. Among the most obvious factors to be assessed are:

- The strategic or tactical objective that would motivate the potential partner institution to work with your institution.

- The quality of the facility, including computer access and libraries.

- The academic *and* business reputation of the institution in the host country.

- The likely compatibility of students at the host institution with those at your institution.

- The ease or difficulty for your students to operate in the locale of the host institution, in terms of language, housing, and the relative difficulty of day-to-day living.

Once an acceptable partner institution has been identified, approached, and found to be amenable, some sort of official agreement delineating the terms of the exchange or provision of service must be formulated. Given the inclination to litigate that typifies the U.S., a sound legal footing is important. You must overcome any inclination to proceed on a verbal agreement and friendly handshake. Agreements should include:

- Eligibility requirements for participation (which students at each institution are eligible for the activity).

- Performance requirements for participants (what constitutes acceptable performance at the host institution by guest students).

- Selection processes for participation at each institution.

- Financial requirements for participants and any institutional payments. There should be a clear demarcation between what students pay for and what the institution pays for.

- Academic issues, such as eligibility of guest students for specific courses at the host institution, credit to be granted by the guest students' institution for work at the host institution, and exchange of academic records.

- Exit provisions from the agreement, including terms for alteration, renewal, and termination of the agreement.

Business schools that are involved in developing international internship programs need to establish corporate relationships for this activity. Precisely how these relationships are developed depends in part on whether academic credit is granted for the internship. Summer interns who do not receive academic credit most likely will be the responsibility of the business school's placement office. However, if a substantial amount of academic credit is granted, and if the internship is required, the business school will no doubt do all of the subjective processing: arranging the internship, evaluating it, and assigning the credit. Additionally, internships require periodic visits for on-the-job performance evaluation and continuity of relationships. Internships with a corporate partner can lead to placement opportunities for other students.

Chapter 10, *Developing International Relationships*, provides more detail about the abundant possibilities of international relationships.

Component 8. Acquire the financial resources necessary for the program activities.

Internationalization of the graduate program can be expensive, particularly if the program involves substantial external activities. Major funding needs include:

- Faculty acquisition and development costs, including research support.

- Program marketing costs.

- Travel expenses for development of relationships with partner institutions and corporations.

- Support for student participation in program activities abroad.

- Payment to other institutions for academic services.

The program design needs to recognize that substantial economies of scale exist in international operations. Repeat visits to the same location on a trip abroad are probably superior to changing the venue every year, as experience indicates how the program can be improved and expenses reduced. The key is to find replicable experiences that meet program needs. On the other hand, the costs of mistakes and problems are magnified by the complexities of the international dimension. Poorly negotiated agreements, lack of specificity about internship arrangements, incomplete insurance coverage of students, and a host of other potential cost exposures enhance the risk of international operations.

There are three broad categories of funds that can be used to support internationalization: internal, private external, and public external. Business schools charge tuition for academic activities, and it is this tuition income and (for public institutions) general subsidies from the supporting government entity that the business school naturally considers a primary source of funds. Private support in the form of endowment and annual giving form the second level of funding. Finally, there are a number of public sector sources of funds specifically available for the internationalization of IB education.

The extent to which the business school's current budget and new allocations can be used for funding IB activities is subject to an enormous array of variables, including the will of the university and business school administration to make significant changes and support these activities. Additional budgetary restrictions may exist in public institutions to limit international expenditures. Study abroad and exchange programs seem to come under significant extra scrutiny, and are often required to be self-sustaining in some fashion. Insistence on strict exchange equality on an institution-by-institution basis tends to result in lack of use and cancellation of otherwise promising agreements designed to gain initial entry into a particular region.

Business schools must compete with other units on campus for allocations of funds, and rarely is there parity between the proportion of credit hours generated by the business school and the proportion of university budget allocated to it. Some universities have recognized this disparity and allow the business school to charge a more market-driven tuition to support graduate programs. Thus, it is important to look at the IB graduate programs themselves as a major source of funding, to the extent that these programs can attract additional students. New students may be non-U.S. nationals drawn to the main campus, or U.S. and non-U.S. nationals located at an overseas center operated by the business school. Sustainable programs need to be positioned to provide academic services in growing markets. Finding the appropriate market position and utilizing growth in numbers can in turn generate substantial cash flow for further international activities. Finally, the link to executive education is important. The business school's internationalization strategy may create important opportunities or a brand identity in sectors of the executive education market, opportunities that have significant revenue potential.

Business schools do have substantial access to private funding for activities, and the internationalization of graduate business education has provided a number of new opportunities for developing potential donors:

- Seeking personal support for a named center, named academic program, or named graduate school of international business.

- Seeking personal support for endowed named faculty positions in international business or in the international dimension of particular functional fields.

- Seeking foundation support for new curricular initiatives, either in international business, or for emerging disciplines with international content (e.g., international entrepreneurship).

- Seeking foundation support for internationally-oriented research for faculty development.

- Seeking foundation, personal, or corporate support for students involved in international activities.

- Seeking general support of international activities by alumni, particularly alumni of international programs.

A particularly useful exercise is to develop a portfolio of funding opportunities for planned international activities. This portfolio can be presented to university or business school development officers. When the university conducts a major capital campaign, elements of the portfolio can be incorporated in case statements and proposals to major donors. Development officers can play a major role. You should support them with creative IB ideas especially at those times when they are particularly focused on corporations.

Cultivation of alumni, particularly those that have international business ties, is another potential approach for generating leads for support. International business leaders are in a position, perhaps more than any other group, to recognize the need for IB education. The U.S. government has a number of grant programs that have as their purpose the enhancement of U.S. global competitiveness through support of internationalization activities discussed throughout this chapter. Chapter 4, *Funding Your Initiatives*, provides additional details on program funding.

The design of a funding strategy is an important part of the internationalization of graduate business education. If the institution needs to make massive curricular or operational changes, or if it needs to start a new venture, substantial new external funding is usually required. A less radical approach may be used if the school can adjust its existing graduate business program by significant but limited changes. Even so, internationalization is an opportunity to acquire external as well as internal resources. The key is to utilize these resources wisely in a course of action that makes strategic sense.

Final Note

Business schools are engaged in borderless competition to prepare managers to operate in a world where borders continue to exist; and conflicts, whether cultural, religious, ideological or racial, continue to divide. Business is often derided for its emphasis on profit and power, and business education is similarly condemned. When colors for academic regalia are handed out, the business M.B.A. graduate dons a color officially defined as "drab." Yet business (and with it, graduate business education) ultimately has a goal of some nobility, the efficient combination of resources to meet real human needs. Graduate international business education has emerged as a force for reducing global conflict and enhancing global prosperity. Business schools need to support international businesses by developing managers who can meet these challenges.

CHAPTER SEVEN

Building a Bridge to Liberal Arts

Steven J.
Loughrin-Sacco

What special skills do modern language and area studies faculty have in assisting business schools in their internationalization efforts?

Today's language educators are trained in communicative and proficiency-oriented language teaching. In addition to offering traditional one-hour-per-day courses, most modern language programs offer tailor-made, on-campus language courses for the business student, immersion courses to condense language study, as well as semester and year-abroad exchange programs with overseas business schools. Modern language faculty can also provide intercultural expertise through the study of literature and civilization.

Area studies faculty can play a major role in internationalizing business students by providing them with the political, historical, sociological, geographic, economic, and religious background to understand their future clientele in Latin America, Europe, Asia, Africa, the Middle East, and North America. Additionally, modern language and area studies faculty can strengthen exporting workshops (such as "Doing Business with Mexico") that business schools offer to small and midsize companies. Businesspeople value the historian's discussion of U.S.-Mexico political, economic, and historical relations, the economist's overview of the Euro and its impact on the strength of the U.S. dollar, and the French professor's discussion of differences between French and Québec business cultures.

But how does one go about working with modern language and area studies faculty? The goal of this chapter is to provide business educators with insights and strategies for developing and maintaining collaborative ties with their modern language and area studies colleagues. Successful collaborations at three business schools are described, demonstrating the payoff to be received by such interdisciplinary cooperation.

Rationale for Business and Liberal Arts Collaboration

Some business school professors and administrators have questioned the need to internationalize their curricula though the infusion of second-language and area studies courses. "English is the world's business language," they say. "It's a waste of time for our students to master a second language. The time they take studying languages and culture would be better spent taking more business courses." A closer look at the role of English in international business suggests otherwise.

English is the *lingua franca* of business in many countries because most U.S. businesspeople cannot speak the native language of clients or coworkers. In a study focusing on the languages used for work-related communication at TRW, Grandin and Dehmel reported that English is indeed the language used most in Germany between U.S. businesspeople and their German coworkers. However, when German employees communicate with their European coworkers, English is *not* the language used. Germans speaking with colleagues in Central Europe most often speak in German; Germans working with their Spanish counterparts typically use French. Grandin and Dehmel's most poignant finding is that European workers at TRW would prefer not to conduct business in English on their own soil. Speaking English at TRW sites in Germany has engendered resentment among German workers who feel that their U.S. counterparts should make every effort to speak at least some German while in Germany. It is highly likely that many workers worldwide share similar feelings.

Additionally, the use of English in business settings worldwide does not preclude the potential catastrophic damage to business activity that cross-cultural blunders can cause. One need only read case studies of the costly cross-cultural fiascoes committed by U.S. companies overseas (such as Disneyland Paris). English may be the world's leading business language, but monolingual English-speaking business practitioners will find it difficult to compete with those who speak the customer's language and who are sensitive to the customer's culture.

Roy Herberger, President of Thunderbird (The American Graduate School of International Management) and the past president of the AACSB, seconds the need for modern language and intercultural study for business students. In a 1998 keynote address entitled "New Corporate Global Strategies and the Impact on Specialized Language Instruction," Herberger identifies the new model under which top management approaches the challenges of economic and cultural globalization. Herberger states that this model "embraces the need for cross-cultural expertise that includes language facility for key personnel." In citing international recruiting trends, Herberger finds that international skills are now as important as functional skills. To illustrate, Exhibit 7.1 shows how top managers rated the following global and functional skills on a scale from one to five. Notice that after quantitative and analytical ability, international knowledge in a functional area and cultural or regional knowledge were the most important skills.

Exhibit 7.1

Most Useful Global and Functional Skills for Managers (1=low to 5=high)	
• quantitative analytical ability	3.90
• international emphasis in a functional area	3.89
• cultural and regional knowledge	3.82
• oral second-language proficiency	3.70
• marketing	3.62
• finance	3.55
• information technology	3.50

Source: Roy Herberger, 1998 keynote address presented at the Eighth Annual CIBER Conference on Language for Business and Economics.

Although previous studies (Machan; Fixman; Bikson and Law; Vande Berg) have questioned the need for second-language expertise, Grosse reported that corporate demand for second-language and cultural proficiency is increasing. Of the 3,000 job ads posted between 1995 and 1997 at Thunderbird and the University of South Carolina MIBS program, Grosse found that 56% of corporate recruiters preferred applicants with second-language skills and cultural knowledge. U.S. marketing majors among others share the corporate demand for second-language and cultural proficiency. Turley, Shannon, and Miller found that 61% of marketing majors believed that courses on a foreign culture should be required, while 53.7% thought that marketing majors should be required to study a second language.

It is clear from these findings that international business education is severely hampered without the study of modern languages and area studies.

Establishing Interdisciplinary Collaboration

It should not be surprising that collaborative endeavors are inherently difficult at most U.S. universities. In the current system, administrators encourage compartmentalization making individual departments the unit of administrative measurement. Each individual department has its own budget, curriculum, policies, and tenure and promotion guidelines. To further complicate matters, administrators set departments against one another in the quest for tenure lines, merit raises, and dwindling resources.

The current model discourages collaborative efforts such as interdisciplinary programs, team teaching, and the development of a cohesive general education curriculum. Administrators generally prefer not to grapple with issues such as determining which department will receive the student full-time equivalents (FTEs) in a team-taught course, in which department an interdisciplinary major will be housed, and how to evaluate interdisciplinary faculty research. Faculty who participate in interdisciplinary projects risk not getting tenure and promotion because these projects often do not conform to the traditional notions of teaching and research output. The result of the U.S. post-secondary administrative model is that philosophers generally work only with philosophers, engineers with engineers, historians with historians, and economists with economists.

Working with Liberal Arts Faculty

The first step in establishing collaborative ties with modern language and area studies faculty is to understand their inner workings. To use an analogy from the business world, you cannot be successful in business unless you possess a thorough understanding of your clientele and the market forces at work. The same holds true in the quest to attain cross-disciplinary collaboration. Before approaching or reapproaching members of the modern language and area studies faculty, you must first understand their background, research focus, problems, aspirations, and feelings toward their business colleagues. "Market forces" here refer to the increasingly difficult situation in which modern language departments find themselves due to dwindling enrollments and new exigencies.

Collaboration between business faculty, modern language and area studies faculty, can be extremely tricky because no two schools are more dissimilar than liberal arts and business. It may be useful to view the dissimilarities as analogous to the plethora of cultural dissimilarities existing between people in the United States and France. It is not necessary for the IB team to conduct a cross-cultural study of their liberal arts colleagues to establish a collaborative relationship, but it would be helpful to identify some of the differences.

The first dissimilarity between business and modern language faculty involves their different perceptions of the rationale for second-language study. Many business professors value second-language acquisition for practical communication, favoring greater emphasis on oral skills than on reading and writing skills. Additionally, they value second-language courses that are highly efficient. Conversely, many modern language professors, trained in literary studies in most instances, continue to view the study of languages as a means to read and analyze literature written by the masters of the language in question. Although the number of professionally-oriented courses such as "Business French," "German for Science and Technology," and "Spanish for Health Care Professionals" have greatly increased in recent years, modern language professors still dream of teaching upper-division courses on the nineteenth-century French novel, medieval Spanish poetry, or modern German drama. The ultimate goal of virtually every modern language department is to possess well-enrolled masters and doctoral programs in literature.

In teaching and research, modern language faculty generally focus on conceptual topics involved in literary criticism, such as post-modernism, hermeneutics, and semiotics, which are light years away from the practical fields of accounting, economics, finance, management, and marketing. Additionally, liberal arts faculty often possess an ideological perspective very different from the business school faculty, who, in their view, represent the negative values of U.S. capitalism. To further complicate matters, most liberal arts faculty are resentful of the higher salaries paid to their business counterparts.

Despite these differences, there are many modern language faculty who are eager to collaborate with their business counterparts. Since 1980, hundreds of modern language faculty have undergone retraining by completing workshops offered by the Paris and Madrid Chambers of Commerce, Germany's Goethe Institute, and many of the twenty-eight U.S. Centers for International Business Education and Research (CIBERs). Thousands of new courses in business Chinese, French, German, Japanese, Russian, and Spanish have sprouted up as a result. Many of the modern language faculty, who teach these business language courses, do so because they believe that a significant part of their departmental mission is to prepare future business practitioners, engineers, and scientists for the international marketplace (see Loughrin-Sacco). In the quest to establish collaborative relationships, the business college will discover that virtually every modern language department houses faculty with a practical bent to language teaching. These faculty tend to possess certain attributes in common, as shown in Exhibit 7.2.

Exhibit 7.2

Strategies for Developing Collaborative Ties

- experienced in teaching international modern languages for professional purposes
- eager to establish collaborative relationships with business and engineering faculty
- adaptable to creating a more practical second-language curriculum
- attuned to market forces to safeguard second-language enrollments
- often talented in securing external funding in support of international education

Returning to "market forces," modern language departments are undergoing significant changes that lend themselves to easier collaboration. First, enrollment figures in most languages have collapsed (Brod and Huber), forcing modern language departments to adopt a more marketable curriculum. For example, between 1990 and 1995, college-level enrollments in French fell 25%, German 28%, Russian 45%, and Japanese two percent. Conversely, Spanish increased 14%, and Chinese increased 36% making them the winners of the decade of the 1990s.

In the face of declining enrollments, many modern language departments risk losing the cherished major programs they have held for decades. One response to decreasing enrollments has been the appearance of courses under the rubric "languages for special purposes" (LSP). LSP courses are increasingly popular among students. It is not uncommon for LSP courses to have the largest enrollments in a modern language department. Surprisingly, business and engineering students are the largest group of consumers of LSP courses despite the lack of a second-language requirement in their respective majors.

Second, in the era of "doing more with less," modern language departments are expected more and more to secure external funding for curriculum development, scholarships, research, and the purchase of high-tech equipment. The U.S. Department of Education (US/ED), the primary provider of external funding, requires interdisciplinary collaboration in most of its funding programs. Thus, there are a growing number of modern language departments initiating the collaborative effort, knocking at the doors of business schools, colleges of engineering, and even colleges of agriculture interested in establishing alliances.

Strategies for Developing Collaborative Ties

In working together on international projects, the strategies presented in Exhibit 7.3 have been found to be especially effective. Collectively, the goal is to locate interested faculty, discover common professional interests, build a working relationship, seek approval from superiors, and develop projects that are successful for all involved.

Strategies for Developing Collaborative Ties

- approach modern language faculty and area studies faculty to discuss potential collaboration

- discover common professional interests and focus on relationship building

- be a guest speaker in each others' classes

- sponsor a regularly scheduled international forum on your campus

- develop collaborative activities that are win-win for all involved

Exhibit 7.3

Approach liberal arts faculty to discuss potential collaboration. Collaborative ties cannot be established without interacting with faculty, but should initial contacts be made between faculty or between administrators? Either strategy is workable. If you are a management chair, for example, it might be best to approach your counterpart in international modern languages, history, or political science. If you are a business dean, discuss possible collaboration with your counterpart in arts and sciences. If you prefer a faculty-to-faculty strategy, contact a colleague or colleagues in modern languages or area studies. If you do not know any modern languages and area studies faculty, get recommendations from your colleagues or department chair as to the person or people you should approach. Do not be discouraged if you meet individuals who are not at first receptive to collaboration. Keep in mind that you need not have the cooperation of the majority of a department's faculty to establish a collaborative relationship. If you fail in your first attempt to find a receptive counterpart, try again. It is a given that there is at least one faculty member in modern languages and area studies who will be interested in collaboration.

Discover common professional interests and focus on relationship building. Once you have made initial contact with modern language and area studies colleagues, discover common points of interest or bring up a project you already have in mind. In one case, a modern language professor saw the advantage of working with the department chair of social sciences and a new tenured faculty member in political science possessing a business background. They began work immediately on coauthoring a U.S. Department of Education-Undergraduate International Studies and Foreign Language (US/ED-UISFL) grant that they received in 1988. In 1990, the same modern language professor approached the business dean and a business faculty member to partner on a second UISFL grant project focusing on Russia and Eastern Europe. The modern language professor's approach in both cases was to describe the grant program and propose possible ways in which faculty members might participate. Using a more conservative strategy, you might simply start by getting to know each other and then discussing problems, aspirations, strengths, weaknesses, and potential future projects.

Be a guest speaker in each others' classes. Being a guest speaker in each others' classes is an excellent relationship-building activity. Business, modern languages, and area studies professors can address a wide variety of topics in each others' classes. Students in "Business French" classes, for example, will be interested in a business professor's discussion of the European Union, the Euro, trade conflicts, and cross-cultural business failures and successes. Conversely, business professors will find modern language and area studies faculty who can discuss the impact of language and culture on doing business abroad.

Sponsor a regularly-scheduled international forum on your campus. Collaborative efforts uniting business and liberal arts faculty at monthly presentations to discuss international issues can be a good way to enhance interdisciplinary cooperation. Faculty can organize the forums in one of two ways. First, the "brown bag" format can bring together internationally-oriented faculty from across campus to listen to each others' research. The second format entails inviting guest speakers to campus to discuss international topics. On one campus, Phi Beta Delta, the Society for International Scholars, sponsors monthly luncheons headlined by an off-campus expert. On another campus, the Office of International Studies sponsors a speaker's series where CEOs and other upper-level administrators from multinational companies are invited to discuss international topics. Either type of forum will facilitate communication among business, modern language, and area studies faculty.

Get your superior's imprimatur before embarking on major projects. Buttress the blossoming relationship by seeking the blessing from administrators such as department chairs and deans. Keep them apprised of your efforts. Your superior's approval is needed to submit new courses, programs, and grant proposals—and, in any case, their good will is invaluable.

Develop collaborative activities that are win-win for all involved. This seems an obvious strategy, but exploitative situations between business and liberal arts faculty are, unfortunately, all too possible and all too frequent. For instance, a grant proposal calling for cross-departmental participation should never be submitted without previous discussion and approval of all potential parties involved. Also, compensation, whether monetary or in terms of release time, should be both worthwhile and equitable.

Effective interdisciplinary collaboration must be long-term. If the liberal arts professor is a major project contributor, consider including him or her as a codirector in grant projects.

Apply together for external funding. Nothing strengthens budding collaborative ties more than the acquisition of external funding for joint curriculum development and research. Grant opportunities abound (see Chapter 2, *Charting Your Course,* and Chapter 4, *Funding Your Initiatives)* for business and liberal arts project possibilities.

Interdisciplinary Collaboration: The Payoff for Business Schools and Colleges of Liberal Arts

By way of example, three successful models of interdisciplinary cooperation between business and liberal arts faculty are presented here. In each case, interdisciplinary cooperation has led to the development of innovative programs and the awarding of major grants. Most importantly, as a result of their collaboration these three institutions have garnered a nationwide reputation in international business education.

San Diego State University

Interdisciplinary cooperation led to San Diego State University's successful CIBER and undergraduate international business program. Informal discussions began in 1985 between Mike Hergert, a professor of management, and Al Branan, a professor of French. While serving as chair, Branan discovered that more business majors enrolled in French and Spanish courses than liberal arts and sciences majors, despite the lack of a second-language graduation requirement for business majors. In response to student demand, "business language" courses were created in French and Spanish.

Building on this successful experience, Branan and Hergert decided to test the validity of an interdisciplinary international business program at SDSU. At first, Branan and Hergert advised their students to create their own special majors by combining a common core of business and international business courses, coupled with a minor in a second language and in regional studies. In its first three years of existence, the number of majors in the "International Commerce" program catapulted from nine to eighty-three. The program was renamed International Business in 1989 and now boasts more than 750 majors. SDSU's international business advisory committee is composed of an equal number of business, modern language, and area studies faculty.

Branan's and Hergert's collaboration in developing an IB program led to SDSU receiving one of the original CIBER grants in 1989. As one of the original six CIBER recipients, SDSU has been a leader in undergraduate international business education, as well as the teaching of business modern languages. Collaboration has made possible the development of MEXUS (a transnational dual-degree program with Mexican and U.S. business schools), and Project North America (a NAFTA-oriented degree with collaborating Mexican, U.S., and Canadian business schools), and the development of the National Business Spanish Examination. Interdisciplinary collaboration among business, modern language, and area studies faculty has transformed SDSU's business program into one of the most widely respected programs in the U.S.

Boise State University

Boise State University's College of Business and Economics and the Department of Modern Languages began in earnest to collaborate on a joint program in 1992. Nancy Napier, professor of management, and Steve Loughrin-Sacco, the incoming chair of Modern Languages, founded the program. Napier, who had served on the search committee for the new chair, met Loughrin-Sacco to discuss the possibility of adding a two-year second-language requirement to the newly established international business major. After this positive first step, Napier and Loughrin-Sacco coauthored and were awarded a two-year $128,000 US/ED Undergraduate International Studies and Foreign Language program grant in 1993.

The UISFL grant funded the development of new and revised courses in international business, new courses in business French, German, and Spanish, and several area studies courses. The grant also funded faculty development, the addition of library resources, and travel for research purposes. The UISFL grant was instrumental in the development of an innovative double major in international business and modern languages at Boise State. The double major, a four-and-one-half-year program, provides Boise State students with a complete business major and a second-language major which requires advanced-level language proficiency through the study of language, culture, literature, and civilization.

In 1994, Napier and Loughrin-Sacco received a two-year $147,000 US/ED Business and International Education (BIE) grant. The BIE grant, one of the few in the country involving business and modern language collaboration, sponsored a unique internship program in which students assist Idaho companies in following up the trade leads that companies have accumulated during trade missions. Interns use both their second-language skills to communicate with potential clients overseas and their business skills in conducting marketing research. The BIE grant also funded a "Doing Business within NAFTA" workshop that comprised a cross-disciplinary team of business, modern language, and area studies professors. In 1995, Boise State received a second two-year UISFL grant to create several second-language-across-the-curriculum courses within the business school curriculum.

Boise State's interdisciplinary collaboration is unique in that the business school houses several faculty who are fluent in a second language and are interested in interdisciplinary teaching. Two business faculty have taught the "Business Spanish" and "Business German" courses, sponsored by the department of modern languages. Their international business expertise, combined with their second-language fluency, provides students with insights that modern language faculty lacking business backgrounds cannot provide. In addition, two marketing professors have taken Boise State students to Mexico and Costa Rica where they have taught business courses in Spanish. A management and an accounting professor offer business courses that provide a supplemental one-hour trailer course that is taught in German for business majors who have at least an intermediate-level proficiency in German. Interdisciplinary collaboration among business, modern language, and area studies faculty has transformed Boise State's IB program into a model curriculum.

The University of Kentucky

Curt Harvey, an Austrian-born economist, encountered unique obstacles in establishing a highly-successful foreign language and international economics (FLIE) major. In the late 1980s, Harvey approached business school colleagues to propose a major combining other modern languages and business. The response of the business school was "We really don't need that." Undeterred, Harvey proposed the innovative major to his economics colleagues who voiced their approval. To solve the second half of the equation, Harvey needed the enthusiasm of his modern language colleagues who were scattered across four separate departments. To further complicate matters, Harvey's modern language colleagues were leading literary scholars who favored a classical literary curriculum (but who faced major enrollment drops). Harvey entered into negotiations with modern language colleagues with one appreciable asset. While serving as a K-8 school board member, Harvey had gained favor with his modern language colleagues by supporting the establishment of a second-language immersion school.

When Harvey proposed the bidisciplinary major, the modern language faculty were receptive, though wary at first. Would the new major lead to the eventual elimination of their current literature-based majors? Would faculty have to abandon their literary research? Would the new major incur new administrative costs? To create the new major in a second language and economics, each modern language department had to cut four to five courses from their existing literature-based majors.

The foreign language and economics major was funded through a BIE grant in 1989-1990. The major encountered obstacles at the chancellor's office and was not officially integrated into Kentucky's curriculum until 1994. Between 1994 and 1998, the number of majors has grown from five to ninety-six. Harvey reports that FLIE has attracted the best students at the University of Kentucky, their cumulative GPA rising a full half point higher than students majoring solely in either economics or modern languages. The modern language faculty are now ecstatic because enrollments in all their languages have increased as a result of FLIE. Currently, Harvey is seeking funding from the UISFL program to add a new wrinkle in the curriculum: the development of economic courses that will be taught in a second language. While the economics department thrives, Kentucky's business school has no immediate plans to incorporate a similar degree in their curriculum.

Final Note

U.S. business schools have been the envy of the rest of the world. Business schools worldwide are patterned in many ways after their U.S. counterparts—with one notable exception. European business schools value the study of several modern languages and their students accumulate cultural proficiency through extensive study of cultures in the curriculum and internships in other countries. Given the unquestionable international nature of business, it is time for U.S. business schools to add the study of modern languages and cultures to the current business curriculum as European business schools have already done.

The opportunities for U.S. business schools to collaborate with liberal arts faculty have never been better. Grant monies, emanating especially from the U.S. Department of Education, abound for programs promoting internationalization. Because of declining enrollments, modern language departments have become more attentive to the language needs of the professional schools. Additionally, more and more modern language educators are entering the field of languages for special purposes and they see the importance of working closely with their business school counterparts. Modern language faculty can provide tailor-made language training, immersion courses for condensed language study, and faculty who have overseas experience can provide instruction on a country's history, politics and government, geography, and economic systems.

The end product is an increased number of U.S. business professionals who are more fluent, more aware, and who commit far fewer blunders than their counterparts of earlier generations. Necessary benefits are increased sales overseas at a time when the U.S. is addressing a major trade imbalance, and an opportunity for the U.S. to preserve its preeminence as it sails on into the twenty-first century.

CHAPTER EIGHT

The Special Role of the Community College

Lourdene Huhra

Two-year colleges address three distinct student constituencies, and business programs offered to each of these groups are now slowly (although in greater and greater numbers) being internationalized.

The first group is students who plan to transfer to a four-year college or university and who are increasingly enrolling in international business courses or transfer programs. A second group is those who seek an associate degree in order to immediately enter the workforce, and who are choosing to enroll in courses or programs designed to provide them with the knowledge and practical skills to obtain an entry-level position in international business. A third group is employees currently in the workforce who are turning to courses offered in two-year programs to improve their global marketplace awareness and increase their international business skills. The community college has a special role to play in assisting all of these students with their international business education, and in this arena the community college is flourishing.

This chapter reflects on the data and extrapolates assumptions based on a survey of two-year colleges, developed and conducted by the author in 1998. The survey was distributed to individuals at colleges which have demonstrated an involvement in international business or international educational programming. The survey was sent to the following groups: recipients of funding from the U.S. Department of Education (US/ED) through the Business and International Education Program (BIE), members of the North American Small Business International Trade Educators (NASBITE), members of the American Council on International Intercultural Education (ACIIE), and respondents to a survey on global education conducted by the American Association of Community Colleges (AACC). There were fifty-four responses to the survey, from twenty-one states. The results of the survey instrument are referenced throughout the chapter as a means to highlight this special role.

Components

The survey responses revealed that outreach to the business community, in the form of short-term workshops, seminars, and contract training is a significant component of the international business programs at the majority of two-year colleges. Certificate programs in international business are offered more frequently than two-year associate degree programs. Colleges are also engaged in infusing international content into existing business courses. Faculty development programs, both in the U.S. and abroad, are a component of most college programs, as are linkages abroad and student internship programs. Exhibit 8.1 provides more detail on the components of international business programs offered at respondent colleges.

Exhibit 8.1

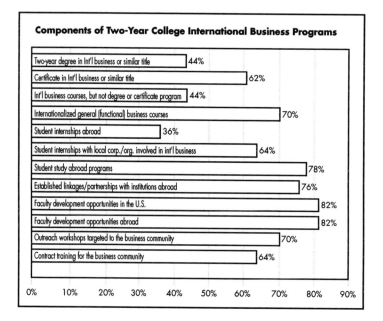

Components of Two-Year College International Business Programs

Two-year degree in Int'l business or similar title	44%
Certificate in Int'l business or similar title	62%
Int'l business courses, but not degree or certificate program	44%
Internationalized general (functional) business courses	70%
Student internships abroad	36%
Student internships with local corp./org. involved in int'l business	64%
Student study abroad programs	78%
Established linkages/partnerships with institutions abroad	76%
Faculty development opportunities in the U.S.	82%
Faculty development opportunities abroad	82%
Outreach workshops targeted to the business community	70%
Contract training for the business community	64%

0%   10%   20%   30%   40%   50%   60%   70%   80%   90%

A review of Exhibit 8.1 reveals that the activities included in the international business programs of two-year colleges are not significantly different from the activities of four-year colleges and universities. The design and implementation of these activities, however, will reflect the specific mission and populations served by the individual college.

Geography is an especially significant factor. In the survey, 74% of respondents were from urban areas, where the presence of international businesses is more likely. Location frequently determines the focus of the program, with colleges on the west coast oriented toward Asia, and colleges on the northern and southern borders of the U.S. oriented toward Canada and Latin America, respectively. The specific industries located in a community often influence the types of programs offered, with colleges developing expertise to meet local needs in diverse areas such as high technology, agriculture, light manufacturing, and tourism.

The presence of other institutions of higher education in the area is also a factor. Two-year colleges located in communities that do *not* have a local four-year college or university often experience significant success in offering courses and programs which are not unlike those offered by four-year institutions, such as international marketing and international finance. On the other hand, two-year colleges in communities served by four-year institutions often distinguish themselves by offering more practical courses and programs not offered by the four-year schools, such as export documentation and international transportation.

Developing an Internationalization Plan

Chapter 2, *Charting Your Course*, addresses the need for and development of a strategic plan for the internationalization of business education. This is the crucial first step. However, the context of this step may be significantly different for community colleges. The reality is that increased attention to internationalization is only a recent phenomenon for most two-year colleges. Therefore, it may be advantageous to consider the internationalization of business as a component of the internationalization of the college as a whole, and not as a "stand-alone" project. It is interesting to note that 96% of survey respondents reported that their colleges are involved in internationalization efforts in general, and 78% reported that internationalization is included in the college's mission statement.

The strategic plan for the internationalization of business education might best be developed as a part of the college-wide strategic plan for globalization. This would have a number of advantages for the business program. Business faculty and staff could take advantage of and build on college-wide efforts to internationalize that are already underway. There would be greater visibility and support for the effort, and it is likely that significantly more human and financial resources would be allocated. The effort would be better connected to other areas of the college, offering greater opportunity for partnerships and synergies with programs such as modern languages and area studies.

Therefore, it is recommended that business faculty and staff who desire to implement an internationalization program expand their initial development activities college-wide. An effective first step would be to advocate for the establishment of a college-wide international education committee. There is a wealth of useful information available through community college international education organizations that could be used to support this activity (some of these bibliographic and organizational resources are included in the *Chapter Reference Notes and Additional Resources* section at the end of this book). Establishment of such a committee would bring together like-minded individuals across disciplines to set the framework for the college-wide internationalization process. Business faculty and staff could then develop their strategic plan within a college-wide context to be consistent with other college-wide activities.

The guidelines for developing a strategic plan described in Chapter 2 are applicable to two-year colleges as well. The role of the champion is crucial to the establishment of an internationalization effort. In most institutions, even the smallest, a potential champion is probably already in place. It may be the person who has demonstrated an interest in international business or in other cultures. It may even be the person who knows nothing about international business but who is always on the forefront of new ideas and enjoys new challenges. In addition to having an interest in pursuing an internationalization strategy, the potential champion must have the personal capability to influence and lead other faculty and administrators in the effort. Ideally, the best person to play that role will emerge in the development process, and the college administration will recognize the person and formalize this individual's role. Survey responses revealed that the leader of the internationalization effort can hold a variety of positions in the college. In 36% of respondent institutions the leader was a faculty member, in 22% it was an academic administrator, in 34% it was a staff person (such as a director of international education), and six percent of institutions took a team approach.

The role of the local business community may be more significant in the development of a strategic plan for internationalization in two-year colleges than it is in four-year colleges and universities. Community colleges often have stronger links to the business community, and most have advisory committees which guide curriculum development and revision. It is important to utilize this expertise throughout the development of the strategic plan. It may be helpful to conduct focus groups or survey advisory committee members to identify their perspectives on the need for internationalization and how they would like to see the program internationalized. Their perspectives are invaluable in guiding the college's curriculum development efforts.

Building Support for Internationalization

Resistance to internationalization is an issue in most two-year college business programs, as it is in four-year institutions, and the challenge of faculty resistance is discussed in Chapter 2, *Charting Your Course,* and Chapter 3, *Winning Collegial Support.* When survey respondents were asked to indicate the top two challenges to their internationalization process, the issue of resistance was the second most frequently cited.

Faculty often initially question the relevance of international business courses in the two-year business curriculum, the need to internationalize functional courses, and their students' capacity to understand international business concepts. One excellent strategy for overcoming these objections is to ask members of the business community, as current and potential employers of the program's graduates, for their perspective. These employers will convincingly articulate how even the most entry-level positions require some level of international competence. Most are also willing to provide guidance on the specific requirements in particular program areas.

Useful strategies to build institutional capacity to counter resistance are also discussed in Chapters 2 and 3. A number are particularly relevant for two-year colleges, as many have only recently embraced the concept of internationalization, and need more time to fully develop and support an international vision. One very significant strategy for two-year colleges is faculty development.

Given that most community college business faculty members have limited education or training in international business, the need to enhance the expertise of faculty is a required first step in most colleges. As indicated in Exhibit 8.1, 82% of survey respondents indicated that faculty development programs both within the U.S. and abroad are in place at their institutions. Faculty take advantage of a variety of formal and informal faculty development activities such as national and international conferences, seminars and workshops, international study tours, guest speakers, and internships with local businesses. Some participate in the programs offered by the Centers for International Business Education and Research (CIBERs).

While these programs are of high quality and are certain to contribute to the participant's acquisition of international business knowledge and expertise, community college faculty must be certain to evaluate their relevance to and potential impact on their own teaching situations. It can be frustrating for the community college faculty attendee when all other participants are from four-year colleges and universities and have different perspectives and needs. The Michigan State University CIBER offers a biannual faculty development program exclusively for community college faculty, which has been very positively evaluated by previous participants. The distinctive feature of this program is that it offers participants the opportunity to use the framework of the community college curriculum as they learn more about international business issues. It would be ideal to have more programs such as these, at international as well as domestic locations.

Colleges should not overlook the potential for faculty development that lies within their local international business community. Many faculty have participated in formal or informal internship programs with local businesses, and all reported that the experience was extremely valuable. They gain not only experience in international business operations, but they also gain a mentor and a resource for curriculum development activities. These experiences often result in subsequent collaborations in a variety of areas. Business professionals can also be invited for in-service workshops, faculty meetings, and as guest speakers in classes.

International travel can have a strong impact on a faculty member's interest in and commitment to internationalization, especially in the case where faculty members have only limited experience beyond the U.S. Therefore, all types of international travel should be encouraged. When the college makes a financial investment in travel, however, the faculty member should be required to meet a specific internationalization objective, such as the revision of a particular course.

Curriculum Development

Two-year colleges have taken various approaches to curricular internationalization, and offer a range of options to meet student and community needs and interests, as indicated in Exhibit 8.1. Some colleges have elected to offer a two-year degree program in international business, either an associate in arts (A.A.) degree or an associate in applied science (A.A.S.) degree. Other colleges offer certificate programs, composed of four to six international business courses. A variation on the certificate offered by some colleges is the international concentration or track within a functional major, such as an international marketing concentration within a marketing program. Some colleges offer only stand-alone international courses as electives, and still others have concentrated exclusively on the internationalization of existing functional business courses.

In determining the optimal approach to employ, it is important that colleges identify and assess the needs of their students and the local business community. One disheartening note from the survey is that respondents indicated low enrollment in courses to be their most significant challenge. While there are a number of obvious reasons for small enrollments, this fact clearly underscores the importance of accurately identifying needs and interests initially, and continuing to assess them regularly. Colleges should examine the profiles and characteristics of their business students. Student intentions after completion of the program—whether they intend to transfer to a four-year college or university or plan to seek immediate employment—will impact the type of program developed.

The potential for articulation of transfer programs to four-year colleges and universities in the local area must be thoroughly explored. Colleges which offer courses that do not transfer credit will experience difficulty in meeting their enrollment goals. Colleges report great variability in their capabilities to secure effective transfer-credit articulation agreements. One frequent comment is that four-year colleges and universities prefer to offer the international business courses themselves, and will accept only lower-level business courses for transfer. Yet some institutions are quite successful in articulating their programs, which suggests that their success has more to do with the character and flexibility of the receiving institutions involved. In general, colleges report greater success in arranging credit transfer with private institutions than with public institutions.

When students' goals are for immediate employment, the needs and perspectives of the local business community are paramount. It is important to ascertain the career path for international business in the local community, and to identify the information and skills that students will need to enter the field. The assistance of an advisory committee of international business practitioners who hire or work with entry-level employees can be invaluable in the curriculum development process. This committee can provide assistance in identifying the type of program to develop, specifying the course titles and content, and providing advice and assistance in program marketing. Some colleges have utilized a DACUM ("developing a curriculum") process, through which entry-level employees in international business describe their responsibilities and tasks and identify the information and competencies they utilize to complete those tasks. This information is then used to determine the type of program to offer and to develop the program and course content.

Many two-year college programs rely on adjunct faculty from the business community as course and workshop instructors. Their expertise and real-world experience are well-received by students, especially those who are currently employed in international positions. Some colleges have paired their adjunct faculty with full-time faculty in a team-teaching situation. The adjunct faculty gain experience in course development and classroom management, while the full-time faculty benefit from the real-world experience of the business professionals.

In addition to the development of international business courses and programs, the internationalization of functional business courses is a significant component of two-year college business programs. A strategy that has worked for many institutions is to recruit advisory committee members with international expertise for all business programs. Their presence helps to educate faculty and other committee members alike on the internationalization of their industries and the topics which should be addressed in the curriculum.

Outreach Programs for Local Businesses

Workforce development is a significant component of the community college mission, and two-year colleges generally have well-developed outreach programs and infrastructures in place. As indicated in Exhibit 8.1, 70% of the survey respondents reported that they offered outreach programs to the business community. Respondents also indicated that business outreach was the second most successful component of their programs, after faculty development.

Chapter 9, *The Far Reach of Outreach*, provides a comprehensive discussion of the development of an international business outreach program, which should be useful to two-year colleges that are currently involved in, or considering, that activity. The most significant question for two-year colleges is the location of the international business outreach function. While Chapter 9 suggests that this function be a component of the business program, that may not be the most effective location within the two-year college. Most two-year colleges have offices or divisions that are charged with the outreach function, and have the infrastructure and resources needed to partner with the business community to develop and market effective programs. Colleges should consider whether there would be greater long-term success if that office were internationalized rather than attempting to develop a parallel outreach function within the business department.

Previous research on effective outreach programs at community colleges, such as the 1995 survey conducted by AACC, has shown that the outreach function is housed in a variety of locations within community colleges, depending primarily on the interest and commitment of the particular individuals involved. There are trade-offs associated with each location. Colleges should examine their own particular circumstances and determine the optimal location for their international business outreach activities. All relevant areas of the college (the business department, the office responsible for outreach activities, and the international education office) should be involved in this decision.

Significant Issues and Trends in Two-Year College IB Programs

Survey respondents were asked to describe the overall success of their internationalization programs. Sixteen percent indicated that their programs were very successful, 44% indicated that programs were moderately successful, and 26% indicated that programs were somewhat successful. Only two percent indicated that programs were unsuccessful, and 10% reported that their programs were struggling. The most successful program components at respondent colleges were domestic faculty development, outreach programs, student study abroad programs, international business courses, and international linkages. The least successful program components were student internships, contract training for the business community, certificate and two-year degree programs, and student and faculty development opportunities abroad.

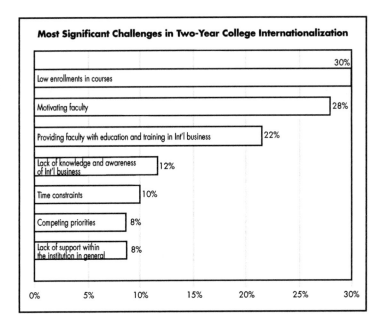

Most Significant Challenges in Two-Year College Internationalization

Challenge	Percentage
Low enrollments in courses	30%
Motivating faculty	28%
Providing faculty with education and training in Int'l business	22%
Lack of knowledge and awareness of Int'l business	12%
Time constraints	10%
Competing priorities	8%
Lack of support within the institution in general	8%

Exhibit 8.2

Two additional questions were included in the survey to challenge and address important issues for the future. Survey respondents were asked to list the most significant challenges they encountered in their internationalization efforts. Exhibit 8.2 summarizes these responses. Respondents were also asked to indicate their perception of the issues that would be most significant to the future of internationalization in two-year colleges. Exhibit 8.3 summarizes the responses to this question.

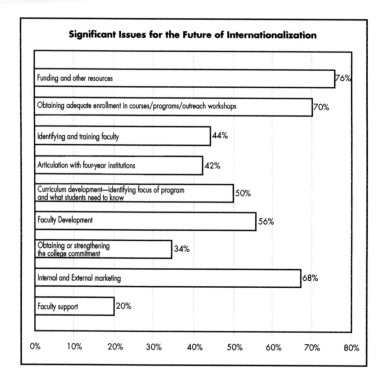

Exhibit 8.3

Significant Issues for the Future of Internationalization

Issue	Percentage
Funding and other resources	76%
Obtaining adequate enrollment in courses/programs/outreach workshops	70%
Identifying and training faculty	44%
Articulation with four-year institutions	42%
Curriculum development—identifying focus of program and what students need to know	50%
Faculty Development	56%
Obtaining or strengthening the college commitment	34%
Internal and External marketing	68%
Faculty support	20%

It is not surprising that funding was the most frequent response, as it often appears as an issue in surveys of this type. While no one will dispute the value of financial support, there are a number of colleges which have done very well without substantial funding, and a number which have done poorly despite an influx of funds. The presence of other resources, may be more significant for the future success of international business programs. These resources include sufficient release time for the person who leads the internationalization effort, adequate clerical and administrative support, and appropriate access to college resources such as curriculum development specialists. The presence or absence of these resources can greatly impact the college's ability to secure external funding, as grant applications will only be successful when the necessary staff and resources are in place to implement the proposed project.

It is important to note that the majority of survey respondents have received federal funds to support their internationalization efforts. Many have received grants from the U.S. Department of Education: 62% from the Business and International Education (BIE) program; 36% from the Undergraduate International Studies and Foreign Language (UISFL) program; and 64% from a variety of other federal, state, local, and institutional programs. Thanks to the effective relationships developed between the two-year college community and US/ED Title VI program officers, two-year colleges now have a level playing field in competition for these seed-money grants. Two-year colleges are regularly encouraged to apply, and are offered useful technical assistance in developing their proposals. Two-year colleges are becoming more competitive in other federal grant programs as well. It is necessary, however, to continue to increase the number of two-year colleges that apply for federal grants. The more that community colleges apply for these grants, the more familiar the program officers will become with the mission and programs of two-year colleges. This will undoubtedly lead to increased funding levels. For further discussion of federal granting possibilities, see Chapter 4, *Funding Your Initiatives.*

Another significant issue raised is the difficulty in obtaining adequate enrollment in programs, courses, and outreach workshops. It is extremely disheartening to develop and market a program and obtain only limited response. Nonetheless, this has happened to many institutions. It may be that they misread the market, or tried a new idea for which the market was not yet ready. If limited response occurs regularly, however, it becomes a serious issue which is best analyzed and addressed at the level of the individual college and community. It may be that full-time employment has negatively impacted enrollment in all programs at the college. It may be that the number of offerings by institutions and organizations within the service area is too great for the more limited demand of businesses. It may be that regular participants in programs no longer have the time and flexibility to attend. Or it may be that programs, courses, and workshops of a competitor institution better meet the needs of the community.

Competition for the relatively small market of students and employees interested in international business education and training is a reality in most communities, especially those in which there are new providers regularly entering the education and training marketplace. Some two-year colleges have reduced the number of their offerings in response to competition; others have developed new programs or revised existing programs or delivery formats; and others have facilitated coordination of offerings among the providers within the community. Those who are experiencing a decline in enrollment are encouraged to address the issue systematically, and should do so with the assistance of members of the business community. A thorough marketing analysis should be conducted, giving attention to market changes and needs, the competition, the types of programs offered, the marketing plan, and the delivery format and location of the program.

A related issue highlighted in the survey is the need for internal and external marketing. There may be a perception within the local community and within the institution itself that it is not appropriate for a two-year college to offer international business programs, or that the college is not capable of doing so. Consistent and regular messages about the college's activities and success will raise the visibility of the program and contribute to future success. The need for public relations activities is an idea that many educators resist, perhaps because they lack experience in this area and the tasks can be very time-consuming. Yet frequently there are appropriate staff in the college who can provide effective marketing assistance. Another strategy is to recruit a representative of a local advertising agency to the program advisory committee. That person can be assigned the task of developing and coordinating a public relations program.

Other issues raised in the survey were curriculum and faculty development. Two-year colleges must continue to assess the needs of local businesses, and maintain an awareness of trends which may impact local businesses in the future. If, for example, local international businesses are moving toward an international product strategy and organizational structure, how will that impact their entry-level hiring and the skills they will be seeking? The presence of an active advisory committee is crucial to the college's understanding of the changes that must be made in curricula to assure that their students will be competitive in the local marketplace. At the same time, faculty skills must be upgraded regularly to insure that they are capable of providing the quality of education and training that is needed.

Final Note

Results from the survey conducted for this chapter clearly indicate that internationalization is becoming increasingly important in two-year colleges. Business departments report considerable success, but face a number of challenges as well. Faculty and administrators are encouraged to seriously address these challenges so that their programs can be even more effective models for those who are just beginning to internationalize. Those who have not yet begun to internationalize, or who are in the beginning stages, are encouraged to take advantage of the expertise and experience of their colleagues by joining appropriate professional organizations and networking. The role of the community college in adding value to international business education is becoming increasingly important because of its special mission. For this reason, the time for international business education in the community college is *now*.

CHAPTER NINE

The Far Reach of Outreach

**Brian Gauler
and Joop Bollen**

Given today's dynamic and lightening-fast business environment, meeting managerial needs reaches back to our academic institutions: and what better way to address these changes and gain an understanding of how to meet them than through an outreach program to the business sector. There are numerous direct benefits that can be realized with such programs. Most importantly, these include opportunities for faculty and students to participate in meaningful ways with business. In many instances, outreach is also a natural extension of already existing facilities that the institution has available. Faculty in the various disciplines of marketing, finance, management, and information systems can often be identified as resources for an international outreach program.

Involving faculty and students in staff support functions, such as market research, can have productive outcomes for all parties involved. Most companies have limited managerial staff, and they are usually totally committed to line functions supporting the sales and marketing effort. As a result, basic staff functions or planning and research are often never accomplished. This can provide an excellent opportunity for faculty and students to assist business with specific secondary (or, in some cases, primary) market research. Such services can be performed through classroom participation, special projects, or other specific means. They provide a real-life experience for the faculty and students, and are usually a much needed form of support by the firm.

There are also potential funding benefits. Businesses are generally willing to pay for services received when they have value. This does not mean that an outreach program should necessarily be run like a business on a fee basis. However, offering programs and services that have value to a firm does create fair income opportunities, while at the same time establishing relationships that can serve as related benefits for the institution, such as job placement for graduating students. In addition, a well-received outreach program can greatly enhance the institution's image both within the business community and with the general public. To take advantage of these opportunities, in this chapter we discuss the integral components to develop and implement an international business outreach program.

The Culture Gap Between Academia and Corporate America

It is very important to the success of any international business outreach program that it be based on the type of business practices that companies are accustomed to receiving from private-sector service firms. This means the outreach program must take a business service approach. It is understandable that those firms that can best be served by an outreach program are the ones that need help *now*. Conceptionally, this can be in conflict with the way in which faculty focusing on research and the administration of education are accustomed to operating. In the business world, time is often truly money, and this is nowhere more true than in the global marketplace.

Another cultural gap that needs to be bridged is that of faculty staffing. When initially establishing an outreach program, there are two faculty issues that must be taken into consideration: that of integrating the program into the institution, and that of best serving the intended clientele. These needs generally require different academic qualifications.

That is, the administration and integration within the institution of such a program can usually best be accomplished by utilizing existing faculty, or a person with standard faculty credentials. The two main functions of this individual, often called the IB champion, generally are fund-raising and integration of internationalization into the institution. Since they will be dealing primarily with faculty and administration, in particular deans and department heads, they should have the same academic credentials as those they are working with. On the other hand, when it comes to teaching, academic credentials are generally not perceived by the business community to be as positive as actual experience and first-hand expertise. This is especially the case with international issues since they generally require technical expertise in addition to knowledge of common standard business practices.

In many cases, particularly for the start-up phase, a faculty member can serve as a program administrator on a time-release basis. Although this might be considered for administrative aspects of the program, it would not be recommended for the service aspects. Whoever is selected to develop and manage the implementation of the program should have qualifications most acceptable to the businesses being served. Generally this is a person with business background, preferably with some international, export and international marketing experience. However, once the outreach program has developed specific export-related programs and services, it may be possible to manage such a program with a minimum of business experience.

Roles and Activities

Types of Outreach

There are many ways that an international outreach program might serve the business community. These include aspects of importing, direct international investments, translations, research, and training. However, most programs start with a focus on exporting, implementing programs, and services to assist firms to start exporting, or to improve existing export efforts.

This is a logical first step for various reasons. Exporting is perhaps the single most effective way for creating economic development within most communities, both metropolitan and rural. It has the most potential for identifying needs in the business community, and is often overlooked as a means for sustaining community development. Interestingly, both state and federal government agencies have identified the need for assisting U.S. firms with exporting, and have created numerous funding opportunities for institutions to serve those needs. In addition, all states will already have some type of existing infrastructure that is available to help firms with exporting, but seldom is it sufficient to meet the demand, particularly in the area of education and training.

Individual Roles

The most readily identified potential roles for faculty and students to assist businesses in international trade are in the area of *staff* functions. These are generally defined as those functions that support the line functions of marketing and sales, and often focus on market research. Other staff functions include aspects of preparation of materials used in exporting, such as international sales programs, various forms that assist the company's efforts, and for promotional materials like news releases, public relations, newsletters, product and sales literature, and other printed materials as determined by the company.

Market Research

There are some very natural roles in which an academic institution can provide assistance to business, and one of these is conducting secondary market research. This can involve faculty, staff, and students, and provide a major contribution to the firm that has limited resources. In addition, there is a wealth of information already available to assist the firm. In fact, there is usually more information than they can initially use. Simplifying market research for a firm can provide a significant service and meet an initial key need.

International market research for local firms leads to numerous opportunities for other types of analysis that students can provide, particularly with the help of faculty. Additionally, this same type of data-gathering can be applied to other areas of interest, such as international marketing reports, CIA country reports, State Department background notes, Foreign Trader's Index, and myriad other information that is readily available, including the National Trade Data Bank (NTDB). In fact, this type of service can be expanded to the point where specific secondary market research reports can be developed for firms by student teams under the direct guidance and supervision of a faculty member, and usually for a fee. Companies that would like to gain more knowledge about a particular part of the world, or specific markets, usually do not have a staff to perform such research.

Training Programs

There are four key areas always considered essential for export training. These are (1) marketing, (2) transportation (shipping and documentation), (3) banking (payment and trade terms), and (4) legal. Most training programs focus on aspects of these four key areas. However, most academic institutions have two other areas that can readily provide resource expertise. Those are in language and culture.

Of these four key areas for exporting, the business school normally can provide expertise in the marketing, finance, and transportation areas. Some aspects of marketing, such as advertising and promotion, are often located in other schools (such as journalism, or arts and sciences). Legal issues usually focus on contracts and intellectual property rights, and if the institution has a college of law, one would look for assistance there. Special industry sector interests, such as engineering and agriculture, are located within their respective colleges. Some areas are often best left to the private sector service providers, such as international bankers, freight forwarders, insurance agents, and legal counsel. If a specific resource for a specific export need doesn't exist within your institution, you may ask faculty to help you network to find a resource for the need. Another excellent resource is the nearest world trade professional organization, since their members are all export-oriented and basically either manufacturers or providers (service companies and organizations).

Modern language and culture resources are generally available at most academic institutions, particularly those that have a large international student population. However, language training can be difficult to provide to business professionals, since both students and managing faculty would like shorter-duration training and less personal commitment. Fortunately, most language schools already have some intensive programs in place that can meet the needs of the business community.

Cultural training has, over the past few years, taken on much more significance for U.S. business. Much of this is attributed to the globalization of business that now reaches all levels. This has numerous repercussions, one of which is an increased number of international visitors that come to the U.S. to attend major national domestic trade show events. U.S. businesses are realizing the importance of these visitors, and are more actively recruiting them to visit their factories and facilities. This has increased the need for knowing more about international interpersonal relationship skills, and many companies are actively seeking help in educating their managers and staff.

Some institutions tap into this market by offering specific country (or area) training, utilizing international faculty and students associated with the school. Generally the training is developed by qualified faculty who use nationals to assist in the actual training. It can be very effective to have a native of a particular country explain to a U.S. business professional just how business is done in their country, and what social graces and business etiquette they should be aware of. When this can be combined with some language training, it meets an important educational and practical need.

Building the Programs

There are numerous ways an international outreach program can be established. In addition to determining what method or combination of methods you want to use, you should also take into consideration two other factors: (1) the institutional strengths available to the program, and (2) the market need.

Depending on the area being served, these factors can vary tremendously.

For example, institutions located in metropolitan areas will find that many business needs are being met by private sector services and state and federal agencies. This is particularly true for those special export needs that tend to be more technically-oriented or require expertise based on experience. Institutions located in metropolitan areas also tend to attract more international students and faculty that can provide the language and cultural expertise often not found in rural areas. Institutional strengths are key to serving market needs. That does not preclude trying to meet needs when expertise is not readily available locally, since experts can be brought in as needed. For the most part, however, ongoing services should be based on available expertise.

For an outreach program to be successful, it must be geared toward what is needed in the market area that is being served. One way to determine what needs are being met is to gather information about the services provided by all the existing export service providers in your area. By initially focusing on what is available, you can more readily determine what services you might want to provide. In addition, identify the types of programs that have been provided by other similar academic institutions in their international outreach programs. This can be done by obtaining abstracts of those receiving federal grants to support their outreach program activities. Simply contact the U.S. Department of Education, Business and International Education (BIE) program office. They will be quite willing to provide you with that information.

Once you have a general understanding of the types of needs that exist, you need to determine the needs specific to your area. One way to do this is to collect brochures from service providers. They will give you a general idea of the programs and services available.

It helps to establish a positive working relationship with other service organizations right from the start. Letting existing organizations know that you are interested in cooperation and not competition creates a positive environment for all parties. It can also lead to the kind of synergistic program development that will best serve the business community and avoid potential problems of "turfdom."

Most state and federal programs that provide export services focus on international trade promotion and overseas contacts. They tend to avoid getting involved with education and training programs, thus providing many collaborative possibilities. This is particularly true of commerce and agriculture agencies which promote their services for the "export ready" firm.

One key way to foster the spirit of collaboration is to always include other service providers in educational events you may be promoting, especially training seminars. By adding them to your list of sponsors, they receive additional recognition and are perceived as being team players supporting your program. Since they are often evaluated on their effort to work with other service organizations, you are also providing them a direct means for better performance results. Second, the established export service providers already know the business community that you intend to serve. By identifying what providers are doing and who they are serving, you can quickly understand where you best fit and what programs and service needs you can provide.

In addition to contacting these service providers directly, to complete the picture it is strongly recommended that you also do primary market research by contacting the business community. This, too, can lead to opportunities for establishing key relationships with other existing stakeholders. For example, working with local chambers of commerce, economic development agencies, and other governmental and private organizations that are currently (and directly) serving the business community are several ways to reach the businesses you want to survey. At the same time, it establishes a cooperative working relationship and positions your outreach program with the already known key players. The section at the end of the book, *Chapter Reference Notes and Additional Resources*, provides a comprehensive list of federal, state, local, and private sector international trade service providers.

Identifying Your Potential Client Base

Since there are a growing number of U.S. businesses interested in international trade, many apparent opportunities of seemingly great potential will present themselves. It is therefore very important for any outreach program to keep in mind the fundamental reason for that program: economic development. With limited staff and budget, the focus must remain on helping established firms research and develop international sales and distribution.

In general, your *client base* is going to be local manufacturers, those firms that are producing a product and already selling successfully in the U.S. This will become even more apparent as you understand the focus of the state and federal agencies which generally concentrate on trade promotion services: making contacts overseas with potential distributors and other international trade representatives. There are obviously more aspects to international trade than exporting (such as importing, joint ventures, and licensing technology). However, as an educational institution, generally the focus will be on providing structured information and training that will assist firms in obtaining a foothold in international markets.

As a start, it is suggested that you determine some type of *company profile* to describe the size of firm that you think you can best serve. For example, some outreach programs have a profile for a firm as follows: sales of $1 million or more, a minimum of twenty employees, and two years of successful domestic sales. By establishing this type of profile, you can usually prequalify those firms that can best use your services. This can also help you avoid spending too much time trying to help home-based businesses, microenterprises, and others which lack sufficient resources (people and money) to enter international markets. Although the above profile suggests a minimum requirement of sufficient resources, it might not be applicable for firms in your specific area and you may choose to adjust it.

Your potential success at attracting clients will not happen overnight. It is very important to stay focused and build your program one service at a time. You will be principally working with companies who are new-to-export, and they will require a lot of time and patience (theirs *and* yours) to work through the export development process. By sticking with them and providing assistance each step of the way, you can establish your program as offering pragmatic services that produce results.

Understanding the Export Development Process

In order to determine what services your international business outreach program might most usefully offer, it is helpful to understand the process that a company goes through as they look beyond their domestic borders. This is referred to as the *export development process*, and can be explained as four basic phases (see Exhibit 9.1).

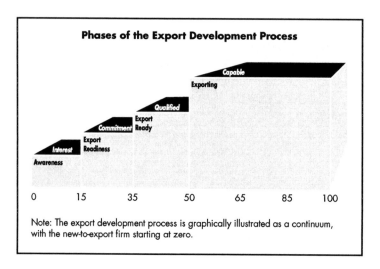

Phases of the Export Development Process

Exhibit 9.1

Capable
Exporting

Qualified
Export
Ready

Commitment

Export
Readiness

Interest

Awareness

0   15   35   50   65   85   100

Note: The export development process is graphically illustrated as a continuum, with the new-to-export firm starting at zero.

(1) *Awareness and interest.* Most firms start by serving their domestic market, either locally, regionally, or nationally. Usually they have not considered their international market potential. Even if they have, they often prematurely conclude that they do not want to participate in exporting because they do not understand it. It is a known fact that most small to medium-size U.S. manufacturers do not explore their global market potential simply because they have very little knowledge of how to go about it.

This first phase of export development, awareness and interest, is generally the prime challenge for an international outreach program.

(2) *Commitment and export readiness.* Once a firm becomes aware of its international trade potential, it needs to prepare to enter international markets. This is referred to as becoming *export-ready*, and represents the *key niche* for an outreach program. In fact, this need for export-readiness is basic to a firm's ability to use the trade promotion programs and services offered by state and federal agencies. Both the U.S. Department of Commerce, and state departments of economic development, promote their services for the *export-ready* firm, yet neither generally have education nor training programs specifically focused on readiness. This phase of export-readiness is often the single greatest opportunity for service by the school's international outreach program.

(3) *Qualified and export-ready.* As a firm begins to learn about aspects of exporting and international trade in general, they reach a point where they are considered to be export-ready. At that time, they are qualified to use the numerous trade promotion services available from the federal and state export service providers. This phase of a firm's export development process tends to be the one that is most visible and creates the most excitement since its goal is to promote the firm overseas and establish sales and distribution. Many international business outreach programs will have select services to assist the firm in this area of their development, but generally this is the domain of the existing federal and state assistance services. It is during this phase that a firm truly becomes involved in exporting. They obtain orders, and begin to face the myriad issues associated with the actual export. For the international outreach program, it is a time to provide specific export training and services of a more technical nature.

(4) *Export-capable.* The *final* phase of a firm's export development is the ongoing process of entering additional markets. In fact, most firms will remain in this phase for the duration of time that they are involved in global marketing

and international trade. The U.S. Department of Commerce refers to this as *new-to-market,* and uses it as a criterion for determining the success of their trade specialists' activities. In practice, all exporting firms will have issues associated with this phase since global markets are subject to constant change.

This phase of exporting provides opportunities for a university-based international outreach program to help the firm keep abreast of world events and further hone their international expertise in disciplines of language, culture, and other relevant contact areas.

Elements of an Outreach Program

Roles for the Service Provider

Three roles that provide a solid base for developing an international outreach program are awareness, networking, and facilitating. These are defined as follows:

- *Awareness.* Alerting firms to their potential for international marketing.

- *Networking.* Helping firms to identify where they can obtain specific exporting assistance.

- *Facilitating.* Assisting firms to understand the basics of international marketing and how to get started, identifying specific export services they need, and helping them obtain those services.

Identifying these roles for your international outreach program can also serve as a basis for establishing the types of services you want to provide.

Creating awareness can be accomplished by providing firms with information about their specific international market potential. This can be accomplished through secondary market research, using students and faculty. Once a firm is alerted to their potential, they will generally want to actively pursue those opportunities, but usually do not know how to get started. They need to understand who is available to help them.

Networking assistance can be another major role for your program as most new-to-exporting firms will not have a working knowledge of the federal and state programs and services available to them. This generally leads to *training* opportunities for your program to initiate once the full extent of the education needs are determined.

Facilitating simply means bringing awareness, networking, and training together in a way that ultimately leads to export readiness. Training programs may, and often do, utilize available private sector expertise. These businesspeople are generally eager to assist, since it is an opportunity for them to gain new clients. While it is important to keep in mind that not every good business professional makes for a good instructor, it is perhaps even more important to keep sight of all the positive factors of such arrangements. The college provides the logistics for the training program, and the private sector provides the expertise for the content. The firm receives the information they need.

Program Development

Once you have determined that you are going to create an international outreach program, and define for yourself the services you plan to offer, it is very important that you establish with the other service providers in the area an understanding of exactly who and what you are. When they are comfortable that you will be working with them (and not competing against them), they will more readily help you establish credentials within the business community by working cooperatively with you. Just having an affiliation with other service providers is a testimonial to their acceptance of your program.

Businesses are accustomed to having easily available information from their service providers, so it is equally important that you create communication tools to let others know about your program. You may want to start rather *low key* with your promotional efforts, at least until you have some successes or greater assurance of the reception for your programs and services. This might be as simple as having desktop-published materials explaining your program and using it to see what kind of response you receive.

Since you will have limited staff and budget to provide your services, it is clearly better to do a few tasks well rather than attempt many tasks and risk failure. Promoting your programs one step at a time will help you to carefully manage your program portfolio. It will also allow you more time to determine actual needs that you can serve, which may be different in practice than what you determined in your preliminary research. Once you can establish a good working relationship with a few firms and service agencies, you will gain credibility which will result in natural growth for your program. Completing one project at a time will often lead to successfully managing multiple projects once you have some experience.

One way to facilitate multi-tasking is with training programs. Those firms who participate in a training program become candidates for other services you might offer (facilitating, counseling, market research, and other training). Recruiting firms to a training program then becomes a first step in providing them with services. As noted in the section on the export development process, your initial efforts might simply focus on creating awareness within the business community that you want to serve. Once a firm becomes aware of their export potential, that interest can be further developed through training. Creating awareness can be a recruiting tool for your training programs, which in turn provides you with clients for your follow-up services.

Working cooperatively with other service providers is perhaps one of the easiest and quickest ways you can build acceptance for your program and service delivery. Developing cooperative efforts with community stakeholders is often the best way to expedite your program's acceptance. This cannot be over emphasized. And it can be as simple as making sure you participate in every activity that includes the other service providers. When you include them in your activities, they naturally reciprocate and invite you to participate in their programs. Keep in mind that it is also beneficial to them to be networked with your institution: benefits flow both ways!

Funding Your Program

Most funding programs available to higher education institutions focus on two components: internationalization of the business school curriculum, and an effective outreach program. Since you will be establishing the outreach component, it is important that you position your program with the curriculum which in turn means involvement of faculty and students.

One of the keys to obtaining funds is your attitude. If you treat funding as *seed monies*, working capital to create self-sustaining programs based on market demands, you will immeasurably increase your chances for receiving funds. Outcome-based funding that creates value and catalyzes development is the most appropriate way to start an outreach program. Chapter 4 and the relevant section in Chapter 2 discuss funding in detail.

Sourcing Your Program

Sourcing your outreach program must take into consideration three aspects: people, facilities, and budgets. Although there is no set minimum for staffing an outreach program, to be effective it should have at least a full-time director, part-time secretary, and access to institutional resources for program support. In order to be effective with such a limited staff, the director must be a self-starter with sufficient export experience to make a positive impression in the business community.

Selecting from faculty for this position can often lead to problems, since a director with a terminal academic degree may be more effective with institutional aspects of integration and fund-raising, but may not be perceived as capable of meeting the needs of the business community. Conversely, a director with business acumen will be readily acceptable to the business community, but may have difficulties integrating the program into the institution.

By creating programs and services that focus on needs of the new-to-export firm that require less initial export expertise, a director with a general understanding of marketing can be effective. Expansion of the program into areas requiring more export expertise can often be accomplished by using outside private sector resources.

Attention should be given to the facilities in which the program is housed. Since the focus of the program is outreach and the service to the business community is off-campus, accessibility to clients should be given priority. Often overlooked, something as basic as a conference room can be a great asset to the program. Most academic institutions have facilities that reflect an educational environment, which is not particularly conducive to working with businesses. Holding a consulting session in a classroom with a business client gives the wrong impression. If the client has to struggle with parking and locating the program somewhere on-campus, this, too, can be detrimental to the credibility of the program.

Developing the operating budget for an international outreach program need not be that complicated. Standard aspects of the budget should include staff salaries and benefits, equipment and operating expenses (printing, postage, telephone, supplies, memberships, and subscriptions), and travel. Do take into consideration some limitations that might exist for normal day-to-day travel expenses. They are often based on faculty participation at conferences, and not always realistic for business expenses. This can be particularly important in the case of international travel, which will probably be a part of your international outreach program at some time. One way you might get a realistic idea for your budget is to ask other comparable organizations what expenses they incur in their programmatic work.

Networking Your Program

Another key element in the development of an international business outreach program is to build your internal support team, often called an *advisory committee*. If carefully chosen, this group of select leaders can provide many benefits. Members of the advisory committee guide the development of the program. This can be done in many ways, and most committees are a balance of individuals with business experience and political acumen.

The advisory committee should not be a *yes* group. Their main task is to provide guidance to make sure that the plans you develop for implementing your programs are accomplished. Often they can even help develop the plan, but their primary role is to help you see that your goals *can be accomplished*, and find ways to assist you in accomplishing them. This may be nothing more than providing help in promoting your programs at the local level. If you have the right people on your committee, their endorsement may be enough to assure your program is credible in the business community.

To be most effective, your committee should be limited to less than a dozen people. Usually the people that you would like to have on your committee are already involved in supporting other programs. In addition, not all members will be able to make all meetings. This means that you will need to appoint more than you would really like to have to make the meetings work, but enough to make certain you have a sufficient number of participants to make the meetings productive.

By selecting a mix of representatives from business (those you want to serve), organizations (those with which you want to cooperate), and stakeholders (those who are already invested in your program and have the clout to advocate), you can establish an advisory committee that will help assure the success of your program.

Networking Your Program Externally

In addition to an internal support team, you need to consider creating key relationships which will provide external support. Although there are numerous people that can be of great benefit to your program, the three key areas for selection include appropriate government export-service providers, the private sector, individuals in the political arena, and vertical interest groups.

The government. There are many people to chose from in the government service category. As previously mentioned, key players tend to be the representatives of the federal and state export assistance programs. Since your program will be closely networked with their programs, it is imperative that they support your efforts in some manner. By developing your program to work in a supportive manner with their efforts, you can work toward creating a synergism and become part of the team that provides statewide services. On the other hand, if they perceive your programs and services to be in competition with their own services, then you create a "turfdom" situation that will impede the development of your program. By letting them know your intentions up front, and asking for their support, you can guide your program to grow in the right direction.

Nationally, there are numerous programs, publications, and people with whom you will want to become familiar. Although you may consider this wide perspective to be distant to your immediate needs, principals in these organizations can often be very helpful since they usually have a good overview of market dynamics nationwide. For example, it is a good idea to subscribe to the U.S. Department of Commerce monthly publication *Business America*. By simply reviewing the table of contents you can quickly get a feel for current and relevant international trade topics.

The same concept holds true with those contacts that you can make with the various agencies with which you will be establishing cooperative efforts. The more you understand the organization and function of the U.S. Department of Commerce in Washington, DC, the more effective you will be at networking at that level. One way to accomplish this is to talk with the staff of the agency office with whom you are working, and you may even consider arranging a visit to the headquarters offices in Washington. It enhances the credibility of your program if you can relate in person to agencies such as the U.S. Departments of Commerce and Agriculture, Ex-Im Bank, and the Small Business Administration (SBA).

The private sector. The private sector export-service providers will be your strongest platform of "experts." They can be instrumental in helping you gain immediate credibility for your program, and equally important in sustaining your efforts. Keep in mind that they are probably already involved with the state and federal agencies, and (since you will probably be using them to support your training activities) you can take synergistic advantage of this in preparing your business clients for government agency services. Also keep in mind that your external experts from the private sector compete against each other to serve the same business clients you are assisting. Be certain that your efforts of working with select individuals are not interpreted by their competitors as *favoritism*. You will need lots of help, so it will be advantageous to get acquainted with all possible private sector resource people you can (and that also helps minimize the favoritism problem).

The political arena. Another area of concern will be political contacts. Your institution already will have a working relationship with those they have determined as most helpful. You need to make sure they are aware of your international outreach program efforts, and this includes key individuals at the local, regional, state, and national levels. Often this requires nothing more than providing key players with copies of the promotional information that you develop. You might even consider inviting them to visit your outreach center. Global marketing and international trade are important issues for your political leaders, and they will appreciate being kept informed, especially when you have an economic development success story to tell (such as how a local manufacturer has successfully exported).

Vertical interest groups. Keep in mind that your program is involved in a network of vertical interest groups, such as engineering, agriculture, or even more specifically defined areas of business such as finance, accounting, or information management, will share that interest. Whenever that occurs, there is a potential for you to serve that need, ally with them, or at least have a powerful onlooker.

For example, most major cities are home to various vertical interest professional associations or organizations, such as transportation (e.g., an international hospitality group), industry sector (e.g., an oil & gas organization), service (e.g., credit managers group), or other type of special interest. By establishing contact with these groups, you can determine if they would be interested in networking with your program when they are involved with international trade issues. This can be an excellent way to expand your program.

Promoting Your Program

The importance of promoting your international outreach program cannot be underestimated. This means much more than creating a brochure and mailing it to potential clients.

It is important to consider that your program can benefit more from straightforward communication efforts than from advertising. You probably do not need to develop a media plan. What is most important is having printed materials that project a professional image of your program, and to inform various audiences about your program. These can range from simple desktop black-and-white brochures to more elaborate four-color professionally prepared catalogs. That, of course, is dependent upon your budget.

In most cases you probably will not even have a budget for advertising, although you should have budgeted funds for developing and printing materials. These can be greatly augmented with a planned public relations effort. One way to determine what can work best for you is to see what is being provided by the other federal and state service providers. Since you want to be perceived as providing professional services, studying what they do can be very helpful in determining how you want to position your program. In fact, it may be important to not be perceived as having spent more money for promotion than other service providers.

Once you have your materials, use your established relationships with other agencies as multipliers to help promote your services. Because you are focusing on establishing supportive roles, they are often glad to help promote your services in the spirit of networking.

In addition to the printed materials that you will want to provide, you will no doubt also want to have a web site. That gives you not only a state-of-the-art method for promoting your programs, services, and materials, but it is also another way to demonstrate your business acumen. Your web site tells the companies you are serving that you understand and use the latest technology in you own business practices. Keep in mind, your web site is a dynamic tool. You can probably find lots of student help in maintaining your site, and may want to make it an ongoing class project. At a minimum, your web site should have two sections: information specific to your own program, and links to other service provider information. There are numerous examples of international business outreach programs that have web sites, and they can serve as excellent examples for developing your own.

Integrating Your Outreach Program with the Business School

An international business outreach program is naturally associated with the college of business, and it is vitally important that the program is well integrated within the school. In essence, the program is an extension of the school serving the business community.

Perhaps one of the most overlooked aspects of integration is acceptance by the faculty. If they perceive that the outreach program is not professionally managed, or that it does not represent the school well, they will not be supportive. One way to prevent this perception is to carefully inform and involve faculty whenever possible. Sometimes this can be difficult if the faculty has limited international business experience or interest. However, determine what specific faculty experience is available and use it in whatever cooperative manner you can.

Some of the most important services you can provide involve students and faculty. From finance to market research, from area studies to product promotion (sales) techniques, you can create successful situations that enhance both the school and your program.

Final Note

Your business school is probably already undergoing an internationalization process of some kind: adding international components to existing curriculum, developing new internationally-oriented classes, providing the international training and experiences for the faculty, or enhancing international student programs.

The development of an international business outreach program is usually just an extension of that internationalization process, and a catalyst for collaborating with all the different stakeholders. More importantly, it serves directly as a conduit for the business school to plug directly into the business community. In addition, it networks the school with the various other agencies that are also working with the business community. There is probably no better method for the school to develop and maintain business relationships and sustain the process of internationalization than can be provided by an international business outreach program.

CHAPTER TEN

Developing International Relationships

Sara D. Tucker

The establishment of relationships with overseas academic institutions is a critical part of a business school's internationalization efforts. These linkages can take many forms: student exchange programs, study tours, solo or joint faculty research, internships, business simulations, or other joint projects across borders. All of these programs contribute to the internationalization process in some way by increasing international teaching and research opportunities for faculty, and by increasing opportunities for students to learn about other cultures and markets through interacting with their counterparts overseas in either the classroom or workplace.

Despite clear advantages that accrue to institutions with international linkages, many schools lack the financial resources for major initiatives—and, unfortunately, those which do have the funds often lack a unified strategy connecting their activities (Altbach and Peterson).

Over the past twelve years, the number of U.S. students receiving academic credit for study abroad as reported in *Open Doors* (Davis) has increased from 48,483 to 113,949. Much of this growth occurred during the late 1980s, but the last three years have seen double-digit growth, including a 14.6% increase from academic years 1997/98 to 1998/99. Participation rates show 9% of undergraduates have studied abroad. Of those going abroad, an overwhelming majority (88.3%) report going for one semester or less. *Open Door's* statistics point to a gradual increase in business students as a percentage of all majors participating in exchange programs over the last decade. In academic year 1998/99, business and management students made up 15.6% of the total. *Open Doors* notes a pronounced trend toward ever-shorter stays overseas. Despite the growth noted above, the U.S. needs to continue to increase participation rates in study abroad programs as part of an effort to educate students about our increasingly networked global community. In this chapter the focus is on how to build these important international linkages and the many forms they can take.

Institutional Considerations in Establishing International Linkages

Prior to establishing a linkage with an academic institution overseas, it is important to have a thorough understanding of your home institution's strategic objectives and financial and human resources (see Chapter 2, *Charting Your Course*). You must also consider what is the most appropriate home for a given agreement: the institution as a whole, the college, or the department.

Robert Green and Linda Gerber of the University of Texas at Austin list ten "keys to success" to consider when establishing linkages with international institutions. The first three key factors are critical to the internationalization process and emphasized repeatedly elsewhere in this book. These are strong support from the dean, the existence of an IB champion, and the formulation of a plan that includes strategic objectives. The remaining seven key factors are specific to the establishment of linkages. Summarized, all ten key factors are as follows:

Keys to Success in Establishing International Linkages

1. *Strong support from the dean*	The dean's support is important to help overcome faculty resistance to the establishment of linkages, as well as to help negotiate the bureaucratic maze at public institutions and at very large institutions. It is important to educate the dean about possible difficulties so that they are prepared for the inevitable hurdles ahead.
2. *A champion*	In the long run, faculty are the foundation for all internationalization activities,

linkages included. Though administrators can handle many aspects of international relationships, early-stage linkages require continuity and the development of institutional memory. It is more likely that faculty members will provide such continuity than more mobile administrators.

3. *A plan*

It is important to develop a plan that includes strategic objectives. In developing this plan, you must consider your school's financial and human resource limitations. Overseas commitments can be expensive because of extra travel and communication costs required to develop and to support them. You should also be well aware of your typical student profile. For instance, institutions where many students work full-time in addition to their studies will find they cannot sustain exchange programs of more than a few weeks duration. Regarding faculty, does your institution's incentive structure support faculty that teach or do research overseas?

4. *Two-way benefits*

It is crucial that both parties to an agreement feel they are benefiting from the relationship. These benefits need not be the same for both parties.

5. *Equality in the relationship*

The partner institution must be considered an equal, and not a "country cousin." U.S. institutions must resist the temptation to view their international counterparts as inferior, but rather must view them as different.

6. *Creativity*

Creativity is needed to deal with the different structures of national educational systems, the differences between institutions, and the many bureaucratic rules that make inter-institutional collaboration difficult. Barriers that can be overcome with creativity range from incompatible academic calendars to large discrepancies in faculty salaries.

7. *Institutions, not individuals*

Linkages should be established between institutions, not individuals. Though many linkages are initiated and sustained by personal relationships, eventually they must rise above this in order to become long-term relationships. All individuals involved initially should consider what systems will be needed to institutionalize the link.

8. *Incrementalism*

Linkages should be developed slowly, as two institutions get to know each other. Many schools start with student exchanges, a relatively low-risk form of collaboration that most certainly benefits students.

9. *Opportunism*

Be opportunistic in seeking possibilities for linkages, and be prepared to act quickly when opportunities present themselves. If your institution is clear about its objectives, it will be far easier to seize opportunities that present themselves.

10. *Centrality within the institution*

The individuals involved in establishing linkages must occupy a central position within the institution. Faculty must be part of the process: they should be consulted about the appropriateness of prospective partners, and provide feedback on issues such as the performance of students from linkage schools in their classes.

Green and Gerber build on the above "keys to success" by differentiating between different types of relationships, and by identifying the various forms of cooperation that partnerships can take.

In evaluating a potential partner institution, William R. Folks, Jr., Director of the CIBER and the Master of International Studies (MIBS) program at the University of South Carolina (USC), cites a list of criteria that you should examine once you are clear about your strategic objectives. Partner institutions should be qualified along the following parameters: commitment to the project, quality of faculty, quality of facilities such as the library, academic reputation in the host country, business reputation in the host country, and in the case of exchanges, compatibility of students, and the host institution's ability to deal with acculturation difficulty (language, housing, and transactional difficulties such as not being able to read signs, or handle simple tasks such as shopping for necessities).

The Office of International Education of the American Council on Education has also published *Guidelines for Colleges and University Linkages Abroad.* This publication touches on many of the same issues that Green and Gerber discuss. It also provides some specific suggestions about the negotiation process, and about the formal agreements or contracts. It reminds institutions to recognize the importance of local customs and laws and the need to impress this on all program participants.

Student-Centered Programs

Student Exchange Programs

Student exchange programs are one of the most common, and the least complex forms, of international linkage. Student exchange programs range in duration from a quarter or semester to a full academic year. Full academic year exchanges are possible at the undergraduate business level, but unlikely at the M.B.A. level because of the already short duration of M.B.A. programs.

Schools can set up their own exchange programs, or can join with a group of other schools in a consortium arrangement. By joining a consortium, schools can provide more opportunities for their students and faculty at less expense than if they formed their own one-on-one relationships. The consortium arrangement also allows beginners to access a network of more experienced institutions. Consortium members generally participate in governance of the organization. The downside of a consortium is that it's more unwieldy and complex because of its combined governance. The following examples illustrate the wide variety of approaches to consortium arrangements.

Thunderbird (the American Graduate School of International Management) sponsors an international campus consortium (ICC) that currently has fifteen members in the U.S., Canada, and Mexico. The ICC's mission is "to provide high quality, globally-oriented, and internationally-located educational programs for graduate students in business." Students at an ICC school can participate in any of the graduate programs offered at any other ICC school. In addition, many member schools also offer nonconsortium sponsored exchanges. By doing this, students can take advantage of other ICC campuses as well as take courses at nonconsortium schools of their choice.

Another example is the University Studies Abroad Consortium (USAC), located at the University of Nevada, Reno. Mostly serving undergraduates, this consortium of twenty-one members and associated universities maintains resident directors at eight campuses located in Europe, Latin America, and China, and has exchange relationships with another nine universities. The obvious advantage of such a consortium is that institutions pool their resources to offer programs that would be much too expensive to run alone.

There are many consortia operating around the country. But the larger the consortium, the less input each participating institution will have. The College Consortium for International Studies (CCIS) is a partnership of seventy-eight two-year and four-year colleges around the country. CCIS sponsors both study abroad programs and professional development seminars for faculty and administrators, designed to strengthen international/intercultural perspectives within the academic community.

Alternatives abound for an institution interested in joining a consortium. Another such arrangement is illustrated by Southwest Missouri State University's (SMSU) experience. SMSU worked with the nonprofit organization Cultural Exchange Network in order to provide exchange opportunities for its faculty and staff. Through Cultural Exchange Network's Magellan Exchange, SMSU joined with several other regional state schools linked to five European universities. Cultural Exchange Network administers the program, handling all paperwork for the exchanges in addition to maintaining parity in campus-to-campus relationships.

Should your institution decide to go it alone, as is typical with study tours, you will need to grapple closely with a number of issues. The Institute of International Education (IIE) publishes a list of consortia in their annual publication on study abroad (*Academic Year Abroad 1999/2000: The Most Complete Guide to Planning Academic Year Study Abroad*). As with any potential partnership, it is important to understand a given consortium's mission and how it dovetails with your institution's mission and needs. One should investigate other questions as well. What is the academic credibility of the consortium's programs? How much control does the consortium exercise over the academic curriculum offered at overseas sites? What is the relationship of consortium members to one another and to overseas partners?

If you are satisfied that a given institution is an appropriate partner for your school, you will want to decide on terms of an agreement. Some institutions have formal legal agreements, while others have less formal letters of understanding that govern their relationships. You will have to determine what is required by your institution. Whatever form the agreement takes, it serves the purpose of focusing the parties on the details that will make your relationship work more smoothly. Such an agreement governing student exchanges should set forth participant qualifications, financial requirements, and academic credit issues, as well as exit provisions governing the agreement itself.

Participant qualifications include such things as the stage in the academic program that must be reached prior to participation in the exchange, by both sides; the level of performance that must be achieved by candidates to participate, on both sides, and admission requirements (such as TOEFL, GMAT, and transcript requirements), with a schedule of performance dates for both sides.

Financial requirements include areas such as tuition and special fees. Many institutions avoid the complex issues that surround international tuition payments by agreeing to tuition waivers at the host school, and tuition payment is made at the home school. Thus, a UCLA student studying at the Hong Kong University of Science and Technology (HKUST) continues to pay UCLA tuition, and the exchange counterpart from HKUST continues to pay HKUST tuition. If there are any special fees that need to be paid, such as computing fees or recreation fees, these should be noted in the agreement. If necessary, outline responsibility for travel expenses, medical insurance, and financial certification.

In terms of academic credit, parties to the exchange agreement should determine the selection of courses to be taken by exchange students, how credit will be granted, what provision will be made for records, and the waiver of degree requirements to participate, should this be necessary.

Lastly, an agreement should state who can amend it and how it can be amended, when it terminates, and what provisions there are for renewal.

Student Study Tours

Study tours are another way to expand student and faculty exposure to the international business environment and practices outside the U.S. The destination and composition of a study tour is very individual to organizers, but will include some combination of lectures and visits to companies and universities in another country. Some schools such as Ohio State University (OSU) and University of Southern California (USC) incorporate the study tour as part of a longer course. Some schools, such as Arizona State University (ASU) West campus, offer the study tour itself for credit. Still other schools do not offer credit for such tours.

The issue of credit is an important one to many students because it has implications for financial aid. Noncredit study tours must be financed outside of the normal financial aid channels, unlike for-credit tours.

Schools organize study tours very differently. Some schools have a staff person dedicated to making all arrangements, some have student organizers directed by one faculty member, and some hire an outside organizer. Links with an academic institution in the country of destination are important in some countries for sponsorship purposes (Vietnam for instance), but not so important in most countries. Setting up the company visits for such trips can be difficult and time-consuming. Where possible, schools should first pursue existing relationships for help in setting up company visits abroad: local alumni, U.S. companies with local subsidiaries, and a local business school with strong ties to the business community. Where such relationships do not exist, a school can begin to cultivate them for the long term, and might pursue the short-term solution of hiring an outside organizer. The Institute for International Management at ASU West organizes study tours to some destinations, but hires International Business Seminars (IBS) of Scottsdale, Arizona, to organize others.

Since 1977, IBS has offered over 150 seminars at both the graduate and undergraduate levels in Europe, Asia, Australia, and New Zealand to thirty universities. Some of these programs are private, arranged for only one university, while others are designed so that a consortium of universities may send students. IBS organizes the company visit itinerary, and makes travel and hotel arrangements. Each university handles its own academic details, such as granting of credit and charging of tuition.

Those schools that organize company visits themselves might contract with a travel agency to manage all logistical arrangements. USC's Pacific Rim Education Program (PRIME) which incorporates travel to one of seven international sites into a four-week, three-credit class, is coordinated overall by one person, who then hires local contractors in each city to make all local arrangements. In addition, one faculty member is assigned as a "desk officer" for each country to assist students and the lead coordinator with country-specific concerns.

International Internships

International internships are an increasingly attractive way for business students at both the undergraduate and graduate levels to gain direct knowledge of the business culture and acquire second-language competency in another country. The duration of the internship depends on both company need and student requirements, but a basic rule is that the longer the internship the greater the knowledge gained, and the more meaningful the work that can be accomplished. Unlike a domestic internship, most international internships will require facility in another language. It is important that language needs, as well as project needs, are part of the internship negotiation process.

It is possible for students to conduct self-directed searches for internship opportunities, but their quest can be made much easier by skillful advising on the part of the academic institution. Internship development is complex, and can be costly, depending on your institution's approach. For instance, the University of South Carolina's MIBS program has three full-time assistant managing directors and track managers dedicated to coordinating internships for the 150 students in its programs in Europe, Latin America, and Asia. In addition, the program director and the program's advisory board actively cultivate internship opportunities.

Another way in which a school can approach the internship process is to develop very close ties with a small number of large multinational firms that agree to take a certain number of interns in their overseas offices each year. To do this, an institution should identify companies with which it already has a strong recruiting record.

The search for an international internship is complicated by distance, time, and visa issues. All of these obstacles can be overcome with persistence. Should your institution wish to develop internships, a good place to start is with alumni, board members of your school who may have overseas connections, multinational companies that currently recruit from your pool of students, and any other local business supporters that have overseas branches or connections. The University of Wisconsin actually has, on loan, an international human resource executive from a local multinational who develops internships for Wisconsin students with the executive's parent company, as well as with other companies.

The process of establishing an internship program is arduous, but not impossible. It is wise to involve the student in the search as much as possible. In this manner, the student clarifies his or her short-term internship goals and long-term career goals internationally, while learning life-long job search strategies. Once a position is secured, you should confirm all previous discussions regarding project, reporting, and compensation in writing. If it is a paid internship, you should be prepared to deal with visa issues, which vary depending on country and company.

If your institution cannot directly support international internship searches, but wishes to encourage them all the same, there are a host of institutions that provide internship placement services. San Diego State University (SDSU) has compiled a list of such institutions. The *Chapter Reference Notes and Additional Resources* section at the back of this book contains listings for these. Be aware that many of these services charge a fee.

Another organization that actively develops internships for undergraduate students is AIESEC (Association Internationale de Etudiants en Sciences Economiques et Commerciales). Since 1948, this nonprofit organization has grown to encompass a network of over 50,000 students in 800 higher education institutions in eighty-seven countries. Students interested in finding an internship abroad through AIESEC should contact the closest local office to learn about information sessions.

International Business Simulations and Joint Cross-Border Courses

International business simulations and joint cross-border course offerings provide cross-cultural exposure without travel. Even though the class does not travel, there is still much that can be done behind the scenes by professors and administrators to make the class experience meaningful. Kathryn Martel at Southern Illinois University at Edwardsville (SIUE) has taught courses that integrate student project teams at SIUE and the Toluca campus of Instituto Tecnológico y de Estudios Superiores de Monterrey (ITESM) in Mexico. The integrated student projects have several components: a chat room, joint research, report writing, critiquing other students' work, and preparing and delivering a professional presentation. Most of student interaction takes place on the Internet, but a teleconference at the end of the semester gives students a chance to meet and interact in person.

It is crucial to the success of such a course that you have a faculty counterpart at the other campus who has the same enthusiasm and commitment that you do. One can more readily identify such a person through home campus faculty who have spent time at the non-U.S. campus. If you do not have such a faculty connection, you should approach the dean or director of the school, explain your goals, and ask for recommendations of faculty members whom you can directly contact. You should be prepared to travel to the other campus in order to set things up, and, ideally, once again to monitor the progress of the program while in session. Careful planning made during the preliminary trip can eliminate months of frustrating e-mail, fax, and disjointed phone calls. Larger technology costs, which many institutions may see as a barrier, can be lowered by using public access alternatives.

Field Study Projects

International field studies, likened to consulting projects, expose students and faculty to a higher level of complexity than they might encounter with a domestic firm since political, social, legal, and cultural issues must all be considered. In addition to the internationalization of both students and faculty participating in such a study, faculty may also establish contacts that lead to future research, and future consulting projects with international dimensions.

Field study projects can range in size and scope from teams of four to five students to groups of sixty, such as the international field studies conducted by students in the Fully Employed M.B.A. (FEMBA) and Executive M.B.A. (EMBA) programs at UCLA. Studies conducted by smaller teams allow more flexibility and direct association with management, but scope is limited by the size of the team. In the larger format, nine to ten teams of six to seven students study all aspects of a strategic issue in more scope, linking functional and cultural perspectives with industry trends and dynamics.

As with international internships, employers of your students and your alumni are the best source of contacts for field study projects because they know your program. Employers can and do use projects to preview future hires.

At UCLA, developing client companies for large-scale international field study projects begins two years in advance of a study. The commitment and participation of top management must be secured in order to ensure that the study has real strategic value for the firm. A reporting infrastructure must be developed with the client at the outset so that all appropriate people receive the relevant information as the study progresses.

Such an infrastructure at the client company should be comprised of a team of cross-functional managers that will devote time, at the start, to determining the focus and scope of the project. This may be modified slightly throughout the course of the study, but consensus among this group is important.

International studies add a level of complexity that you do not have with a domestic firm. Differences in distance, time, and culture must all be factored in when devising a time-line for an international project. Strong communication systems, and firm but flexible planning are crucial to their success.

Faculty-Centered Programs

Faculty-centered programs are both essential and critical to the long-term internationalization of any business school. As faculty become more sensitized to and knowledgeable about international issues through travel and research, this information will find its way into the curriculum. There are various ways to expose faculty to international issues: by providing overseas teaching opportunities, by supporting joint curriculum development with colleagues at an institution abroad, by encouraging and supporting participation in faculty development programs offered by institutions more experienced in international research and teaching, and by offering incentives for joint faculty research across campus and across borders.

Joint Faculty Research Across Campus and Across Borders

Faculty research interests are so highly individualized that it is difficult to devise programs that promote joint faculty research across borders. Cross-border research tends to arise out of personal contacts developed by professors who discover common interests while attending academic conferences, or who establish direct contact with a colleague abroad after reading their work in an academic journal, and subsequently develop a relationship based on mutual interests. You can increase faculty opportunities to make such contact by promoting and supporting faculty membership in organizations such as the Academy of Management (which has an international management division), the Academy of International Business, and by attending conferences sponsored by these organizations.

Joint faculty research can also be encouraged by offering research grants to those professors who are collaborating with colleagues in other countries—or in other departments on your campus such as modern languages, geography, anthropology, political science, economics or history, on international research topics. These grants can support research assistance or international travel necessary for data collection.

Cross-campus faculty ties are often more easily established and maintained because they do not face the difficulties of communicating across time and distance. Granted, there will still be cultural differences among campus departments. An example of such cross-departmental ties is the CIBER Cross-Cultural Collegium (C4) at UCLA. C4 has encouraged collaboration across departments and disciplines among many schools in the western United States since 1989. Faculty from twenty-two colleges and universities gather three times a year to present and discuss their research. From C4 many collaborative research and writing projects, sharing of syllabi for courses, and professional collaborations have evolved. The UCLA CIBER supports the collegium's modest meeting costs. As with other internationalization efforts, the presence of a faculty champion is critical to the group's ongoing success.

Overseas Teaching Opportunities and Faculty Exchanges

As with student exchange programs, one of the most effective ways to internationalize faculty is to support overseas teaching opportunities. This is easier said than done as many institutions encounter difficulty in sustaining a regular exchange of faculty. Such opportunities might be created as part of an agreement with an overseas institution. In general, it is easier to convince faculty to take advantage of such openings if they are short-term assignments that do not necessitate long separations from home institutions and family, ideally lasting several weeks at most. Such short-term assignments are usually connected to executive education programs, rather than full-time M.B.A. programs.

Pacific Lutheran University (PLU) in Tacoma, Washington, has provided development opportunities for faculty through an ongoing partnership with the School of Management at Zhongshan University in Guangzhou, China. This partnership arose out of a relationship formed by program director Thad Barnowe when he was a Fulbright lecturer at Zhongshan in 1982-83. PLU students and faculty travel to Zhongshan as a group for a semester of study and teaching, and Chinese students and faculty have reciprocally visited PLU. The teaching opportunities in China are made more attractive to faculty because the relationship with Zhongshan allows them access they might not otherwise have to companies for research projects.

Another way to internationalize faculty is by bringing international scholars to your campus. If you would like an international scholar to teach a specific course or undertake a specific project, you might post this position in the *Academy of International Business Newsletter* or other professional journals. You might also attend professional meetings widely attended by international faculty to seek out and interview potential candidates. Whereas faculty positions tend to be paid, scholars often arrive through funding from their home institution, or are sponsored by federal agencies of the U.S. government, and can be attracted with offers of library access and office space. Once an international scholar arrives on campus, you should be proactive about creating opportunities where the visitor and your permanent faculty, students, and staff can learn from one another.

Joint Curriculum Development

As with faculty research, efforts at joint curriculum development depend on a strong working relationship between faculty at the participating institutions. Perhaps the easiest way to start is on your own campus. What faculty resources are already present in other campus departments that could contribute to a course? For example, do you conduct business in Latin America? Do you have a center for Latin American studies? What faculty outside of the business school are affiliated with the center? You can draw on faculty from anthropology, economics, modern language, and political science departments in developing such a course. As these faculty mix with one another and with business school faculty, opportunities for joint research as well as future curriculum development will more readily present themselves. As always, it is important that the effort be supported by the dean of the business school by providing faculty release time for curriculum development, and by vocally supporting such efforts in communications with the school's faculty.

Based on campus strengths, the University of Oregon's Lundquist College of Business decided to concentrate on enhancing the level of Asian expertise among its business school faculty and subsequently expanding curriculum in this area. It was able to do so because the business school built mutually beneficial ties with the campus center for Asian and Pacific studies. A grant from the U.S. Department of Education's BIE program helped underwrite the development of a six-month on-campus training program for faculty that integrated cultural and business studies, followed by a three-week study tour of Southeast Asia. All participants were then required to integrate Southeast Asian materials into their course work and contribute to the university's outreach activities.

Overseas Campuses and Programs

Another method for encouraging faculty involvement outside of the U.S. is through the establishment of a satellite campus in another country. Although a complete description of this type of program is beyond the scope of this chapter (and there are many details to attend to including accreditation issues, budgeting, and scheduling), many colleges of business are offering executive education programs and complete M.B.A. or undergraduate degrees for non-U.S. nationals in their home countries. Students from the U.S. campus can usually also attend the classes at the non-U.S. location for credit.

This type of arrangement is typically accomplished not by building a new campus, but by partnering with a host institution in another country or with an overseas government by delivering the program in an already existing facility.

Benefits from this type of program include opportunities for the U.S. faculty to teach abroad while working for their own university, providing classes in an international environment for students of the U.S. college of business, providing a service for host-country national students, establishing contacts in another country for research projects and internships, and generating revenue for other international programming. Wright State University illustrates this type of program.

Since 1994, Wright State University (WSU) in Dayton, Ohio, has been delivering its M.B.A. program on the campus of the H. L. Stoutt Community College in Tortola, British Virgin Islands (BVI). The program's genesis was based on a request from the government and college officials in the BVI. After a needs assessment, WSU began this lock-step program with a single M.B.A. concentration in management and the first cohort of students graduated in 1996. Because the population of the BVI is small, it took three years for the queue to fill with enough qualified candidates to start the second cohort with a concentration in finance.

As a result of the program, WSU's Raj Soin College of Business was able to provide authentic international teaching experiences for its faculty in an English language environment, to provide a service to students in the BVI, to generate income for other programs, and to develop and implement new methods of teaching which have been utilized on the main campus in Dayton. The WSU business school is currently working with H. L. Stoutt Community College to deliver the last two years of an undergraduate degree with a major in management in the BVI for local students.

Faculty Development Programs

Faculty development in international business (FDIB) programs are plentiful. The CIBERweb, resident at Purdue, maintains a comprehensive list of FDIBs offered by universities in the CIBER network. The target audience for these programs is wide: from K-12 teachers, to community college faculty and administrators (such as the biennial Institute for International Management offered by Michigan State University CIBER), to university faculty in general and in specific disciplines (such as the pedagogy workshop offered by the Indiana University CIBER), to the many specific graduate programs offered by the Thunderbird CIBER, the University of South Carolina CIBER, and the University of Colorado at Denver CIBER. The aim of many of these FDIBs is to provide faculty with the tools to either teach a general course in international business, or to add international topics to functional courses. Some programs deal with international research issues as well, exposing faculty to the different topics, journals, and methodologies.

Full Partner Institution Programs

As an institution becomes more experienced in developing and administering international relationships with international partners, it might decide to take a giant leap forward and investigate double or joint-degree programs with an institution abroad.

Reciprocal Recognition Programs

"Reciprocal recognition" agreements allow graduates of partner institutions waivers of specified courses which will apply toward a second masters degree in business. This arrangement is predicated on the idea that similar programs will have a certain amount of overlap in course content. A student might seek a second degree in order to open more doors internationally, and possibly even choose to work and live abroad.

Double Degree Programs

Two institutions can take reciprocal recognition one step further by integrating degree programs to create a "double degree" program. Students enrolled in a double degree program earn degrees from both institutions in a shorter period of time than would be required to study for the two degrees separately. Each school participating in a double degree program might waive the M.B.A. core for students from the other institution and apply some of the elective credits earned in overseas study toward its own degree. Overlapping electives, and the demand that students fulfill the requirements of both institutions in order to graduate, differentiate the double degree program from the reciprocal recognition program. The double degree program at the University of Texas at Austin, is distinguished by a number of features: (1) the number of student participants each year is limited by agreement, (2) the applications of students from the partner institution are processed separately from other applications, and (3) it is expected that roughly equal numbers of students will flow in both directions.

Fusion Programs

"Fusion programs" take the reciprocal recognition and double degree programs even further. Fusion occurs when partner institutions jointly plan and offer an integrated degree for a group of students. Such a program might be offered 50% at the partner institution outside the U.S., and 50% at the U.S.

institution. A fusion program creates a much more intense and culturally integrative experience than other models as the students from the partner institutions study together for the length of the program.

Final Note

International relationships between business schools in the U.S. and those overseas come in myriad forms. Therefore, before deciding what sort of relationships your institution would like to develop overseas, it is important to examine institutional goals and financial and human resources as part of an overall strategy. What works for one institution does not necessarily work for another.

Once you have a clear idea of your assets and your goals, a wealth of resources is available to schools pursuing international relationships. It is helpful to explore what other institutions have done in this area. A good place to start is by reading the abstracts for grantees of the U.S. Department of Education's BIE and CIBER programs where you will find many interesting and instructive models.

Though many relationships may come through serendipitous events such as a chance meeting on an airplane or at a conference, there are many concrete steps you can take to establish ties. In the process of deciding whether or not to develop independent programs, you should investigate the various established consortia that handle student exchanges and internships. You should look to your school's alumni, current employers of your students, and other interested businesses in your home community. You should consult with faculty who are members of international academic organizations, and see what meetings and conferences they regularly attend.

Above all, it is important that the dean of the business school or business program supports the internationalization plan and is enthusiastic about establishing international relationships.

CHAPTER ELEVEN

Welcome to Virtual Business Education

Jamie Alonso Gómez and Germán Otalora

Change has been a constant in the evolution of humankind but never has change been so intense and rapid as we see it now, and in the areas of business and technology never has the acceleration been more difficult to clock and as challenging to contemplate.

As we move into the new millennium, we will continue to see a more globalized society including regional trade blocks such as the North American Free Trade Agreement (NAFTA), the European Union (EU), and the Mercado Común del Sur, or Southern Common Market (MERCOSUR). There will be more mergers and acquisitions (Kotabe), and more investment funds flowing literally from one corner to another corner of the world, in a matter of nanoseconds. Furthermore, we are already seeing political, social, technological, and economic systems that interrelate in a way that gives genesis to many new market variables that were not considered in the past (Brugger). And finally, increased complexity and uncertainty in human activity requires the reconceptualization of public and private management systems which will undoubtedly give rise to new economic paradigms and dynamics. In short, we now live in an environment that is more global, yet highly personal (think of the ways in which we participate daily in the marketplace of the world) than ever before.

There are several names to describe this phenomenon. It has been called the "post-modern society," "the knowledge economy," "the information age," and "the digital economy," to mention just a few (Crawford; Oblinger and Rush). Consequently, life styles and workplaces across world societies are being transformed. This transformation is demanding new skills, new knowledge, new ways of delivering information and making decisions, new ways of learning, and new attitudes about the whole notion of education. This chapter is devoted to describing how technology is playing a role in this transformation with respect to business education within an international environment.

New Alternatives for Education and Business

Executives and managers must be able to adapt, learn, and respond effectively to what takes place in their organization and its environment. They must continuously compete in a quickly changing world, and must manage adult workers who cannot afford to stop learning, and who cannot afford to stop working to learn. Fortunately, the velocity of change and the tremendous dissemination of information and communications technology have enabled institutions of education to provide new learning alternatives for people who are immersed in workplaces.

Schools around the globe are under pressure to improve educational quality, to cover a wider network of students and academic markets, and to respond to changing customer expectations without going over budget. Perhaps the biggest question learning institutions are facing is exactly how learning is to take place in a computerized, technological, and multipoint environment: how to design it, how to present and retrieve conceptual and applied knowledge, and, equally important, how to make it cost-effective and learning efficient.

Institutions such as Athabasca University (Canada), Walden University (U.S.), Thunderbird (U.S.), Instituto Tecnológico y de Estudios Superiores de Monterrey (ITESM, Mexico), The Open University (UK), and a wide variety of corporate universities around the world as well, are already offering distance-learning options, based on telecommunication linkages and systems to satisfy the needs of individual professionals, companies, and institutions around the world. They are developing new learning models, which are increasingly being enriched by information technology (IT), electronic networking, and multimedia technologies to improve delivery of education and learning effectiveness.

Information technology (IT) has shown the potential to support schools in these ventures by promoting learning-based approaches (as opposed to teaching-based), enriching and expanding the impact of faculty (frequently a limited resource), and creating meaningful alliances with corporations and institutions in both the private and public sectors. Progressive changes in IT such as digitalization, storage capacity, and processing power have also allowed for paperless learning materials, electronic access to remote libraries, external databases and networks, and rapid student-professor interaction across national borders.

The Information Technology/IB Education Experience

At ITESM's Graduate School of Business Administration and Leadership, information technology allows for the creation of a learning environment that brings together exploration and progressive construction of knowledge under the mentoring and tutorial guidance of professors and a group of technical and pedagogic staff (the course development team). Information technology also permits the design of learning environments that simulate real-life situations (problem-based learning), and Internet or videoconference student-student and student-professor interaction that brings many business and cultural perspectives together from different places (distance-learning).

These and other similar initiatives involving technology and learning processes have been managed at ITESM since 1987, since it started its first television course. Below we describe our experiences using technology to meet these new educational challenges.

Establishing the Virtual University

We have shifted the educational focus from teaching to learning, from the traditional transfer of academic content from professors to students, to active groups of students and professors seeking relevant knowledge. A consequence of this strategy has been the formal establishment of a Virtual University (VU) with satellite-linked on-line courses, continuous student-student interaction and student-teacher feedback, and electronic lounges for informal talk. There are considerable advantages to this strategic shift:

- learning processes that are independent of space and time

- targeting of lifelong market niches

- research activities across regions and cultures without abandoning the researchers' place of origin

- efficient management of course logistics and academic materials

- groups of faculty, from different places, working synchronically and asynchronically to enrich courses and test for local relevance

- continual access to learning materials, students, and professors located at different institutions

- developing business neural networks which make competition and collaboration viable and compatible

One of the principal advantages of IT learning through the VU is that while it is highly stimulating it is also much more relaxed than the conventional university environment. This relaxation means that the educational experience typically includes:

- self-motivation, self-discipline, and self-management skills

- participation of students in space and time that are convenient for the learner, not for a class schedule

- time for students to prepare and organize their thoughts and questions before sending them to an electronic chat room

- enough time for students to present questions and explain concerns without being interrupted or being inhibited by other students or a professor

- opportunities for discussion in an environment not monopolized by one or a few individuals

The amount of lecturing has been reduced to the time necessary for introducing the subject matter of the session and outlining some of the basic concepts and tools of the discipline. Lecturing is largely replaced by self-initiated student learning activity and mentor responses to the student's performance. Virtual visits to companies, virtual experiments, virtual keynote speakers, computer-based business simulations, electronic and face-to-face debates, group assignments, and field projects take the place formerly occupied by formal in-person presentations.

Evaluations are not solely designed to test for knowledge acquisition. Evaluation is more integral and includes critical thinking skills, knowledge, and values. This approach is much more broadly based and greatly enriched by a humanistic use of information technology.

We have thus implemented both behavioral and structural changes in support of student-centered learning and faculty-centered administration processes. These are aimed at developing academic strengths and embedding them in resources both tangible and intangible.

Consolidating the VU Curriculum

Technology has also greatly helped us to consolidate our curriculum of graduate studies across the twenty-eight campuses of the ITESM system and the more than 1,500 distance sites in Mexico, Latin America, Europe, and the United States. Frequent communication of students interacting in collaborative teams across regions and countries is a key element of this consolidation. Under the guidance of a homogeneous faculty and staff team, students report research, participate in business simulations, analyze cases, discuss critical issues, solve problems, and identify challenges. They become coauthors of their educational processes and critical actors in the decisions of their current and future companies and communities. This is coupled with state-of-the-art lectures given by internationally recognized experts via teleconferencing. Parallel to all the events in this learning process, students are exposed to advanced research problems and conceptual material through a variety of applied experiences.

Some of the peripheral IT tools that we use to support communication are the Internet for most direct communication and also for chat, video links, data mining, fax, and telephone (for those places where technology infrastructure is limited). All of this technological collaboration results in multiple learning outcomes for students:

- competency in a second language

- deeper understanding of other cultures when solving problems in internationally delivered courses

- greater knowledge of how multinational companies operate by working with students from other countries and different organizations

- development of skills to creatively solve problems

- increasing comfort working in virtual, technology-enhanced environments

ITESM has already consolidated many of its educational activities in the creation of its Virtual University. The VU portfolio of services includes:

- high quality graduate (master's and doctoral) programs delivered worldwide

- nondegree customized educational programs for institutions and organizations in developing economies

- executive education programs delivered via cable

- special programs responding to the objectives and needs of institutions such as the World Bank, the governments of Venezuela, Panama, and Colombia, multinational corporations, and the teachers union in Mexico

The adoption of the learning-oriented paradigm at ITESM and the deliberate incorporation of technology into undergraduate, graduate, and executive business education programs encourages reflection at three different but interrelated levels: the school's new mission, the dean's concerns and opportunities, and the faculty's role.

The School's New Mission

Once the portfolio of technology-assisted educational services is free of problems due to technical delivery and redesign, schools are able to develop competencies that are attractive to many institutions and corporations. One in particular is the expertise to deliver distance-learning programs which can easily take the form of programs across academic fields, across education levels, and across borders.

The fundamental question is whether the school or the university should set up an educational branch to take advantage of these institutional and business ventures. If so, what should the school's role be? What is the potential for revenue? Deans and academic administrators ought to have a clear understanding of their role, their mission statement, and the school's strategy in order to make the right decision. They must reflect on the scope, their existing and potential portfolio of services, and the markets in which the business school already operates and might operate in the future.

The use of technology allows the school to go beyond its traditional markets and borders. Students from distant regions with needs and expectations that have not been previously considered are now the school's potential students.

This brings a tremendous wealth of perspectives, skills, and learning styles that can enrich the whole academic community. It also brings the need to know more about the distance-learning students themselves and their native regions. ITESM has greatly benefited from this aspect of technology use, and has students "attending" from many countries who study at home or in the office (not in the classroom). Because of technology, ITESM is able to continually invite faculty who add value, and is able to maintain a high standard of service regarding academic and administration issues.

The newly developed mission of the school allows for many new partnerships and strategic alliances to develop. Our program has captured the attention of sister universities such as Carnegie Mellon University, Thunderbird, the University of British Columbia, the University of Waterloo; the governments of Venezuela, Mexico, and Panama; and institutions such as the World Bank. A number of joint projects and ventures are under construction or already in progress.

Decisions concerning diversification, partnering, and brokering in program design and distribution, joint research, team teaching, and executive development are now part of daily activity between committees configured by people from ITESM and other universities, ITESM and company executives, and ITESM and government officials. An example of partnering is the Master of International Management for Latin America, MIMLA, a program that ITESM is offering with Thunderbird and that will also soon include partner universities and companies in South America.

The Dean's Concerns and Opportunities

The adoption of the learning-oriented education philosophy, the incorporation of information technology in the education process, and the inclusion of instructional and graphic design experts require deans to focus their attention on issues which go well beyond outreach, research promotion, academic disciplines, and academic administration processes. The key issues are fiscal concerns, opportunities, and technical experience.

Fiscal Concerns. Technology is a new item in the budget. Computers, servers, software, and staff to keep them in working condition, and the management of all these processes including design, implementation, and delivery of the entire learning dynamic require a large capital investment initially and over time.

Opportunities, often very profitable, can arrive at the school's doorsteps. In the case of ITESM, the school has been invited to provide education for technicians, junior and senior high school teachers, potential voters, and employees of public institutions. All opportunities can, and many times do, positively modify the institution's primary task or mission statement.

Deans need to build new technical expertise to design strategy, articulately discuss adult-learning didactics, synchronic and asynchronic interaction, and competently address issues of server and computer configurations, delivery formats, satellite links, and fiber optics, among others. This does present a new challenge to make adequate investments in technological developments and innovations that emerge so quickly and impact upon so many aspects of a school's life. In fact, some schools have already created a new position, chief technology officer, as a way to cope with this new vector in academic life.

The Faculty's Role

Professors as Designers of Learning Dynamics. In the delivery of learning-oriented and technology-enhanced courses and seminars, professors at ITESM's Graduate School of Business Administration and Leadership engage in a new and holistic activity. They have become designers of learning dynamics, moving away from their prior role of content transmitters.

Professors migrate from the teacher-based delivery of content into engaging with a team of instructional design staff, a TV producer, a teaching assistant, an information technology expert, and a graphic designer. The ultimate goal of this team is to design experiences, exercises, and activities that are aimed at maximizing learning of the subject matter and of those values, attitudes, and skills that are elements of ITESM's mission statement. The professors become more than just teachers; they become designers of learning processes, facilitators as well as mentors.

The International Dimension. Faculty challenges not only include working collegially in a team but also require incorporation *of global dimensions* into courses. To do that, professors travel to those countries where the course is delivered, conduct interviews with private and public decision makers, conduct short executive education seminars or consulting projects, talk to locals, make company visits, and receive international profiles (economic, political, and social). The goal is to make locally relevant what is academically pertinent to the curriculum.

Instant Research Opportunities. With the use of information technology, the relative ease of access to large numbers of students, and the enrollment of international students and executives, professors can easily obtain data from questionnaires, surveys and other data collection instruments in order to extend and enrich their current research interests beyond geographic boundaries. Experiences have been very positive and a growing number of faculty members are already engaged in research activities across regions in both the Americas and Europe.

Final Note

Technology as a tool to achieve educational objectives has been utilized for decades. In our classrooms we have moved from overhead projectors, filmstrips, and movies to interactive video, online discussion groups, and satellite downlinks. This new educational paradigm includes a shift from professor-centered courses to student-driven collaborative learning communities. The model encourages a shift from learning at specific and narrowly scheduled times to education available anytime and anywhere. Technology facilitates learning which is holistic and interdependent, not disconnected and compartmentalized. The virtual university encourages extensive use of multiple and complementary distance-learning technologies.

For international business educators, technology offers a means to make the world a real-time classroom. Technology offers a means to design classes driven by creative problem-solving and interaction among learning teams. Use of instructional technology does not solve all of the problems of course design and delivery. Rather, it creates new challenges to meet the demands of business professionals, students, and other stakeholders. As you continue your technological explorations and chart your international courses, we say "welcome to virtual business education."

CHAPTER TWELVE

Evaluating Your Program

Lorraine A. Krajewski

What do you think of when you read the word *evaluation*? A high school essay exam? Your first college course in statistics? Does the word make you think of a dental examination or a tax audit? These are the images many faculty and IB team members conjure up when they first consider the word *evaluation*. The process seems mystical, smoke and mirrors, and fraught with intimidation, as though some degree of failure was a most natural consequence.

The purpose of this chapter is to demystify evaluation and focus on the positive and integral way in which evaluation provides usable information for IB program managers. Much has been written about conducting the ideal evaluation (and some of it is summarized here), but the focus of this chapter is on what Wholey, Hatry, and Newcomer call "practical program evaluation," that is, evaluation that can be accomplished at reasonable cost, without extensive involvement of highly-specialized personnel, and for the purpose of helping to improve program performance.

Answers to the following questions form the organizing framework of this chapter:

- Why is evaluation avoided?
- Why is evaluation needed?
- How is evaluation conducted?

- Who conducts the evaluation?
- When should evaluation occur?
- How is evaluation conducted?
- What does evaluation cost?
- What is the format of the evaluation report?

Why is Evaluation Avoided?

The term "evaluation" can be defined in both simple and complex ways. A simple definition is "the process of determining whether what was planned to be done was achieved, and whether what was actually achieved had the anticipated impact" (U.S. Department of Health and Human Services). A more complex definition states that evaluation is the "systematic application of social research procedures in assessing the conceptualization and design, implementation, and utility of social intervention programs" (Rossi and Freeman). A synthesis of these two definitions suggests that evaluation is a planned process that determines the extent to which objectives were met, and assesses the impact of the described outcomes.

Evaluation and assessment are not simple tasks, which is one reason why evaluation is often an afterthought in the internationalization process. It requires knowledge in an area with which most business school faculty are not familiar. It requires attention to very specific outcomes (objectives), as well as to general outcomes (goals). And, it requires objective, empirical evidence based on activities and results.

Another reason why evaluation is often avoided, if it is even thought of, is because it is sometimes perceived as being less creative, less interesting, and less important than developing and implementing IB programs. Furthermore, an element of fear may be present: the fear of failure. After all, if one has devoted substantial effort to create and implement a new program, does one really want to face the possibility that it may not be effective? But the most common reason that evaluation is overlooked is simply that it was not thought of when plans for internationalization were first developed and implemented.

Why is Evaluation Needed?

According to Tuckman, "The purpose of evaluating an instructional program is to provide the means for determining whether the program is meeting its goals; that is, whether the measured outcomes for a given set of instructional inputs match the intended or respecified outcomes." Another perspective on the purpose of evaluation is given by Steffy and English. They view evaluation as the basis for informed decision-making that will capitalize on effective practices and eliminate ineffective approaches.

Evaluation is a way to describe and then judge the value of IB programs, and with the increasing emphasis on educational accountability, evaluation and assessment are necessary components of internationalization efforts. In addition, for international business projects that are funded through federal government grants, such as the Title VI-A UISFL program and Title VI-B BIE program, evaluation is required. The Government Performance and Results Act of 1993 (GPRA) focuses on accountability that is demonstrated through the establishment and measurement of performance goals. *Results* of activities are emphasized in this accountability, rather than mere description of such activities.

But measuring results is only one aspect of evaluation. Equally important is the use of evaluation for continuous improvement of internationalization efforts. If faculty are committed, they will want their work to continue and their IB program to improve. Assessment is a means to that end. In summary, the answer to the question "Why is evaluation of international business programs needed?" can be answered in a simple and straightforward way. Aside from any grant mandate, evaluation is needed to assess effectiveness so that worthwhile internationalization activities can continue, and ineffective activities can be discontinued.

How is Evaluation Used?

Evaluation is conducted for many different audiences. Those who will use the information are typically the program developers, managers, implementers, supervisors of these individuals, funding agencies, and program participants— that is, all parties with a vested interest in the internationalization process and all parties with decision-making responsibilities.

A distinction is often made concerning the use of evaluation, with the key words being *formative* and *summative*. Each type of evaluation has a different audience, and different purposes. Furthermore, each occurs at different times in the duration of a program or project. Exhibit 12.1 summarizes the key aspects of formative and summative evaluation.

Exhibit 12.1

A Comparison of Formative and Summative Evaluation

Type of Evaluation	Purposes	Audience	Occurs
Formative (Process evaluation)	1. Monitors and provides continual information flow regarding procedural design and program implementation 2. Examines conduct of program to determine whether processes are consistent with the planned outcomes 3. Looks at relationship of program activities to overall program effectiveness 4. Gives immediate feedback so that program managers can identify and rectify problem areas during project's duration	The program's planners and managers	Throughout the program's duration
Summative (Product evaluation)	1. Determines degree to which stated objectives have been achieved 2. Looks at extent to which accomplishment of objectives can be attributed to the program 3. Provides a final assessment of the program's effectiveness	The school's administrators; funding agency; other program constituencies	At end of program

Who Conducts the Evaluation?

Obviously and logically the question arises: can the evaluator be someone who is already involved in the school's internationalization efforts, or must the evaluator be someone from the outside? Each type of evaluator, internal and external, has advantages; and the type of evaluation, formative or summative, is also a factor in answering the question. However, general agreement is that external evaluators are more effective because they are more likely to be objective and to have an independent perspective. Furthermore, their findings are more likely to be accepted by stakeholders because of this objectivity.

Internal Evaluators

Internal evaluators are individuals who are employed by the institution being evaluated; they may be, for example, faculty, staff, or administrators. An advantage of internal evaluators is that they are usually closer to the program than are external evaluators; consequently, they are usually less obtrusive (Fink and Kosecoff). They are, however, less likely to be objective than are external evaluators. Internal evaluators should be used for formative evaluation only.

What qualifications should internal evaluators have? They must be objective (insofar as that is possible) and have strong observational, analytical, and critical thinking skills. Good oral, written, and interpersonal communication skills are also necessary. Finally, the evaluator should possess technical skills; that is, the evaluator should have knowledge of evaluation, and, preferably, evaluation experience. Although the evaluator will need to acquire knowledge of the particular international business program being evaluated, this individual should not have a vested interest. For example, the program director might seem to be an ideal choice because of program knowledge, but the vested interest would disqualify the director.

Although an internal evaluator might be found within one's own department or college, often a faculty member from another unit might be a better choice. For example, if international business curricular activities are to be evaluated during the first year of a program, a colleague from the college of education might have the requisite knowledge. If international business outreach activities are to be evaluated, a colleague from a campus unit that is involved with outreach activities might be suitable.

What is the role of the internal evaluator? The internal evaluator is, of course, involved with data collection and analyses of ongoing activities. However, the internal evaluator might also be involved with the project during its planning stage. The evaluator is an excellent resource person to assist with the setting of goals and objectives for the internationalization evaluation efforts.

External Evaluators

External evaluators are individuals hired as outside consultants. They have the advantage of being objective and of having a fresh perspective (Fink and Kosecoff). Furthermore, they are professionally independent of any institutional political concerns. External evaluators are responsible for both formative and summative evaluations.

A good external evaluator needs a variety of skills, all of which are the same as for the internal evaluator: objectivity; strong observational, analytical, and critical thinking skills; and good oral, written, and interpersonal skills. For the external evaluator, evaluation experience is essential. So too are the technical skills of evaluation, such as, a solid knowledge of evaluation design. Ideally, the evaluator should also have experience with internationalizing the business school. Finally, as Popham emphasizes, the evaluator should be a "sensitive and sensible person. If an evaluator's style of interacting with people is discordant, then all the technical wizardry in the world will prove insufficient. An insensitive boor, camouflaged in technical regalia, is still an insensitive boor."

The best way to find a good external evaluator is through recommendations from other people, preferably from those who have been involved with internationalization efforts. Seeking recommendations from former and current BIE project directors is an efficient way to obtain names. Other suggested sources of recommendations are faculty at schools with strong IB programs, and individuals at the federally-funded CIBERs.

Once a list of potential individuals has been compiled, the next step is to request and obtain their curriculum vitae, and determine their general availability. Vitae are one source of information, and telephone interviews are strongly advised. A ranking of qualifications may then be made based on what is important to one's particular situation. For example, what might be most important for a formative evaluation of a BIE project is that the evaluator has had experience working with BIE projects.

Although the evaluator is a crucial component of an objective, finding the "perfect" evaluator is probably an impossible quest. Wholey et al. stress the idea of "practical program evaluation," and this concept is worth mentioning again. A well-done, useful evaluation can be conducted by someone who is not "perfect." Less than ideal does not mean useless.

When Should Evaluation Occur?

A plan for evaluation and assessment should be developed when the international business project or program is being planned. During the initial development of goals and objectives, *how* these outcomes are to be measured needs to be determined. Performance measures are characteristics used to assess performance aspects of a program or project. Performance indicators are target levels of performance expressed in measurable terms against which actual achievement can be compared.

One of the barriers to a complete, usable evaluation is the lack of agreement between intended users and evaluators on the goals, objectives, and performance criteria that will be used in evaluating the program (Wholey et al.).

In addition, program goals and objectives are sometimes found to be unrealistic once the evaluator begins the evaluation process. If the evaluation plan had been developed during the program planning stages, the weaknesses will likely have been already revealed.

Another difficulty can be the establishment of objectives that are not measurable. This problem can be eliminated during the developmental phase if the evaluator is involved early on. Since the evaluator will be assessing the accomplishment of performance indicators, he or she will be able to determine whether performance indicators can be written for the objectives. For example, if an objective states that "students will develop an awareness of international business," the evaluator might discuss the need to operationally define "awareness." How will "awareness" be measured? Without the means to measure an objective, an accurate and meaningful evaluation cannot be conducted.

To illustrate the points made in the preceding three paragraphs, Exhibit 12.2 presents three examples of goals, objectives, and performance criteria for international business projects.

Exhibit 12.2

Project Goals, Objectives, and Performance Criteria (Examples)

Goal	Objective	Performance Measure	Performance Indicator
Increase students' knowledge of international business	New senior-level elective IB course will be developed	Percent of business seniors enrolled in course; course grades earned	50% of business seniors enrolled; 70% of these students earn "B" or higher course grade
Increase business faculty members' knowledge of international business	Faculty will attend Faculty Development in International Business (FDIB) programs	Percent of faculty who participate in FDIB programs during two-year period	80% of faculty participate in FDIB programs over a two-year period
Increase awareness of local businesspeople concerning international business	One-day seminar on "Doing Business Internationally" will be presented	Number of people attending; attendees' evaluation of seminar	Minimum of thirty attendees; 80% evaluate seminar as "effective" or "very effective" in increasing their awareness of IB opportunities

As shown earlier in Exhibit 12.1, formative evaluation should be ongoing throughout the project. This type of evaluation, formative evaluation, is designed to monitor the program or project while it is in operation in order to determine strengths and weaknesses of the activities, as related to the program's objectives. The evaluation needs to occur while adequate time is available to make any adjustments in the project's operations. Orlich explains that when people associated with a program realize they are being constantly monitored and helped, they are more likely to keep their focus on measurable objectives and performance indicators. Thus, they are more likely to think, "Is this working the way we believed it would?" and "Are we obtaining the results we anticipated?"

If formative evaluation has been built into a program, then the evaluation at the end of the project, known as summative evaluation, can be conducted easily and efficiently. As shown earlier in Exhibit 12.1, the task of the summative evaluator is to determine the degree to which goals and objectives were attained.

Additionally, another reason exists for working with the evaluator to design the evaluation plan during the initial program development: this inclusion will remind the planners that evaluation is needed. By expanding one's approach to planning so that it is more than just developing goals and objectives and designing activities, evaluation will be viewed as an integral part of a project from its inception to its completion.

The question of when should evaluation occur may be answered simply: it should occur *formatively* throughout the project or program's lifetime, and it should happen *summatively* at its conclusion (or periodically, as determined at the outset, if it is an ongoing program).

How Is Evaluation Conducted?

Two important points that have already been presented in this chapter are worth emphasizing again: evaluation and assessment should not be an afterthought, and evaluation must be tied to measurable objectives. Another key point must also be stressed: if objectives change, then the evaluation plan must reflect these changes. Orlich stresses that formative evaluation often shows weaknesses in the program plan: "If a program, course, or project needs to be modified because of unrealistic expectations (objectives), then why not alter it?"

Ideally, the evaluator should be an external evaluator, but in some cases an internal evaluator can be the more appropriate (and certainly the most cost-effective) person to be involved in the planning stages and in the ongoing formative evaluation. Often, in fact, an external evaluator cannot be hired for the planning phase. For example, if the project is one that is being submitted to a funding agency, the agency will not usually pay for costs incurred in planning. In such a case, evaluation should still occur during the developmental phase, but it would involve internal evaluators who would be performing the services as part of their regular job duties. An external evaluator could be planned for and brought in to do a final summative evaluation.

Focusing the evaluation is a crucial step that occurs during the planning of the evaluation. The evaluator and the client program director need to clarify three key items: evaluation questions, procedures, and costs (Stecher and Davis). Evaluation questions should relate to the program objectives. Exhibit 12.3 illustrates examples of this relationship.

Exhibit 12.3

Program Goals, Objectives, and Evaluation Questions

Program Goals	Program Objectives	Evaluation Questions
To internationalize the business faculty	80% of the faculty will attend Faculty Development in International Business (FDIB) programs	What percent of the faculty attended FDIB programs?
To create an IB major	To recruit thirty students for the major and retain half after the first year	1. How many students are enrolled in the IB major in year one? 2. What percent of first-year enrollees have continued in the major in year two?
To add international content to existing business courses	To integrate IB material into five courses	In which courses are IB materials integrated?
To assist local business with international trade	M.B.A. students enrolled in IB courses will serve as consultants to companies seeking to begin exporting	1. How many companies sought assistance? 2. How many companies began export activities as a result of this assistance?

Sometimes the evaluation questions will be broad. For example, a goal might be to establish a study abroad program, and one measurable objective might be that at least ten students will participate in the program each year over three years. However, perhaps the project designers also want to know what resulted from these overseas experiences. To discover such information, an evaluation question would have to be framed more specifically, such as "What are the consequences of establishing a study abroad program?" in addition to the specific question of "How many students participated in a study abroad program each year?"

Second, the procedures that will be used to carry out the evaluation need to be clarified. The evaluation questions form the basis for what is often referred to as the *evaluation design*. "A design is a plan which dictates when and from whom measurements will be gathered during the course of an evaluation" (Fitz-Gibbon and Morris). The evaluator needs to determine whether complex procedures are needed, or if perhaps simpler ways of obtaining the necessary data might exist. Determining the procedures to be used is crucial, because the procedures dictate the length of time for the evaluation, the costs involved, and other aspects.

Tuckman emphasizes that the design depends on whether the evaluation is formative or summative. Once again, *formative* design seeks to assess the ongoing program activities in relation to program objectives, but does not seek to demonstrate the program's relative superiority or inferiority compared to alternatives; whereas *summative* design looks at whether the program being evaluated accomplishes its purpose better than alternative means. Exhibit 12.4 presents data collection methods often used in, but certainly not restricted to, *formative* evaluation.

Summative evaluation can be quantitative or qualitative. *Quantitative* evaluation is usually more precise and less likely to be questioned if the results are not as favorable as program planners, administrators, and other involved parties would like them to be. However, quantitative evaluation appears to be underutilized in IB programs.

Because this chapter is an overview of evaluation and not an in-depth presentation, quantitative evaluation design is not discussed in detail. The reader is referred to the sources cited and additional texts listed in the *Chapter Reference Notes and Additional Resources* at the end of this book for additional avenues to information.

Since summative evaluation seeks to determine whether change has occurred as a result of the program, a logical question is "Could other factors, not the program, have resulted in change?" This question relates to what is known as *internal validity*; that is, the validity with which any effects can be attributed to the program. Ideally, the data-gathering design should help to rule out explanations, other than the program, for measured effects.

A second important issue involves the *external validity* of evaluation. External validity refers to the generalization of findings from one specific evaluation to other programs. This validity can provide useful information for future programs.

Internal and external validity need to be differentiated because different information may be required to establish each one. A design that increases internal validity might weaken external validity. The emphasis that is placed on internal or external validity will vary, depending on decisions agreed to between the evaluator and the program planners.

Typical Formative Evaluation Data Collection Methods

Exhibit 12.4

Method	Description	Example
Focus groups	Small group participants present their reactions to program activities	Students in a new IB course discuss their reactions
Observation	Watching the delivery of an activity, or videotaping the delivery	The actual teaching of a new IB course and the students' reactions are observed
Open-ended interviews	Asking open-ended questions of program participants on an individual basis	Businesspeople who have received export assistance are interviewed
Message analysis	Seeking participants' reactions to written or other types of communication	A selected sample of the recipients of an IB pro-motional brochure are surveyed
Expert judgement	Asking individuals with extensive experience to offer expert opinions	Faculty at other colleges with an IB major are asked to give their ideas about yours
Equipment trial	Physical trial testing for possible program purchase or use	A database system being considered for international finance research is tested
Activity or participation log	Determining the actual use of a facility or the participation in an activity	The sign-in log of a multimedia modern language laboratory is analyzed
Organizational records	Examining records kept by an organization for purposes other than evaluation	Student rosters are analyzed to determine the number enrolled in a new IB course
Written questionnaires	Using structured questions for written or telephone surveys	Faculty complete surveys about their participation in FDIB programs

Two techniques are generally incorporated into evaluation designs to eliminate problems with internal and external validity. These techniques are the use of control groups and the randomized assignment of subjects to the groups. From an ideal perspective, these techniques are a necessity. However, from a practical perspective, sometimes these techniques cannot be employed. To ensure the best possible evaluation design, the evaluator and the program manager need to discuss thoroughly the evaluation design and reach an understanding of the ramifications of the chosen design. Fitz-Gibbon and Morris present a useful explanation of six types of research designs. A qualified external evaluator should be familiar with these designs and be able to use the most appropriate approach.

An alternative to, or supplement to, the quantitative aspects of summative evaluation is the qualitative approach. Tuckman describes qualitative research as having the following features: (1) the natural setting is the data source, (2) description is the primary focus, (3) both process and product are considered, and (4) the essential concern is with what things mean, that is, the "why" as well as the "what." Common questions studied in qualitative evaluation are:

- What was intended?
- What was actually done?
- What were the results?

Exhibit 12.5

	Possible Evaluation Procedures
Evaluation Questions	*Procedures*
What percent of the faculty attended FDIB programs?	The evaluator obtains a list of all faculty and then determines which ones participated in FDIB programs. This determination could be made by reading reports from all faculty who attended programs or by asking the project director for a list of faculty who participated. A percentage is then calculated.
1. How many students are enrolled in the IB major? *2. What percent of first-year enrollees have continued in the major in year two?*	Student rosters for years one and two are analyzed. All students with a declared IB major are counted, and the list for year one is compared to the list for year two. A percentage is then calculated.
In which courses are IB materials integrated?	Faculty are queried, and the number of courses with new IB materials is tallied.
1. How many companies sought assistance? *2. How many companies began export activities as a result of this assistance?*	Organizational records or participation logs are analyzed. Open-ended interviews or questionnaires provide information to answer question two.

Data sources that are usually used in qualitative evaluation are interviews with program managers, administrators, professors, students, and others; additional data sources include documents such as proposals, public relations material, curriculum units, and observations of the program in action.

Exhibit 12.5 uses the evaluation questions shown in Exhibit 12.3 to illustrate possible evaluation procedures.

What Does Evaluation Cost?

Estimating the general cost is an important step in focusing the evaluation. Indeed, the choice of procedures might depend on the cost of each alternative. For example, costs associated with questionnaires include the time involved in writing and field-testing, printing and postage, follow-up with nonrespondents, and data analysis. Personal interviews are labor-intensive, and these costs may be high. The evaluator and the program manager might, therefore, decide to use methods that are less costly than questionnaires or personal interviews.

In addition to the costs incurred for data collection, other costs will be incurred. The external evaluator will have to be paid for the initial consulting, whenever that may be. Ideally the external evaluator should be involved during the initial program development, in which case the same evaluator can perhaps be involved in formative evaluation, and definitely should conduct the summative evaluation.

Fees for the time involved in the data collection, analysis, and report writing must also be considered. These fees, which are usually grouped together as "consulting fees," should be agreed upon before the evaluator begins the data collection. No standard fee has been established for evaluation consulting, but several points need to be emphasized:

- The evaluator needs to propose an acceptable fee based on the evaluation procedures and the estimated time that will be involved in carrying out these procedures and with writing the evaluation report.

- If the program director views the fee as too high, the director and the evaluator will need to discuss whether alternative, less costly procedures might be employed.

- To avoid misunderstanding, specific agreement needs to be reached between the evaluator and the program director concerning the evaluation procedures and the length and depth of the evaluation report.

- Both parties must keep in mind that the evaluator should receive fair professional compensation.

- In addition to the evaluation consulting fee, travel and *per diem* expenses are usually included in evaluation costs.

- A properly conducted evaluation should be carefully planned as an interactive cooperative process that involves both the client and the evaluator. Never assume that an evaluator will be ready at a moment's notice, and will necessarily accept whatever fee the project director cares to offer.

What is the Format of the Evaluation Report?

The evaluation report answers the evaluation questions and explains the procedures that were used to determine the answers (Fink and Kosecoff). The report should be clear, concise, and correct. It should explain what was done, how it was done, and why it was done. As is true with all other aspects of evaluation, one must be careful to distinguish between a formative report and a summative report because each type contains information specific to its purpose.

The overall purpose of both types of evaluation, however, is action. "An evaluation report that is received and placed on a shelf, with no action taken, is reflective of a poorly conceptualized, executed, and reported design" (Steffy and English).

During the formative evaluation period, several reports might be written. They could be issued on a regular basis, such as monthly or quarterly, or on an as-needed basis. If the evaluation is summative, then the report is issued at the conclusion of the project or program. Hendricks, writing in Wholey et al., presents six overall principles to guide reporting:

- The burden for effectively reporting the evaluation results is on the evaluator, not the audience.

- The evaluator should be persistent and actively look for opportunities to report results.

- The report should be simple and create interest.

- The report should be targeted for the specific audience and not be generic.

- The focus of the report should be on actions.

- Reporting should be done in many different ways: in writing, in personal oral briefings, with computer-generated presentation graphics, and with videotapes.

The focus of the remainder of this section is on the written report. Wholey et al. and Morris and Fitz-Gibbon present useful information about oral reporting and briefings. A credible printed evaluation report should include the following components (Fink and Kosecoff; Morris and Fitz-Gibbon):

1. *An executive summary.*

2. *An introduction* that puts the evaluated program in context. The program should be briefly described, including goals and objectives; and the evaluation questions should be presented.

3. *A description of the evaluation design.* This section should explain why the evaluation was conducted, its intended outcomes, and the limitations on the scope of the evaluation. The remainder of this section should describe the methodology, that is, how the program was evaluated. Samples of all instruments should be included in the appendix and referenced in the text. "It is important that this description be detailed; if people are to have faith in the conclusions of the evaluation, they need to know how the information was obtained."

4. *The evaluation findings.* This section, presents the results of the various measurements. The answers to the evaluation questions are also provided. Additionally, the results may be interpreted and discussed in this section or alternatively, the discussion of results and the conclusions may be presented in a separate section following the findings. Tables and graphics make the data more understandable, and their use is highly recommended.

5. *Recommendations.* Although most evaluation reports contain recommendations, not all clients ask for or want recommendations. Sometimes they might prefer to calculate changes or alternatives for themselves. The evaluator needs to know in advance whether recommendations are wanted, and if so, how extensive they should be.

Hendricks, writing in Wholey et al., recommends the use of action-oriented reports. In this type of report, which is often structured as a series of short reports, very little attention is given to a description of the study's background and methodology. The findings are the most important part of an action-oriented report, with analysis limited to key points that give an overall picture. Graphics are extensively used, and conclusions and recommendations are always included.

Because the evaluation report is a professional document, the program manager should expect high quality in both format and writing, as well as in content. A title page containing the title of the program and its location, the name of the evaluator, the name of the receiver, the period covered by the report, and the submission date should always be included. If the report is formal and long, a transmittal letter and table of contents might be included. If the report is less formal, shorter, and of the action-oriented type, the transmittal letter is not needed and even the table of contents is optional.

For ease of reading, the text should be double-spaced. Headings and subheadings should be used. A twelve-point serif font is recommended; and although right margin justification has a clean look, it takes longer to read than nonjustified material. The report should be printed on high-quality paper and bound with a cover; spiral binding is good in that it allows the report to lie flat during reading.

The writing style used depends on whether the report is to be formal or more informal. If it is formal, third person should be used, and the report will have a more detached, less personal tone. If the report is more informal or of the action-oriented type, first-person is acceptable and the report will have a more conversational tone.

All evaluation reports should be written with clarity, which means that accessible vocabulary, short sentences (mixed with sentences of medium length for variation), and short paragraphs are recommended. The evaluator should strive to make the report highly readable. Jargon and technical language that might be unknown or confusing should also be avoided. Probably the most obvious aspect of a well-written report is that it is easily understood the first time that it is read.

Final Note

Evaluation is a planned process that determines the extent to which objectives were met and assesses the impact of the described outcomes. Evaluation is a necessary component of internationalization efforts. Evaluation can be formative (to monitor the program's activities) or summative (to determine the extent to which objectives were attained).

Although internal evaluators may be used for formative evaluation, external evaluators are preferred. For a fully researched and highly respectable summative evaluation, an external evaluator is truly essential.

A plan for evaluation should be developed when the program or project itself is being developed. Program objectives must be measurable, for evaluation must be tied to outcomes that are measurable. Evaluation questions, procedures (evaluation design), and costs need to be clarified during the planning of the evaluation. With thoughtful preparation, you can look forward to an evaluation report that is a professional document that is clear, concise, accurate, and, above all, useful.

While evaluation is sometimes viewed as one of the more unpleasant aspects of internationalization, it is one of the most essential. Evaluation results can serve as a set of coordinates for changing course, staying the course, or abandoning the journey. Moreover, results from evaluations of IB programs and projects form the basis for seeking new funds and justification for continuing funds. In reality, evaluation is the historical account of IB programs and the foundation for building and growing.

CHAPTER THIRTEEN

Tips from the Field

Margarete M. Roth

The objectives for your IB programs have been defined. Financing has been secured and it appears as though you are building the team and overcoming resistance. Overseas partnerships have been established. But how do you move from paper to practice, from objectives to activities? This chapter discusses ways to implement your programs based on tips and experimentation from colleagues in the field. The approach taken here views the implementation process as a complex web of interconnected management functions and project management activities necessary to add value to your programs to achieve your objectives in the following areas:

- Faculty involvement and development
- Curriculum development
- Administration involvement and development
- Business and finance office involvement
- Business community involvement
- International champion and support staff involvement and development

Faculty Involvement and Development

Faculty development is the primary objective to be achieved in order to ensure program implementation. Exhibit 13.1 shows the required inputs, value-added components, and desired outcomes from this process. The primary task to accomplish this objective is to establish a working committee of faculty and graduate assistants who will actively support and implement parts of the internationalization activities. Crucial for success are people who have some background in international matters or have shown a strong interest and who can be expected to perform. Ideally, they have already helped with the conceptionalization of the program and their roles have been outlined in the strategic plan. This group should be kept small, but people with different skills and from different backgrounds are needed for implementation. Major decisions need to be shared with them and they need to feel that their ideas are honored and will be incorporated into IB projects. This group also needs to be constantly rejuvenated. When situations or conditions change, new people should be invited to join.

Exhibit 13.1

Faculty Involvement and Development

Inputs	Value-Added Implementation	Desired Outcomes
Expertise and experience of existing faculty Strategic plan for faculty hiring and faculty development Existing faculty exchanges Financial resources	Team-building • within business school • across disciplinary lines Internal working committee Faculty development programs through • FDIB • research • overseas trips and teaching/research • seminars/workshops Faculty hiring Reward system	Creation of a "critical mass of faculty" • who have knowledge about IB • who have had overseas experience • who will infuse their courses with international business questions, examples, and case studies

Generally, members of this group do not receive release time or stipends. Therefore, to ensure their continued involvement, incentives need to be developed. These might include:

- Implementation of ideas brought forth by group members or explanation why suggestions were not implemented

- Group access to resource materials and training possibilities

- Formation of subgroups to carry out specific activities

- Development and implementation of a reward system

- Communication with members on a regular basis

- Demonstration of how team members benefit their own area and themselves

It is also useful to remember that no other individual is as concerned about this particular academic endeavor and its individual programs as the IB champion or director of an internationalization grant. The tendency of a knowledgeable champion to skip steps that are important for others' understanding should be avoided. Therefore sharing of thoughts is very important.

Besides the working committee, there is the larger group of faculty members who will be directly involved in the execution of activities or who will receive training. It is worthwhile for smaller colleges to go through the whole roster of faculty and for universities to go through the roster of the business school to see who could benefit from direct involvement in the international aspects of business teaching and research, and in turn benefit the university. This list of faculty will include people who already have an international background and experience as well as those who are interested and are able to move into the international arena. The larger the group of faculty who feel that they will benefit, the more successful implementation will be, and this group will almost certainly include faculty from other departments.

While the strategic plan includes a time schedule, the first thing a director will notice is that time frames will most likely have to be adjusted. This can be done efficiently by breaking activities down into smaller time units, assigning work related to these units, and negotiating deadlines with people. It is a good idea to provide those involved with a reminder of a deadline, including a reason for its importance. This is especially true if other people have to wait until one part of the planning or implementation process is completed before they can begin or complete their own. Negotiating for deadlines across national borders becomes more complex because the attitude toward time can differ by culture.

The adage "time is money" does not apply neatly to cultures where leisure is thoroughly woven into business. Building international alliances in such cases will take longer and, while these alliances are being worked out, planning should be done on other U.S. internationalization activities which do not rely on decisions from overseas partners. On the other hand, even within the U.S., time problems arise: answers are not forthcoming, priorities shift, people are not available when needed or can't commit themselves.

Here are some of the criteria for selecting faculty for involvement in the internationalization process:

- preexisting international background and experience

- motivation for new training in the international area

- people skills, including cross-cultural communication skills with people from different backgrounds

- flexibility

- proven record of bringing programs and activities to fruition

- proven research, teaching, curriculum innovation, or outreach skills

Determine Costs

Internationalization is expensive, and in most cases cannot successfully be implemented without outside funding. Costs of different approaches to internationalization should be estimated and hard decisions made on what can realistically be achieved with limited funds and resources. Once this is accomplished, approval of an internal budget is important before applying for outside funding (the next important step) because many funding agencies insist on matching institutional commitment. Unfortunately, many projects start with great enthusiasm by dedicated faculty only to be abandoned due to lack of funds.

Provide Incentives

It may be difficult to get new faculty members interested in rearranging their priorities for such IB training, so it is very important that incentives are given up front when at all possible. Generally, release time is a better incentive than stipends. Release time allows a faculty member time for research or other activities. Faculty should be given the choice, however, and in either case there should be a clear understanding (spelled out in writing) of what is being paid for and specifically what the expectations are.

Universities have come up with a variety of other creative incentives: extra stipends, travel money, domestic and overseas projects, competitions for research grants, fully-paid conference and workshop attendance, discretionary funds for instructional materials, provision of better office space, freeing faculty from short-term teaching or committee responsibilities, international travel and setting up faculty discussion groups or seminars on internationalization, and promise of the latest technological support. If the library and computer center's holdings of international business resources are not adequate, this is the time to negotiate with the dean and the directors of these facilities for a pledge that more money will be earmarked for international acquisitions, especially in the early stages of internationalization.

The involvement of the dean or other appropriate person on campus is paramount for both completion of the agreed upon performance and for the rewards given to faculty.

The dean should be informed when a faculty member has performed well. A short unsolicited note to be put in the faculty member's file is always appreciated. Promotion and tenure committees do look at recommendations and letters of support from people other than those who normally evaluate a faculty member. This type of recognition is also most appreciated by younger faculty who are not tenured or can still apply for promotions. Rewards will depend upon an institution's needs and what motivates individual faculty members to do an outstanding job. Money is not the sole incentive.

Build the Team

By nature, international business is interdisciplinary, and departmental cooperation is crucial. Besides the modern language, political science, modern history, and anthropology faculty, those in the computer science and communication departments have much to offer for international education. This diversity necessitates team-building activities between faculty, department chairs, and deans of disciplines that have been traditionally separated by different philosophies, disciplinary subject matter, and teaching methods. Team-building activities can take a variety of forms:

- paying for political scientists to go to Academy of International Business (AIB) meetings and business professors to go to anthropology meetings

- giving guest lectures in each others' classes

- team-teaching, for example, "Introduction to International Business" by a business professor and an anthropologist or world geography professor

- developing programs with faculty from other departments

Faculty from the various departments will be involved in every step of the team-building, and in every activity of the internationalization process. This leads to a natural tension with the administration, who would like to centralize functions for efficiency, and faculty who want to decentralize for ownership purposes. To overcome this natural tension, dialogue between the two groups should try to forestall any attempts at "empire building" and should concentrate on solutions that provide positive solutions for all involved. For example, a centralized study abroad office can handle all technical considerations, like financial aid, passports, and visas, while individual departments retain the right to select the host universities and curricula for their students.

Develop Communications

Many well-planned projects break down during implementation because problems with international communications have not been understood and addressed. Generally, faculty members from other countries are interested in the internationalization of U.S. business programs and, therefore, will play a major role in the planning and implementation, but some cross-cultural training may still be necessary before engaging in projects that necessitate the input of people of different cultural backgrounds. Do the partners come from cultures that value fast-paced or slow-paced, formal or informal interaction; do they prefer direct or indirect, ornate or down-to-earth messages? Messages need to be translated into a style that is communicable and accessible to all parties. Allusion to situations, literary quotes, idioms, historical events should be of a global nature and have a universally accepted meaning or they should be explained or simply omitted. The chosen medium of communication needs to make all partners comfortable. Not everyone is as enamored of the fast and informal messages of e-mail as their U.S. counterparts.

Curriculum Development

To develop a cohesive IB curriculum, different objectives must be discussed, and compromises have to be made. Very practical questions (e.g., what level of competency in a second language will be required of students?) have to be traded off against a larger or smaller number of international business courses. Can some business courses be taught in a modern language other than English to fulfill both a second-language and a business requirement? These kinds of questions will arise and need to be answered. Exhibit 13.2 reviews the necessary inputs, value-added components, and the desired outcomes for curriculum development.

Exhibit 13.2

Curriculum Development

Inputs	Value-Added Implementation	Desired Outcomes
Existing international courses	Development, approval, and delivery of:	Increase of business majors with an introduction to the IB environment
Existing courses that need to be internationalized	• modules, examples, case studies for courses	Increase of business majors who have an in-depth knowledge of the IB environment
Existing international majors/minors/concentrations	• related courses in Political Science, Anthropology	Increase of business majors who can synthesize knowledge or related fields and different world regions crucial for work in an IB environment
Strategy/goal determination	• International Business major, minor, or concentration	
Faculty expertise	• interdisciplinary majors (with second-languages/international affairs/technology)	
Student demand		
Business demand		Increase of language and other disciplinary, majors with a knowledge of international business
Business expertise		
Financial resources		

Internationalization of courses, majors, minors, and internationalization across the curriculum takes a lot of time. Release time is therefore of the utmost importance. Many smaller universities cannot afford release time for planning the internationalization of a single course, but they may be able to ask a faculty member in business to internationalize all courses and grant a one-course release to do this. The reason that it takes time even to restructure an existing course is that many of the functional textbooks merely append an international chapter to the end, instead of weaving the material through all chapters. In addition, many faculty members have little understanding of the importance of cultural differences in international business. These problems will slowly disappear in the future, but they are very present today.

Initial Development

Curriculum development requires patience and great negotiation skills. The college should determine whether in an allotted time period (determined by a grant, or a mandate from the administration) it wants to simply make as many students as possible aware of international business, or whether it wants to reach for full implementation of an IB program. This will determine what kind of curriculum will be developed.

Because many curricular changes include changes in requirements, approval for new courses and overseas activities is necessary. To move a minor, major, or concentration from paper to practice can take years due to departmental, committee, school, and even state deliberations. To speed up the process of exposing students to international business in the short run, individual courses or modules can be offered. These can later become part of the full curriculum. This process is complicated because the IB curriculum integrates courses from other departments which may have to drop one of their courses to accommodate new courses for the IB major, like "Business French" instead of a French literature course or "International Political and Business Negotiations" instead of another political science course. It is therefore important that specific needs be communicated to the other departments and their input be sought on how best to fulfill them.

Approval of curriculum development or changes may run the gamut from simple approval by a department chair, to approval by faculty committees, or the faculty at large. Approval may even be required from state and regional accreditation agencies. The IB champion should find out the mechanics of and the time needed for the approval process, and the political reality of getting changes approved, before spending inordinate time on curriculum development.

Cost estimation and cost control for curriculum development will include stipends for personnel and the purchase of materials from outside the university, sometimes overseas. Cost estimates are complicated by exchange rate fluctuations and longer delivery times. Costs occur in different departments and, therefore, funding should be distributed to different departments based upon developmental needs. Thus, budget reallocations are a necessary reality.

Pay Attention to Detail

Curriculum development can have many goals and can take many forms. After the strategic plan has established what level of competency will be expected of the graduates, these goals will be implemented by different departments, including departments in overseas universities. Continuous quality control takes on an international flavor. To insure quality across the curriculum, the dean or department chair and the IB champion will have to work in close cooperation with other departments, including business departments at overseas universities. The champion is often not in a position to interfere when quality education is not provided by any of the interlinked departments, but this person should be ready to exert whatever pressure is available to keep quality the highest priority.

One of the most frustrating aspects of an international curriculum is the translation of U.S. course content, grading, and requirement systems into overseas academic policies and vice versa. Articulation agreements must be understood by all parties, and issues need to be addressed: who determines the final grade; will certain courses overseas count toward electives, core, or major requirements; how will credit equivalencies be determined? Every country has developed its own terminology and it's desirable to spell out equivalencies at the beginning of an agreement rather than determine them on a course-by-course basis. Universities can use the guidelines that their international student office has developed, while smaller colleges can engage the services of Educational Credential Evaluators (ECE).

One of the most frustrating aspects of starting to internationalize is the fact that not all activities have a demand. This reality can be both psychologically depressing and financially ruinous. If the demand is not present, an activity should not be pursued or it should be modified. If internationalization of the curriculum is a relatively new venture, there is a risk that the new courses or programs will compete with existing programs for scarce students. A separate major competes for potential business students and can slow down the internationalization of functional business areas.

Administration Involvement and Development

Due to academic evolution, as well as increasing competition, many universities and colleges are presently engaged in rewriting their mission statements and strategic plans and restructuring their administration. It is important that people who champion the internationalization of the business curriculum—and, in fact, the whole campus—participate in that process. Exhibit 13.3 outlines the key components for administration involvement and development.

Exhibit 13.3

Administration Involvement and Development		
Inputs	**Value-Added Implementation**	**Desired Outcomes**
Expertise and experience of administration International components of strategic plan and mission statement Administrative champion Financial resources	Cooperation of faculty and administrators Creation of interest in and dissemination of knowledge about international business affairs to decision-making administrators Offer of incentives to administrators	Creation of a "critical mass" of administrators who will support the internationalization effort with: • increases of human and financial resources • help to get international programs and activities approved within the university and by government agencies

A determination of which administrators can be of greatest help with the successful implementation of the internationalization process should precede the estimation of time needed to gain the full support of the administration. If administrators have little international expertise or experience, it may take considerable time to convince them that internationalization is important for survival. It is useful to apply for grants which allow administrators to go overseas, or to attend seminars such as those offered by some CIBERs. A more formidable obstacle is the fact that internationalization costs money: faculty salaries, transportation, mailing, telephone costs, instructional materials, and guest speakers are all more costly for activities abroad than for domestic projects. Establishing exchange programs means travel money will be needed. Monitoring students overseas is complicated, needs staff, and can be quite expensive.

An added problem arises for the IB faculty team with respect to undergraduate programs. Many administrators are convinced that a student with only a bachelor degree will not be hired in an international capacity, and therefore the high costs of internationalizing the business school are not justified. This is a myth. Many jobs that are not classified as international *do* have international dimensions, especially in purchasing and marketing. Because there are still few internationally-trained businesspeople, B.A. graduates move into international departments in a surprisingly short time. A recent survey of students (at Benedictine University) who graduated with an International Business and Economics B.A. degree over the last fifteen years showed that 60% now work in an international capacity, either in the U.S. or overseas.

Structure

Since the international dimension of faculty and curriculum development involves personnel from many departments and areas, reporting responsibilities can become sticky. Changes in organizational structures can be negotiated with administrators. Communication flows more freely and support is given faster when administrators are integrated into specific working committees, such as study abroad, faculty governance, or curriculum development.

If administrative support is not forthcoming in the short run, a change in strategy is warranted. However, if the relevant administrators are not interested in internationalization, only a long-term approach may yield results. Faculty with strong international background or interest should be recommended to serve on search committees for administrators. In state universities, suggestions by legislators can influence decisions to seek internationally-minded administrators.

Business and Finance Office Involvement

Part of the internationalization process involves internationalization of the business and finance office. It eases frustration greatly if charging and reporting procedures are worked out with the business office well in advance of any planned activity or curricular need. Expenses for overseas trips, purchase orders for overseas materials, stipends to be paid to overseas guest lecturers, salaries for extended overseas stays to be transferred, discounted tuition rates—all of these need to be worked out in a timely fashion. Exhibit 13.4 details the components for involvement and development of business and finance office personnel.

If internationalization is carried out with the help of a grant, one of the big concerns is the budget. It is easy to prepare a budget with a few categories when applying for funding, but it is much more difficult to divide the budget into smaller categories and to fit the expenditures into neat categories. A special problem arises when a grant includes a matching funds clause. Many times only part of the revenue or part of the salaries are used for matching funds. It is very important that at the beginning of the implementation process the office which handles budgets be involved in the process.

A detailed budget needs to be developed with line items both for the funded and matching expenditures. The grant directors, their assistants, the grants office, and the financial office of the campus have to be clear about how money is to be charged and allocated. If the grant is from the U.S. Department of Education, everyone should be familiar with the rules and double-check on what can or cannot be used as matching funds. This permission is also necessary when monies are to be used for budget items that were not in the original application or for certain items like overseas travel. It's better to spend some time up front getting permission than to try to justify expenditures at the end of the grant when memories are weak. In smaller colleges, the grants office is not set up to administer the financial part of the grant. Hiring a person who is knowledgeable about budgets and accounting procedures is money well spent.

Exhibit 13.4

Business and Finance Office Involvement and Development

Inputs	Value-Added Implementation	Desired Outcomes
Financial resources: • internal • external grant Expertise in international financial transactions Expertise in international business transactions	Training of personnel in: • international financial and business matters • financial accounting and reporting requirements of external grants	Cost-effective and efficient handling of international business and financial transactions in: • purchasing • marketing • cost determination with consideration of fluctuating exchange rates

Another related challenge with grant budgets are the requirements for keeping records and reports. The finance office can help in monitoring revenues and expenditures. If business and finance personnel are familiar with international rules and regulations of cross-national transactions, their expertise should be accepted and their leadership followed. If they are not, the administration should be asked for money for training sessions. Besides the financial knowledge, the two offices also have to be informed about the extra time needed, the different bureaucracies for approval and implementation of any activity, the complex distribution channels in purchasing and selling, and the different standards for advertising and publicity.

A good working relationship with the business and finance office is crucial to having programs which run smoothly.

Business Community Involvement

The business community is both a resource and a potential client for university services, and agreements and alliances (both formal and informal) will only further the internationalization process. In this environment there is the continuing opportunity to ask businesspeople what they would like us to teach our students, their future employees, and what kinds of outreach programs they need. Exhibit 13.5 shows the factors involved in making business community involvement and development effective.

Exhibit 13.5

Business Community Involvement and Development		
Inputs	**Value-Added Implementation**	**Desired Outcomes**
Expertise and experience of business-people from: • university board • advisory committees • part-time teachers • alumni • friends of the college • parents of students Willingness of business people to contribute to internationalization effort	Work with business community on: • domestic/overseas internships • joint research • guest-speakers • materials to be used in case studies • fundraising • workshops/seminars • business/faculty overseas tours • tours by students of internationally oriented businesses • export/import/investment training and mentoring of small business	Business community which is: • well-informed about internationally educated graduates • involved in the process of internationalization • has increased awareness, understanding, and competency of international business

In exchange for information and expertise given to the university, the business community can also receive valuable services from the university. The determination of what services the university can offer to the regional, national, and international business community must be constantly reevaluated in light of existing expertise at the university and the changing business environment.

Opportunities to Reach Out

If businesspeople are to be involved in presentations, consultations, joint research projects, and curriculum design, then time management becomes crucial. Businesspeople will commit themselves in advance, but they are also more likely than academicians to cancel at the last minute (through no fault of their own, but due to unforeseen circumstances). If a guest speaker cancels a few days before an event, the other speakers will often be willing to extend their presentations somewhat if asked before they arrive on campus. An even more productive approach is to negotiate ahead of time for the company to send a replacement if it becomes necessary.

Business outreach programs demand a certain sophistication on the part of the academic institution. A time frame may be developed to integrate increasingly more complex academic/business joint ventures: from using business professionals as guest speakers, to organizing and running a trade mission to other countries, or hosting an overseas trade mission. The further the internationalization process progresses, the more in-depth services the university can offer businesses. Costs and pricing of services to and from the business community take on an added complexity in the international arena. Costs for offering private export/import consulting and financial consulting to business clients are often very high, while the demand for these services can be quite elastic because they are mainly needed by medium and smaller sized businesses with limited budgets.

If the university has established a good working relationship with a wide network of regional multinational businesses, expenses can be controlled by engaging business professionals who will provide their services at no cost in a workshop setting. Low pricing of university services is especially crucial at the beginning of the internationalization process to ensure a sufficient demand and establish goodwill and a positive reputation. One way to attract participants to university-sponsored programs is to offer a discount rate to alumni, board of trustee members, and business faculty from regional institutions. However, take care that low pricing does not jeopardize the quality of programs.

Businesspeople who are motivated and knowledgeable are a powerful tool to speed up the internationalization process at all levels. Together with faculty, they can become a strong advocate for state legislatures to provide money for international trade centers at universities and community colleges, or to pass legislation to change educational requirements on the primary and secondary level, thus laying the groundwork for more globally-educated college freshmen.

To involve qualified businesspeople in all aspects of the implementation process, incentives have to be developed. They can range from free access to federal government international materials like the National Trade Data Bank that is updated every month, easy access to university research, access to highly qualified graduates, accessible and affordable trade consultations, and low-cost organized overseas trade missions.

Among the most mutually beneficial programs for the business school and the business community are workshops and seminars. They bring together academics and businesspeople from the U.S. and overseas, both as presenters and as participants. While planning, running, and evaluating any workshop involves many time-consuming details, a few extra steps need to be taken when the workshop deals with international speakers and participants:

- Determine the composition of U.S. and overseas businesspeople as participants and presenters and strike a good balance.

- Find the appropriate overseas guest speakers and always have other guest speakers as backup.

- Check for English oral proficiency.

- Provide translation services, if necessary.

- Create promotional services with international appeal.

- Engage overseas presenters for other international activities, such as a class presentation or an open forum to discuss possible internships.

Every detail has been planned. So what could go wrong? Titles of topics can have different meanings in different countries. Time constraints on a speaker may be perceived differently and can upset the timetable of the rest of the program. International flights are often delayed. All of these problems can present themselves in running domestic workshops, but they are more prevalent and more complex when dealing with international participants. It is useful to work out the logistics beforehand by staying in communication with the presenters about the timing, the topics, and the presentation techniques.

International Champion and Support Staff
Involvement and Development

The role of the IB champion is crucial to the implementation of the international-ization activities. This person, however, is usually not in a decision-making position like a dean or a department chair, and therefore must establish networks with the decision-making personnel at the school and the different stakeholders (faculty, students, businesspeople, and support staff) in the planned activities.

Multiple Roles and Tasks

Becoming visible at departmental and university-wide meetings, on advisory committees, and at local trade organization activities is a good way to advertise your program. Taking a leadership or sponsorship role in off-campus events will further publicize your program. It also gives the university access to off-campus resources. In Illinois, international champions from many public and some private schools have formed a consortium—the Illinois Consortium for International Education (ICIE)—which advocates state legislation that would speed up internationalization across the curriculum, and has established a partnership with business and industry.

Being an IB champion or the director of the internationalization process is time-consuming for both the faculty member and the supporting staff. Release time must be negotiated and approved for people from different departments and offices within the school. Since many of them will not be under the direction of the champion, monitoring their time involvement and quality of work becomes more complex. The monitoring will be facilitated if a good network with their supervisors has been established.

An investigation into how costs can be shared by different offices and departments in the school will minimize the cost involvement of the business school. For example, the technical aspects of study abroad, international internships, and exchange programs may be carried out by a university-wide international office; costs for a faculty member can be shared by two departments which teach cross-listed courses, such as upper-level business courses in a second-language.

A decision has to be made up front whether any of the support staff has to speak another language, and what level of international sophistication is necessary. The champion will have to be able to manage support staff services from different offices and, occasionally overseas, while at the same time communicating with administrators in different areas. These administrators should know what is expected in terms of time involvement, quality of service, and financial resources from their areas. The goals of other departments do not always fall nicely into the strategic plan of business school internationalization. Realistic compromises need to be pursued by the IB champion. Thus, conflict resolution skills are extremely useful.

Final Note

Perhaps the only way to fully understand the implementation aspects of an IB program is to go ahead and start one. Through the first-hand experiential process of trial and error, learning and trying new things, your IB team can develop a style and earn the respect of faculty colleagues, administrators, and staff. However, you and your team can also learn from the experience of earlier explorers, and this chapter has been an effort to gather together many of those invaluable tips from the field.

CHAPTER FOURTEEN

Title VI-B BIE Funding, a Survey of Success

Linda V. Gerber

The U.S. government has long recognized the role of international education programs in furthering our national interests. International education enhances cultural understanding and exchange, which in turn promotes positive relationships between the U.S. and other nations and provides a foundation for peaceful interaction. This perspective has led to the establishment of numerous and varied educational activities, including scholarship and grant programs, programs to enhance language skills and cultural competence, and the creation of institutional centers of international expertise.

Over the last several decades, the U.S. congress has acknowledged that national interests are related not only to international relationships, but to international commerce as well. Accordingly, federal funding has been established for educational programs directly related to international business and commerce.

A number of these programs related to international education are administered by the U.S. Department of Education (US/ED). It is the US/ED which oversees some of the well-known and highly respected Fulbright programs, which, in various forms, provide funding to institutions of higher education and individuals in support of international research and academic experience abroad. In addition, the US/ED directs several programs aimed at institutions, particularly in higher education. Some of the most important grant programs funded through the US/ED are the Title VI programs. These programs, which span a variety of specific purposes, have provided vital funding to schools seeking to internationalize their business programs. There are currently ten programs authorized under Title VI legislation, four of which are described below.

The National Resource Centers (NRC) program. NRC grants provide for the establishment of centers of expertise in specific geographic regions (such as Latin America, Asia, or Eastern Europe). The academic scope of the NRC is cross-disciplinary, and funded activities include student and faculty scholarships in support of international study, creation of curricular programs, scholarly academic research, the collection of scholarly reference materials, and delivery of educational programs for the larger community (high schools, business, governmental agencies). The aim of the program is to create and maintain repositories of knowledge and information related to key geographic regions of the world. Currently, NRC grants are awarded for a three-year period, and it is common for institutions to receive continuous funding over many years.

The Undergraduate International Studies and Foreign Language (UISFL) Program. This grant program aims to provide seed money for the development of curricular programs in international studies and foreign languages. Common activities that are funded under the UISFL program are course development, the foundation of study abroad programs, the creation and revision of curricular programs such as majors and minors, and the development of learning resources. It is common, though not required as with the NRC, for programs supported by UISFL grants to have a specific geographic focus. UISFL grants are typically short-term, with funding provided for up to two or three years.

The Centers for International Business and Education (CIBE, more commonly referred to as CIBER, the "R" standing for Research) program. The CIBER program is similar to the NRC program in that the aim is to create and maintain a resource for expertise in international business. However, unlike National Resource Centers, CIBERs are required to have a more global focus, though many are characterized by an emphasis on one or more geographic regions. CIBER funding supports a wide array of activities including scholarly research, curricular design, support for international study and exchange programs, language programs related to business and economics, and the development of support materials. CIBERs are required to provide extra-institutional educational programs for other higher education institutions. CIBER funding is awarded in three-year cycles, and again, like the NRCs, often provides continuing support for successful programs.

The Business and International Education Program (BIE). BIE grants are similar to UISFL programs, but with a stronger business focus. BIE grant recipients must engage in faculty and curricular development activities, and must partner with community organizations for the delivery of programs to local business constituencies. A wide range of activities is encouraged. BIE grants are awarded for up to two years. While some institutions receive multiple grants over time, the BIE program is designed to establish very specific programs which can be sustained without ongoing federal government support, so repeat awards are made only for the development of new initiatives.

It is an evaluation of the last of these, the Title VI-B Business and International Education Program, which is the focus of this chapter. Since its initial funding in 1983, the US/ED has awarded 300 two-year BIE grants to colleges and universities across the U.S. in support of the program's authorizing purposes. As is the case for many federal grant programs, there has been no comprehensive evaluation of the operation and impact of the BIE program. However, increasingly the federal government has placed a priority on ensuring that federal programs meet their intended purposes. This trend has been established through the Government Performance and Results Act of 1993 (GPRA) which requires all government agencies to develop strategic plans, establish performance goals, and measure performance relative to those goals. An outcome of the GPRA is that governmental agencies are now developing measures for long-term performance evaluation and are attempting to assess the impact of their past activities. The Title VI-B BIE program has the following performance objectives related to international education:

1. Enhance the expertise of faculty in business-related disciplines.

2. Create undergraduate and graduate curricula and programs in business-related disciplines.

3. Maintain a diversity of institutions of higher education offering instruction in business-related disciplines.

4. Foster and strengthen linkages between institutions of higher education and the U.S. business community.

5. Increase the number of outreach programs to the regional business community that provide the United States with the ability to engage in international economic activities.

6. Increase the number of study abroad/internship programs with international business content.

This chapter reports on a historical impact assessment of the efficacy of the BIE grant program in meeting its objectives. The evaluation project described here was undertaken partially in response to GPRA requirements. While the US/ED has established mechanisms to monitor activities and performance of grant recipients on an annual basis, there has also recently been a desire among program administrators to examine the grant program from an historical perspective. An evaluation of the impact of the Title VI-B BIE grants over time can serve as a benchmark for current annual measures of program activity and as a means to observe trends in the utilization and impact of specific federal funds. In addition, an historical assessment can provide program administrators with information about the relative usefulness of the various types of activities and programs undertaken by BIE grant recipients, both in terms of long-term impact and sustainability. This information can be used as a guide for institutions planning future BIE projects, to assist program administrators in advising BIE applicants and recipients, and to assist in shaping policy recommendations. Specifically, the study had five primary objectives:

1. To identify the range and frequency of various activities conducted as part of BIE projects.

2. To determine the direct impact of these activities on their targeted populations.

3. To ascertain the degree to which BIE awards have had a lasting impact on the internationalization efforts of funded institutions and the extent and nature of that impact.

4. To identify problem areas in project implementation and administration.

5. To evaluate internationalization activities in terms of their relative effectiveness and efficiency in meeting the purposes of the BIE program.

The CIBER at the University of Texas at Austin provided support for this study. The evaluation is consistent with the CIBER mission to provide direction for the internationalization efforts of higher education institutions across the United States.

Results of the evaluation indicate that the BIE program has been highly successful in meeting the intended goals of congress in establishing and funding the program. Further, BIE funded projects have not only demonstrated high impact on targeted populations in education and business, but have proved to be highly sustainable. The balance of this chapter describes the study methodology, results, and implications.

Methodology of the Study

The evaluation was completed in four phases consisting of an initial assessment of the scope of previous BIE projects, a pilot study to provide a foundation for developing a questionnaire, a pretest of the questionnaire, and a final survey. Based on both the pilot study and the survey pretest it became clear that it would be very difficult to obtain data from older grant projects due to the lack of availability of records and the turnover in personnel associated with the projects at recipient institutions. As a result, the final survey included only those institutions receiving BIE grants since 1989. The study concluded with the 1995 grant recipients who completed their funded projects in 1997. Thus, seven years of BIE grant awards were included in the survey—a total of 152 awards (although due to repeat awards this represented only 126 separate institutions). Questionnaires were sent to all recipients in the designated grant period.

A total of seventy-three questionnaires were completed and returned, representing a 58% response rate. Given the length and detailed nature of the questionnaire, this level of response is quite acceptable. Further, this number represents a full 27% of all BIE grants awarded over the history of the program. Finally, over 95% of the questionnaires were completed by someone directly involved in the funded projects which indicates that information is likely to be both accurate and reliable.

The questionnaire was organized around five typical BIE project activity areas: faculty development, course development, curricular development, business outreach, and academic outreach. In each area, the questionnaire was constructed to establish general impact, specific activities utilized in the project, the direct impact of those activities, the degree to which the activity area has been sustained at the institution beyond the grant period, and finally, the long-term impact of continuing programs.

Survey Results

Faculty Training and Research

Most academics are in agreement that faculty development is a fundamental aspect of internationalization, and one which has long-ranging impact. The BIE projects confirmed this. All the survey participants reported at least some activity designed to increase faculty expertise in international business and there was a high level of participation in faculty development programs (thirty faculty on average at each grantee campus). This level of faculty training naturally resulted in a very high level of student impact over time. As evidence of this, when asked to estimate the number of students who would have been affected by faculty who participated in faculty development programs, the survey respondents projected a total of over 350,000 students to date, for an average of over 5,400 students at each institution. Extrapolating this rate to the 270 BIE grants awarded would yield an estimate of *well over one million students* impacted by just this aspect of the BIE program alone.

The most common faculty development activity was faculty participation in workshops and seminars, followed by faculty attendance at professional conferences, and participation in international study trips and in internship programs. An indication of the significance of faculty development programs is that 68% of the institutions indicated that they are continuing some sort of faculty training activities. Faculty development was considered by many respondents to be one of the most important activities in their projects.

Another very encouraging finding of the survey was the high level of participation in Faculty Development in International Business (FDIB) programs offered by the CIBERs. Over 60% of the institutions surveyed reported sending faculty to CIBER-sponsored programs during their grant periods, and nearly 50% supported faculty participation in CIBER-sponsored FDIB programs subsequent to the grant.

In addition to training faculty, individual research projects were supported by over 60% of the institutions, with an average of over six projects each. Even more impressive is that nearly 45% of the projects resulted in publication of the research findings. Further, over 30% of the programs which funded individual research on international business topics during their projects continued to do so after the end of the grant period.

Course Development

Because course development is a required component of the BIE program, all participants reported some degree of compliance, with a high percentage (over 80%) resulting in course revision or new course development. Particularly encouraging is that over 85% of the institutions continued to offer at least some of the courses developed or revised under their BIE grant, and nearly 90% of the courses involved were still being offered at the time of the study. Naturally, this resulted in a very high number of students being exposed to new material in international business as a result of the BIE course development initiatives. The total number of students enrolled in courses which were either developed or revised as part of the BIE program, as reported by the survey participants, was nearly 130,000, representing an average of almost 1,900 per institution.

Curriculum Development

Nearly 70% of the BIE projects went beyond developing or revising courses and engaged in work on curricular programs with most of these (65%) developing new programs. A wide variety of curricular programming was undertaken, the most common of which were the development of specialized concentrations such as "International Accounting" or "Global Technology Management," followed by international business "majors" and then the development of "minors" and general "concentrations" in international fields. Minors and general concentrations were most common at the graduate level (usually in M.B.A. programs and in "Executive Education"), while majors and specialized concentrations were more common in undergraduate programs. Community colleges were the most likely to develop new degree programs— usually "associate" degree programs in international business or trade.

One particularly interesting insight from the survey was the very diverse and institution-specific nature of the curricular work undertaken. Of the programs noted, over 30% could not be classified as graduate or undergraduate, or, be easily fit into any common categorization. For example, those surveyed described a number of highly specialized summer programs, many involving international travel and language study. Other programs included certificate programs for the business community, and even curricular programs designed for faculty development and academic outreach. It appears that the BIE projects reflect clear understanding, by the institutions, of the particular needs of their students and target populations, and of their institution's resources.

Business Outreach

All approved applicants for the BIE program are expected to develop programs for the business community and establish formal alliances with a company, groups of companies, or other types of business and economic development organizations. Most of the grantees reported multiple partners on their projects, with an average of over three community partners on each grant project. One of the most encouraging findings in the evaluation study was the degree to which the institutions had maintained relationships with their business and professional communities after grant funding ended. Over 80% reported that they had continued to work with at least one of the affiliates from their BIE project. Moreover, the respondents indicated *even greater activity* with the business community after the conclusion of the grant.

Categorizing the types of organizational affiliates proved problematic. The wide variety of organization titles and the ambiguity regarding the private or public nature of the organizations made clear classifications sometimes impossible. Nevertheless, by far the most common type of affiliation was with trade promotion organizations, both governmental entities (such as the U.S. Department of Commerce Export Assistance Centers and state World Trade Centers), and quasi-governmental organizations (such as World Trade Councils and District Export Councils). The next most common were federal, state, and local economic development organizations such as the Small Business Administration, and the Massport Trade Development Center. Despite the important role of these business promotion organizations to the BIE projects, there was also a very high incidence of the respondents partnering with private industry. Many respondents named specific businesses as partners while others noted that "many" businesses were "affiliates."

In addition to questions regarding the formal affiliates in their BIE projects, survey respondents were further questioned about the organizations to which they provided services as part of their project activities. Not surprisingly, the business targets of BIE activities were often the same companies with whom the institution established formal affiliation for the purposes of the grant proposal. The exception was the many schools who focused on delivering services (such as workshops, company assistance, and trade directories) to a large market of entrepreneurs and small and medium-sized businesses in their geographic region.

The extent to which the BIE projects sought to respond to their specific business environment was clear. Overall, more than 4,000 different events and activities involving the business community were reported, and a very high number of companies and individuals were reached (over 45,000).

The most common activity delivered to the business community was individual company consultation and assistance on trade and exporting issues, followed by business internships for students and faculty, and student or faculty consulting projects. While direct individual assistance may be the most high-impact activity in terms of deep effects, the greatest impact in terms of numbers of individuals and companies affected were through seminars and workshops. Technically, however, the single activity which purportedly reached the greatest number of individuals in the business community was trade publication—two projects included development of trade directories for their business constituencies, and together over 30,000 of these two publications were distributed.

Academic Outreach

While academic outreach was not a required component of the BIE grant, many schools reported engaging in activities designed to benefit other academic institutions (68%). Sponsoring seminars, workshops, and conferences which included participants from other institutions, was both the most common and the highest-impact activity. BIE recipients also conducted faculty development programs, offered research grants, and shared instructional materials as part of their BIE activities. Moreover, over 80% of the programs engaged with other institutions reported they were continuing to carry on such activities.

While it is nearly impossible to gauge the possible effects of these efforts on faculty, students, and institutions, it is clear that the BIE awards have produced benefits for educational institutions well beyond the campuses of those schools who received funding.

Program Self-Evaluation

When asked to evaluate the overall success of their BIE projects, the respondents were strongly positive. The survey asked for a rating of the degree to which their BIE award had enhanced "the international academic program of the institution" and provided "appropriate service to the business community which will expand its capacity to engage in commerce abroad." Eighty-five percent of respondents believed that the grant had been either extremely successful or very successful in improving such international outreach business programs, and over 95% indicated at least a predominantly successful outcome. Nearly 70% believed their projects were either extremely successful or very successful in meeting the BIE program mandates in the business community—with nearly 100% rating the program as at least somewhat successful or better.

One particularly important and revealing self-evaluation question in the survey asked recipients to indicate which aspects of their projects had been most effective in meeting the BIE program objectives. All respondents answered this question and many noted multiple projects as being particularly effective. Overall, 130 different projects were mentioned, and, as might be expected, they were quite diverse. Some patterns, however, were evident. Two very different types of projects were most commonly cited: those which increased the international expertise and perspectives of the faculty, and those which forged strong links and delivered vital services to the business community. Curricular programs and course development were also commonly cited.

Noteworthy was a tendency for the respondents to select projects which have a more permanent nature as being the most effective. That is, the respondents had the highest regard for activities which established infrastructure (such as the initiation of a trade assistance center), made permanent changes in programs (such as curriculum development) or for individuals (such as international exchanges for faculty which result in appreciable shifts in perspective and understanding), or developed a permanent resource (such as databases, software, trade directories). In addition, a number of the programs noted as effective could be roughly-termed "hybrid" activities, in that they combined objectives and constituencies. Examples are projects where faculty or students consult with individual businesses, applied research for companies conducted by faculty members, faculty and student participation in trade missions, and courses or course sections taught by members of the business community.

Other responses regarding successful projects are notable. First, several respondents noted that BIE programs had established credibility for their programs with the business community and with university administrators. The respondents believed that this added credibility allowed them to establish relationships and programs which would not have been possible otherwise. As one respondent said, "This allowed us to prove ourselves." Next, a number of responses alluded to the relationships that their project established as having a lasting impact on or for the institution: relationships with the business community, relationships across the campus of their institution, and relationships with other educational institutions, both international and domestic. Some respondents referred to their projects as having established a "core" of faculty committed to or enthusiastic about internationalization. The clear implication seemed to be that establishing a "critical mass" of individuals was pivotal in the achieving of lasting effects in their projects and continued enhancement of their activities beyond the grant period. Finally, some of the respondents chose to comment on the general impact of the BIE award, rather than specific activities. Typically these responses noted the transforming role of the overall project in building a platform for ongoing international activities.

A second important self-evaluation question asked grantees to describe projects "which were particularly difficult to implement." Of those who responded (84%), two general types of problems were indicated. The first related to coordination among diverse constituencies such as academia and business, or between academic units within business or between businesses and other academic departments. These coordination problems ranged from the most basic implementation issues, such as scheduling specific events so that all targeted populations could be reached, to very profound cultural differences such as the differing priorities and orientation between business and other disciplines. The second general difficulty in implementation pointed toward an initial failure to calculate need for, or interest in, the proposed project. Many of the responses indicated concern that the projects did not generate greater response from the targeted populations and noted that many specific activities either were canceled, failed to achieve expectations, or required unanticipated marketing efforts to succeed. Whether these difficulties were due to a fundamental lack of planning, a lack of understanding of the true needs of constituencies, or simply unrealistic expectations on the part of the project proposal was not clear. What was clear is that some activities failed, as perhaps should be expected. Some rationales offered for failure that seem worth mentioning include insufficient support from faculty or administrators, bureaucratic delays in establishing curricular programs, and significant hurdles in developing internships (both domestic and abroad).

One measure of the general impact of the BIE grant program was the extent to which projects led to other grants. In this regard the responses indicated that the BIE program has been effective. Nearly 80% had applied for subsequent grants to fund the continued internationalization of their programs, and of these a 79% success rate was reported with many having received multiple awards. Most often these subsequent awards were BIE grants, although several received CIBER or UISFL grants. The remaining awards identified were either from other governmental agencies or from specific businesses. Although it was somewhat difficult to interpret the actual levels of funding received from the grants noted, a best guess is nearly $13 million or approximately $200,000 per award. A majority (56%) indicated that they planned to apply for other grants in the future with US/ED administered grant programs being the most common target.

A concluding section for the survey asked respondents to indicate the helpfulness of key parties in the development, application, and implementation of the BIE projects: their US/ED program officer, the US/ED grant office, faculty in their own institution, and their own administration. In general, respondents were pleased with the support they received during their grant project. The highest level of satisfaction was with the US/ED program officer who assisted the project directors, both during the preapplication process and on through the administration of the project (89% of the responses cited the program officer as being either extremely helpful or very helpful). The institutions' faculties were rated next most helpful (82% indicated that the faculty was extremely or very helpful). The US/ED administration and academic institution administration were evaluated lower, with "extremely" and "very" helpful ratings at 70% and 67% respectively. Still, satisfaction levels were generally positive for all parties.

Discussion of Survey Results

Limitations

In drawing general conclusions of the findings from this evaluation study, the limitations of the survey approach must be kept in mind. First, the study targeted only a specific time window of BIE grantee programs and projects, although there is no particular reason to expect that this would materially affect the conclusions of the study. If anything, this factor could serve to underestimate the overall impact of the BIE program, since the multiplier effect of early grants is not captured in the measures of long-term effects, as for example, in the number of students affected by course development activities.

A second concern relates to the inherent factor of nonresponse bias. Despite a response rate of 58%, the potential for self-selection may color the responses to make the impact appear more favorable: those who did not have successful grant experiences may not have responded. Nevertheless, the overwhelmingly positive assessment of the BIE program by those who did respond would indicate that any nonresponse bias would affect only the degree, and not the essence, of the benefits of the BIE grants to the internationalization process of educational institutions.

Outcomes and Implications

Meeting BIE objectives. Although it would be a gross overstatement to attempt to directly link the success of U.S. business in world markets to the BIE program, the magnitude of some of the effectiveness measures implies that the program has played some role in impacting U.S. competitiveness. Clearly the program has enjoyed a high degree of success in bridging the gap between business and academia. Considering the increased number of students exposed to international dimensions of business, and the number of individuals in the business community reached in just the limited number of projects included in this study, it is apparent that the program has been successful in its approach. Through its multiplier effects, it has clearly achieved results consistent with the aims of the program.

Developing high-impact activities. In terms of the sheer numbers of individuals reached, the activities which have had the greatest impact are course development, faculty development, seminars, conferences, and workshops for the business community. Depth of impact is much more difficult to gauge. But the tone of many grantees in their responses to the open-ended questions included with the surveys indicate that one-on-one programs for the business community (such as consulting projects and directed research, and direct international experiences for faculty and students), were the most influential in internationalizing efforts.

Platform-building. An extremely impressive finding of the study was the very high level of continuation of activities after the funding for the project had ceased. Clearly the BIE awards have had an impact far beyond the specific direct effects of the projects and activities undertaken.

Cross-fertilizing grant programs. Another important conclusion from the study is the degree to which seed grants to one institution have secondary effects in other institutions. This was evident in the number of academic outreach activities undertaken by the reporting institutions. It was further seen in the cross-fertilization between the BIE and other grant programs and particularly the CIBER program, both in terms of the faculty involved in BIE projects who attended CIBER faculty development programs, and also in the number of schools who have received or plan to apply for other US/ED grants.

Maintaining flexibility. Across the major activity areas, the projects reported represented a wide diversity of programming. This further demonstrates the advantage of flexibility in the BIE program guidelines. The lack of rigid performance and activity requirements allows each institution to target their project to the specific needs of their region, institution, faculty, resources, and students.

Bridge-building. The requirement that project proposals include formal affiliations imposes an implicit accountability on the education institutions to follow through on their proposed activities involving the business community. Because there can be significant cultural differences between academia and the business communities, without this requirement it is all too likely that such associations might be avoided or would be abandoned during points of tension or frustration. The specific business component requirements of the BIE programs encourage a level of cooperation which can be embraced by those who have forged these long-term relationships.

Based on the survey results, future applicants and policy makers would do well to consider the ingredients for success:

- *Stress faculty development.* Faculty development activities are highly important to building a base for internationalization. Further, these initiatives should be designed to create a core or critical mass of faculty members committed to international business activities.

- *Conduct pre-proposal needs assessment.* Project design should include assessment of demand for various potential activities. Many programs which appear to be appealing may not actually generate demand.

- *Customize project activities.* Successful projects must build on the specific resources of the institution and tailor programs to their specific constituencies rather than employing boilerplate programs.

- *Set achievable goals.* Having realistic expectations and achievable goals for project activities, maintaining focus, and not attempting too many tasks, particularly when initiating internationalization efforts are all important for success. This is particularly true for activities which require interaction and coordination across many individuals and groups.

- *Be incremental within a long-term plan.* Internationalizing a business program is a long-term process. Schools can build on initial efforts with subsequent grants, so think of an internationalization effort in terms of phases of development and seek funding for consecutive phases.

- *Institutionalize project activities.* Though not feasible for all project dimensions, activities which lead to permanent change or create tangible output have long-term results. Where possible, international activities should be woven into institutional systems and structures.

Final Note

The last two decades have brought enormous change in the U.S. perspective on international trade and business. Educational programs, funded by the U.S. government, can be given partial credit for this expansion of business horizons, and in particular the BIE grant programs surveyed and discussed in this chapter show how relatively small investments can achieve substantial returns. Most BIE awards are funded at between $50,000 and $90,000 each year, and the total annual program cost is approximately $4 million. For this expenditure, which is matched by the funded institutions dollar for dollar, the government is able to leverage immediate benefits, build a framework which continues to yield returns beyond the grant period, and has a multiplying effect through the human capital which is developed. Clearly this has been a successful program, one which continues to deliver sustainable and significant results. The Title VI-B BIE Program continues to prepare us for the future, and the future is now.

Afterword

Eugenio Oblitas Díaz

In lectures to his students, Marshall McLuhan advised that they only read the even-numbered pages of books which describe techniques because the odd-numbered pages were redundant. This book, with its focus on internationalizing business education, clearly dispels McLuhan's half-serious caveat as it provides a clear vision for profound changes in business education, in a world where it is more important "to be in business" than "to do business." This distinction is not one of semantics, but rather one which allows us to distinguish between traditional and cutting-edge educational and professional practices.

Traditional business education programs have focused on training students to be both effective and efficient, to be "all business" with respect to obtaining positive results in their future business careers. In other words, students have been instructed to create value for their organizations. This type of education has focused almost exclusively on "things to do" such as managing operations and budgets. Only superficial attention, at best, has been given to such areas as the role of language, culture, and regional identity and their relationship to conducting business. Almost no attention has been given to the effect these factors have on doing business beyond the limits of national borders, an area where they are the most important.

The growing transformation of the world into a global village—and on this point McLuhan did not error—forces even the most reluctant university administrators and professors to reflect upon the modifications necessary to advance business education. This change, which requires an acknowledgement of our currently ethnocentric curricula, can be facilitated through the concept of internationalization of the business school. A vision such as this requires an appreciation of the value of cultural plurality, rather than mere assimilation. For this reason, education for adjusting to multiculturalism is necessary to succeed in doing business in the global village. What is needed in international business education are methods and courses which prepare our students to recognize and appreciate the value of differences among people—in attitudes, beliefs, and behavior. Therefore, the generalized belief that people want to be assimilated into a homogeneous culture and cast off their cultural norms, and that globalization will ravage the old traditions, comes under acute scrutiny. What occurs in the McLuhanistic village is pluralism, or in other words, an appreciation of the nearness in diversity.

In this context, internationalizing business education means training for efficacy in human interaction across cultures and geographical boundaries. The changes that need to occur can be distilled into three main points: training in the understanding of individuals who live in the global village; training in understanding one's own conduct in interpersonal transactions; and technical training to be effective in executing the tasks necessary to conduct business abroad. Training of this nature facilitates the imperative of "to be" rather than simply "to do." Simultaneous education and training in these three essential components assures lasting international business relationships, effective intercultural communication, and tolerance for individual and cultural differences.

The process of internationalization of the business school obligates us as professors and academic administrators to jump from the pages of this book to the work of implementation. Professor W. Gudykunst, a specialist in intercultural communication, has repeatedly pointed out that to be effective in multicultural relations it is necessary to reduce cognitive uncertainty, and the fear of being accepted by others. There is no doubt that the most effective way to realize the goals put forth by Gudykunst is to encourage ourselves, our colleagues, our business professionals, and our students to experience international business *in situ*, by going abroad, to experience other ways of doing business, in other cultures, in other languages, with our international business counterparts. Only this will allow us to visualize and embrace the ideas contained in this book. Only this will allow us to jump from theory to practice. This is the merit of the message contained in this book.

Chapter Reference Notes and Additional Resources

Compiled by Todd Trickler

All of the texts referred to by authors in individual chapters are fully noted here. When the reference is site-specific (such as with a quotation, or statistical fact), page numbers are indicated in order of appearance in the chapter.

Additional texts, which may be of interest to those interested in exploring specific subject areas, have also been included in the *Bibliography* sections. *Organizations* referred to by authors are also fully noted, and annotated with contact information: and they too have been incorporated into a larger, expanded list arranged under subject matter and chapter title.

Beyond authorial references the compilation is composite and selective (by no means complete) and it is only as current as *A Field Guide to Internationalizing Business Education* itself. Nonetheless, the editors hope that this compilation will provide a readily accessible and useful resource tool for further research.

Contents

Strategic Development

(Chapter 2: *Charting Your Course;* Chapter 3: *Winning Collegial Support*)

Bibliography

Aggrawal, R. "Strategies for Internationalizing the Business Schools: Educating for the Global Economy." *Journal of Marketing Education* (Fall 1989): pp. 59-64.

Arpan, Jeffrey S. "Curricular and Administrative Considerations–The Cheshire Cat Parable." *Internationalizing Business Education: Meeting the Challenge*, S. Tamer Cavusgil, ed. East Lansing, MI: Michigan State University Press, 1993.

Arpan, Jeffrey S., William R. Folks, Jr., and Chuck C.Y. Kwok, eds. *International Business Education in the 1990's: A Global Survey*. Honolulu, HI: Academy of International Business, 1993: p. 42.

Bartlett, Christopher A., and Sumantra Ghoshal. *Transnational Management*, 3rd ed. Boston, MA: Irwin McGraw-Hill, 2000.

Beck, John, et al. "Internationalising the Business Student." *Journal of Teaching in International Business*, v. 7, n. 4 (1996): pp. 91-105.

Beer, M., R.A. Eisenstat, and B. Spector. "Why Change Programs Don't Produce Change." *Harvard Business Review* (December 1990): pp. 158-166.

Bikson, Tora. "Educating a Globally Prepared Workforce: New Research on College and Corporate Perspectives." *Liberal Education* n. 82 (Spring 1996): pp. 12-19.

Blodgett, Steven A. "A Research Agenda for the Internationalization of Higher Education in the United States: Some Thoughts on Next Steps." *International Education Forum*, v. 16, n. 1 (Spring 1996): pp. 37-41.

Calleja, James, Dumitru Chitoran and Ake Bjerstedt, eds. *International Education and the University*. Paris: UNESCO, 1995.

Cavusgil, Tamer, ed. *Internationalizing Business Education—Meeting the Challenge*. East Lansing, MI: Michigan State University Press, 1993.

Cima, Lawrence R., and James M. Daley. "Internationalizing the Business School Curriculum by Internationalizing the Business School Faculty." Paper presented at the 9th Conference on Languages and

Communication for World Business and the Professions, (Ypsilanti, MI: April 5, 1990).

Developing the Global Work Force: Insights for Colleges and Corporations: How American Colleges and Companies View the New Global Economy and its Impact upon the Human Resources Function. Bethlehem, PA: College Placement Council Foundation, 1994.

De Wit, Hans, ed. *Strategies of Internationalization of Higher Education: A Comparative Study of Australia, Canada, Europe, and the United States of America.* Amsterdam: European Association for International Education, 1995.

Dunning, John H. "The Study of International Business: A Plea for a More Interdisciplinary Approach." *Journal of International Business Studies,* v. 20, n. 3 (1989): pp. 411-36.

Doz, Yves L., and C.K. Prahalad. "Headquarters Influence and Strategic Control." *Transnational Management,* 2nd ed. Christopher A. Bartlett, and Sumantra Ghoshal, ed. Boston, MA: Irwin McGraw-Hill, 1995.

Echternacht, Lonnie, ed. *A Global Look at Business Education.* Reston, VA: National Business Education Association, 1991.

Educating Americans for a World in Flux: Ten Ground Rules for Internationalizing Higher Education. Washington, DC: American Council on Education, 1995.

Ellingboe, Brenda J. "Divisional Strategies to Internationalize a Campus Portrait: Results, Resistance, and Recommendations from a Case Study at a U.S. University." *Reforming the Higher Education Curriculum: Internationalizing the Campus,* Josef A. Mestenhauser and Brenda J. Ellingboe, eds. Phoenix, AZ: American Council on Education and The Oryx Press, 1998.

Gallo Villee, Pat A., and Curran, Michael, eds. *The 21st Century: Meeting the Challenges to Business Education.* Reston, VA: National Business Education Association, 1999.

Hallmarks of Successful International Business Programs. New York, NY: Council on International Educational Exchange, 1988.

Harari, Maurice. *Internationalization of Higher Education: Effecting Institutional Change in the Curriculum and Campus Ethos.* Long Beach, CA: Center for International Education, California State University, 1989.

Internationalization for Higher Education. Paris: Organization for Economic Cooperation and Development, 1996.

Islam, Iyanatul, and William Shepherd, eds. *Current Issues in International Business.* Cheltenham, UK; Lyme, NH: Edward Elgar, 1997.

Ivancevich, John M., and Thomas N. Duening. "Internationalizing a Business School: A Partnership-Development Strategy." *Selections,* v. 10, n. 1 (Autumn 1993): pp. 23-35.

Kameoka, Yu. "The Internationalization of Higher Education." *Organisation for Economic Co-operation and Development Observer* 202 (October/November 1996): pp. 34-36.

Kwok, Chuck, et al. "A Global Survey of International Business Education in the 1990s." *Journal of International Business Studies,* v. 25, n. 3 (1994): pp. 605-623.

Leadership for a Changing World: The Future Role of Graduate Management Education. Los Angeles, CA: Graduate Management Admission Council, 1990.

Lim, Gill-Chin, and Michael Miller, eds. *Strategy for a Global University: Model International Department Experiment.* East Lansing, MI: International Studies and Programs, Michigan State University, 1995.

Oblinger, Diana G., and Anne-Lee Verville. *What Business Wants from Higher Education.* Phoenix, AZ: Oryx Press, 1998.

Ostheimer, Sondra. "Internationalize Yourself." *Business Education Forum,* v. 49 (1991): pp. 131-140.

Sartoris, William L. *MBA International Bench Marketing Study Report.*
International Programs, School of Business, Indiana University, 1999.

Scott, James C. "Providing Instruction for and about International Business."
National Business Education Yearbook V. 1996: pp. 194-203.

Serey, T., W. Lindsay, and M. Myers. "Internationalizing Colleges of Business:
Applying a Strategic Planning Framework." *Journal of Teaching in
International Business,* v. 2 (1989): pp. 5-25.

Thullen, Manfred. "A Research Agenda for the Internationalization of Higher
Education in the United States: Comments, Observations, Suggestions."
International Education Forum, v. 16, n. 1 (Spring 1996): pp. 47-50.

Toyne, Brian, and Douglas Nigh. *International Business: Institutions and the
Dissemination of Knowledge.* Columbia, SC: University of South
Carolina Press, 1999.

Toyne, Brian. "Internationalizing Business Education." *Business and Economic
Review,* v. 38, n. 2 (January/March 1992): pp. 23-27.

Toyne, Brian. "Internationalizing the Business Administration Faculty is No Easy
Task." *Internationalizing Business Education: Meeting the Challenge.*
S. Tamer Cavusgil, ed. East Lansing, MI: Michigan State University
Press, 1993.

Tye, Kenneth, and Barbara Tye. "The Realities of Schooling: Overcoming
Teacher Resistance to Global Education." *Theory into Practice,* v. 32
(Winter 1993): pp. 58-63.

Vanderpool, Christopher K., and Roger E. Hamlin. "Building the
Global/International University for the Future." *Strategy for a Global
University: Model International Department Experiment,* Gill-Chin Lim,
and Michael Miller, eds. East Lansing, MI: International Studies and
Programs, Michigan State University, 1995: p. 144.

Organizations & Online Resources

Academy of International Business
TEL: 808.956.3665

FAX: 808.956.3261
WEB: www.aibworld.net

American Council on Education
TEL: 202.939.9300
FAX: 202.833.4760
WEB: www.acenet.edu/

Business and International Education (BIE)
TEL: 202.502.7626
FAX: 202.502.7860
WEB: www.docp.wright.edu/bie/main.html

The Coalition for International Education (CIE)
WEB: www.docp.wright.edu/bie/cie.htm

College Placement Council Foundation
TEL: 610.868.1421 or 800.544.5272
FAX: 610.868.0208
WEB: www.naceweb.org

European Association for International Education
TEL: 31.20.525.4999
FAX: 31.20.525.4998
WEB: www.eaie.nl/

International Association of Universities (IAU)
TEL: 33.1.45.682.2545
WEB: www.unesco.org/iau/

NAFSA: Association of International Educators
TEL: 202.737.3699
FAX: 202.737.3657
WEB: www.nafsa.org/

National Business Education Association (NBEA)
TEL: 703.860.8300
FAX: 703.620.4483
WEB: www.nbea.org/

Curriculum Development

(Chapter 5: *Crafting the Undergraduate Curriculum;* **Chapter 6:** *Crafting the Graduate Program;* **Chapter 8:** *The Special Role of the Community College;* **Chapter 13:** *Tips From the Field***)**

Bibliography

A Resource Guide for Internationalizing the Business School Curriculum: Organizational Behavior and Human Resource Management. St. Louis, MO: Joint Publication of the American Assembly of Collegiate Schools of Business (AACSB), the Academy of Management, and the University of Michigan Center for International Business Education and Research, 1993.

Ahmed, Zafar, ed. *International Business Education Development.* New York, NY: Harworth Press, 1996.

Ambrose, David, and Louis Pol. "The International Research Experience: Executive MBA Distinctiveness." *Journal of Teaching in International Business,* v. 7, n. 1 (1995): pp. 1-18.

Anderson, Charlotte, Susan Nicklas, and Agnes Crawford. *Global Understandings: Framework for Teaching and Learning.* Alexandria, VA: Association for Supervision and Curriculum Development, 1994.

Aubrey, Robert, et al. *International Educational Perspectives on Business: An Analysis of a New MBA Course Alternative at the University of Wisconsin.* Sandvika: Handelshoyskolen BI, Norwegian School of Management, 1991.

Bigalke, Terance W. *What Works in International Education.* Beliot, WI: Beloit College, 1998. WEB: www.beloit.edu/~i50/whatworks/index.html

Building the Global Community: The Next Step. American Council on International Intercultural Education and The Stanley Foundation. Warrenton, VA: 1994.

Burns, Jane, and Belverd Needles, eds. *Accounting Education for the 21st Century: The Global Challenges.* Elmsford, NY: Pergamon Press, 1994.

Cavusgil, Tamer, and Nancy E. Horn, eds. *Internationalizing Doctoral Education in Business.* East Lansing, MI: Michigan State University Press, 1997.

Chase, Audree M., and James Mahoney, eds. *Global Awareness in Community Colleges.* Washington, DC: Community College Press, 1996.

Comprehensive Guide to International Trade Terms. Washington, DC: U.S. Commerce Department, Updated Periodically. WEB: www.ntia.doc.gov/lexcon.txt

Country Reports on Economic Policy and Trade Practices. Washington, DC: U.S. State Department, Updated Periodically. WEB: www.state.gov/www/issues/economic/trade_reports/

Cowton, Christopher, and Thomas Dunfee. "Internationalizing the Business Ethics Curriculum: A Survey." *Journal of Business Ethics,* v. 14 (May 1995): pp. 331-338.

Davis, James. *Interdisciplinary Courses and Team Teaching: New Arrangements for Learning.* Phoenix, AZ: Ornyx Press, 1995.

Developing the Global Work Force—Insights for Colleges and Corporations. Bethlehem, PA: College Placement Council Foundation, 1994.

Dlabay, Les R. "Integrated Curriculum Planning for International Business Education: Analysis of Global Business Trends." *Delta Pi Epsilon,* v. 40, n. 3 (Summer 1998): pp. 158-165.

Echternacht, L., ed. *A Global Look at Business Education.* Virginia: National Business Education Association, 1991.

Educating for the Global Community: A Framework for Community Colleges. American Council on International Intercultural Education and The Stanley Foundation. Warrenton, VA: 1996.

Feldman, Daniel C., William R. Folks, Jr., and William H. Turnley. "Mentor-Protégé Diversity and Its Impact on International Internship Experience." *Journal of Organizational Behavior,* v. 20, n. 5 (September 1999): pp. 597-611.

Fifield, Mary L., and Lourdene Huhra, eds. *Training for Trade: Community College Programs to Promote Export.* Washington, DC: Community College Press, American Association of Community and Junior Colleges, 1991.

Fifield, Mary L., and Lourdene Huhra, eds. *Strengthening America's Competitiveness: Profiles of Leading Community College International Trade Centers.* Washington, DC: Community College Press, American Association of Community and Junior Colleges, 1993.

Franco, Robert W., and James Shimabukuro, eds. *Beyond the Classroom: International Education and the Community College. Volume IV. Working with Local Business to Enhance Asian-Pacific Understanding.* Honolulu, HI: Hawaii, University, Kapiolani Community College, 1992.

Gibbs Jr., Manton C., ed. *Internationalization of the Business Curriculum.* Binghamton, NY: International Business Press, 1994.

Hawkins, John N., ed. *International Education in the New Global Era.* Proceedings of a National Policy Conference on Higher Education Act, Title VI, and Fulbright-Hays Programs. Los Angeles, CA, 1997. WEB: www.isop.ucla.edu/pacrim/title6

Hoopes, D.S., and K.R. Hoopes, eds. *Guide to International Education in the United States.* Detroit, MI: Gale Research Inc., 1991.

Internationalism and Multiculturalism in Management Education: A Curriculum Development Handbook. Ann Arbor, MI: Center for International Business Education, University of Michigan, 1992.

Internationalizing Higher Education—A Shared Vision? Association of Universities and Colleges of Canada, 1999. WEB: www.aucc.ca/en/international/shared-vision.html

Journal of International Business Studies. Published jointly by the Academy of International Business (AIB), Copenhagen Business School (CBS), and the McDonough School of Business (MSB) at Georgetown University,

Quarterly. TEL: 808.956.3665; FAX: 808.956.3261; WEB: www.jibs.net

Journal of International Marketing. Published quarterly by the American Marketing Association. TEL: 800.AMA.1150; FAX: 312.993.7542; WEB: ciber.bus.msu.edu/jim

Journal of Teaching in International Business. Published quarterly by Haworth Press. WEB: bubl.ac.uk/journals/bus/jtiib/

Journal of World Business. Published quarterly by JAI Press. WEB: www.elsevier.com/

Kaser, Kenneth J. "The Importance of an International Marketing Class." *Business Education Forum,* v. 53, n. 2 (December 1998): pp. 32-33.

Kaynak, Erdener. *International Business Teaching.* New York, NY: International Business Press, 1995.

Kelleher, A. *Learning from Success—Campus Case Studies in International Program Development.* New York, NY: Peter Lang, 1996.

May, Robert G. "Internationalizing Business Doctoral Education: Bringing Down the Barriers." *Selections,* v. 11, n. 1 (Autumn 1994): pp. 1-3.

Mestenhauser, J.A., and B.J. Ellingboe. *Reforming the Higher Education Curriculum—Internationalizing the Campus.* Phoenix, AZ: Oryx Press, 1998.

Milton, Tom. *International Program for Undergraduate Business Majors.* Dobbs Ferry, New York, NY: Mercy College, 1994.

Moffit, G. *Internationalizing the Curriculum: Spring 1993 Fellowship Report.* WEB: www.language.brown.edu/LAC/Administration/Fellowship_Report.html

Moore, Frank. "You Can Globalize Your Curriculum." *Business Education Forum,* v. 51 (February 1997): pp. 16-17.

Muuka, Gerry N., Dannie E. Harrison, and Seid Y. Hassan. "International Business in American MBA Programs—Can We Silence the Critics?" *Journal of Education for Business*, v. 74, n. 4 (March/April 1999): pp. 237-242.

New Expeditions: Charting the Future of Global Education in Community Colleges. American Council on International Intercultural Education, Community Colleges for International Development and The Stanley Foundation. Warrenton, VA: 1999.

Ostheimer, Sondra. "Internationalizing the Business Education Curriculum." *Business Education Forum*, v. 50 (February 1996): p. 41-44.

Phillips, Mary, and John Muldoon, Jr. "The Model United Nations: A Strategy for Enhancing Global Business Education." *Journal of Education for Business*, v. 61, n. 3 (January/February 1996): pp. 142-146.

Pickert, Sarah, and Barbara Turlington. *Internationalizing the Undergraduate Curriculum: A Handbook for Campus Leaders.* Washington, DC: American Council on Education, 1992.

Raby, Rosalind L., and Norma Tarrow, eds. *Dimensions of the Community College : International, Intercultural, and Multicultural Perspectives.* New York, NY: Garland Publishing, 1996.

Ray, Russ. "Internationalizing the Business School Curriculum." *International Studies Notes*, 15 (Fall 1990): pp. 83-84.

Rugman, A.M., and W. T. Stanbury, eds. *Global Perspective: Internationalizing Management Education.* Vancouver: University of British Columbia, 1992.

Sarathy, R. "Internationalizing MBA Education: The Role of Short Overseas Programs." *Journal of Teaching in International Business*, v. 3, n. 4 (1990): pp. 101-118.

Schechter, M. "Internationalizing the Undergraduate Curriculum." *International Education Forum*, v. 10 (1990): pp. 14-20.

Schmotter, James W. "An Interview with Roy A. Herberger." *Selections*, v. 15, n. 2 (Winter 1999): pp. 25-31.

Schwindt, Richard, Compiled By. *International Business I: Multinational Management and the International Environment.* Chapel Hill, NC: Eno River Press, 1995.

Sepe, Thomas D., and Marta Kaufman. "College Uses Virtual Business to Prepare Students for Global Economy." *Community College Journal*, v. 69, n. 2 (October/November 1998): pp. 26-29.

Shannon, J. Richard, et al. "Preparation of Careers in International Marketing: An Empirical Investigation of Students' Attitudes and Perceptions." *Journal of Teaching in International Business*, v. 7, n. 3 (1995): pp. 17-32.

Shao, Lawrence. "Techniques for Improving Student Performance in International Finance." *Journal of Teaching in International Business*, v. 7, n. 3 (1995): pp. 33-44.

Spinelli, E. *Languages Across the Curriculum: A Postsecondary Initiative.* ACTFL Professional Issues Report, 1998. WEB: www.actfl.org/public/articles/index.cfm

Sypris, Theo, ed. *Internationalizing the Curriculum.* Kalamazoo, MI: Midwest Institute; [Washington, DC]: U.S. Dept. of Education, Office of Educational Research and Improvement, Educational Resources Information Center, 1993.

Sypris, Theo, project director; contributors, L. Abshear-Seale, et al. *International/Intercultural Education: Internationalizing the Curriculum, Volume II.* Kalamazoo, MI: Kalamazoo Valley Community College, 1996.

Tennyson, R.D., et al. *Instructional Design: International Perspectives—Volume I: Theory, Research, and Models.* Mahwah, NJ: Lawrence Erlbaum Associates, 1997.

Tye, Kenneth, ed. *Global Education: From Thought to Action.* Alexandria, VA: Association for Supervision and Curriculum Development, 1990.

Wallace, Steve. "Adding International Themes to a Community College Curriculum: A Review of the Southwest Consortium for International Studies and Foreign Languages." *International Studies Notes,* 14 (Winter 1989): pp. 21-23.

White, Steven D., and David A. Griffith. "Graduate International Business Education in the United States—Comparisons and Suggestions." *Journal of Education for Business,* v. 74, n. 2 (November/December 1998): pp. 103-115.

World Trade Center Institute, Coastline Community College. *International Business Curriculum Guides.* Fountain Valley, CA: Coastline Community College, 1990.

Organizations & Online Resources

AACSB—The International Association for Management Education
TEL: 314.872.8481
FAX: 314.872.8495
WEB: www.aacsb.edu

American Council on International Intercultural Education (ACIIE)
TEL: 847.635.2605
FAX: 847.635.1764
WEB: www.aciie.org

Association for Supervision and Curriculum Development (ASCD)
TEL: 703.578.9600
FAX: 703.575.5400
WEB: www.ascd.org/

Association of Universities and Colleges of Canada
TEL: 613.563.1236
FAX: 613.563.9745
WEB: www.aucc.ca/index.html

@brint.com The BizTech Network
TEL: 954.916.1585
FAX: 954.916.4812
WEB: www.brint.com

Community College for International Development, Kirkwood Community College
TEL: 319.398.5517
FAX: 319.398.1255
WEB: www.ccid.kirkwood.cc.ia.us

Educational Resources Information Center (ERIC)
WEB: www.accesseric.org/

Harvard Business School Publishing
TEL: 800.988.0886
FAX: 617.496.1029
WEB: www.hbsp.harvard.edu/hbsp/samples/index.asp

Internet Resources for International Economics & Business
WEB: dylee.keel.econ.ship.edu/econ/index.html

Marketing & International Business Links
WEB: www.wtfaculty.wtamu.edu/~sanwar.bus/otherlinks.htm#Syllabi

North American Small Business International Trade Educators (NASBITE)
TEL: 937.775.2814
FAX: 937.775.3545
WEB: www.nasbite.org

The Stanley Foundation
TEL: 319.264.1500
FAX: 319.264.0864
WEB: www.stanleyfdn.org/

SyllabusWeb
TEL: 800.773.0670
FAX: 408.261.7280
WEB: www.syllabus.com/

Virtual International Business & Economic Sources
WEB: www.libweb.uncc.edu/ref-bus/vibehome.htm

Funding

(Chapter 4: *Funding Your Initiatives*)

Bibliography

Annual Register of Grant Support, 2000: A Directory of Funding Sources. New Providence, NJ: R.R. Bowker, 2000.

Belcher, Jane C., and Julia M. Jacobsen. *From Idea to Funded Project: Grant Proposals That Work.* Phoenix, AZ: Oryx Press, 1992.

The Big Book of Library Grant Money 1998-1999: Profile of Private and Corporate Foundations and Direct Corporate Givers Receptive to Library Proposals. Prepared by The Taft Group for the American Library Association. Chicago, IL: ALA, 1998.

Blake, G., and R. W. Blyt. *The Elements of Technical Writing.* Macmillan, 1993.

Blum, Laurie. *The Complete Guide to Getting a Grant: How to Turn Your Ideas into Dollars.* New York, NY: John Wiley & Sons, 1996.

Blum, Laurie. *Free Money for Foreign Study: A Guide to More Than 1,000 Grants and Scholarships for Study Abroad.* Facts on File, Inc., 1992.

Blum, Laurie. *Free Money from the Federal Government for Small Businesses and Entrepreneurs.* New York, NY: John Wiley & Sons, 1996.

Brisbois, Matthew, and Pamela M. Kalter, eds. *The Directory of Corporate & Foundations Givers, 2000.* Detroit, MI: The Taft Group, 1999.

Cantarella, Gina-Marie, ed. *National Guide to Funding for Libraries and Information Services.* New York, NY: Foundation Center, 1999.

Catalog of Federal Domestic Assistance. Washington, DC: The Office of Management and Budget: U.S. Government Printing Office. WEB: www.gsa.gov/fdac/

Corporate and Foundation Grants. Rockville, MD: The Taft Group. Annually.

Corporate Giving Directory. Washington, DC: The Taft Group. Annually.

Directory of Grants for Study and Research in the USA. Merrick, NY: Overseas Academic Opportunities. Annually.

Directory of Research Grants 2000. Phoenix, AZ: Orynx Press. Annually.

Dumouchel, Robert J. *Government Assistance Almanac 2000-2001.* Detroit, MI: Omnigraphics, Inc., 2000.

Feczko, Margaret Mary, ed. *The Foundation Directory.* New York, NY: Foundation Center, 1996.

Federal Assistance Monitor. Silver Spring, MD: CD Publications. Semimonthly.

The Federal Register. Washington, DC: National Archives of the United States. WEB: www.access.gpo.gov/su_docs/aces/aces140.html

The Foundation 1000: In-Depth Profiles of the 1000 Largest US Foundations. New York, NY: Foundation Center. Annually.

The Foundation Grants Index 2000. New York, NY: Foundation Center, 1999.

Government Research Directory. Detroit, MI: Gale Research Co. Annually.

Guide to Federal Funding for Education. Washington, DC: Education Funding Research Council.

Guide to Federal Funding for Governments and Nonprofits. Washington, DC: Government Information Services.

Guide to US Foundations, Their Trustees, Officers and Donors. Compiled by the Foundation Center. New York, NY: Foundation Center.

Hall, Victoria, ed. *Foundation Grants to Individuals.* New York, NY: Foundation Center, 1997.

The International Foundation Directory 1998. Detroit, MI: Gale Research Co. London: Europa Publications, 1998.

Miner, Jeremy T., ed., and Lynn E. Miner. *Funding Sources for Community and Economic Development 1999: A Guide to Current Sources for Local Programs and Projects*. Phoenix, AZ: Orynx Press, 1999.

Morehouse, Ward, and G. Gutierrez, eds. *International Studies Funding and Resources Book*. Westboro, MA: Apex Press, 1990.

New, Cheryl C., and James A. Quick. *Grantseeker's Toolkit: A Comprehensive Guide to Finding Funding*. New York, NY: John Wiley & Sons, 1998.

Offerman, Susan. *Directory of Grants for Graduate Study Overseas*. Overseas Academic Opportunities, 2000.

Orlich, Donald C. *Designing Successful Grant Proposals*. Alexandria, VA: Association for Supervision and Curriculum Development, 1996.

O'Sullivan, Marie, ed. *Financial Resources for International Study: A Guide for U.S. Students and Professionals*. New York, NY: Institute of International Education, 1996.

Rand, Morgan. *National Directory of Nonprofit Organizations 1997(1998 Edition)*. Roseville, MD: The Taft Group, 1997.

Reif-Lehrer, Liane. *Grant Application Writer's Handbook*. Boston, MA: Jones and Bartlett Publishers, 1995.

Schwartz, Samuel M. *A Guide to NIH Grant Programs*. New York, NY: Oxford University Press, 1992.

Stein, Edith C., ed. *Environmental Grantmaking Foundations: Directory*. Rochester, NY: Environmental Data Research Institute, Annually.

Weber, David R., and Gail A. Schlachter. *Financial Aid for Research and Creative Activities Abroad: 1999-2001*. Reference Service Press, 1999.

Organizations & Online Resources

Business and International Education Program
TEL: 202.502.7700
WEB: www.ed.gov/offices/OPE/OHEP/iegps/bie.html

Council on Foundations
TEL: 202.466.6512
WEB: www.cof.org

Federal Sources of Grants & Funding Information
WEB: www.creighton.edu/Grants/federal.html

Financial Aid Information Page: Grant Information
FAX: 412.422.6189
WEB: www.finaid.org/otheraid/grants.phtml

The Foundation Center
TEL: 212.620.4230
FAX: 212.691.1828
WEB: www.fdncenter.org/

Foundations On-Line
WEB: www.foundations.org

Fund for the Improvement of Postsecondary Education (FIPSE)
WEB: www.ed.gov/offices/OPE/FIPSE/index.html

Grants in Graduate Studies
WEB: www.nyu.edu/gsas/fininfo/gigs.html

The Grantsmanship Center
TEL: 213.482.9860
FAX: 213.482.9863
WEB: www.tgci.com/

GrantsNet
WEB: www.dhhs.gov/progorg/grantsnet/

GrantsWeb
> TEL: 202.857.1141
> FAX: 202.223.4579
> WEB: sra.rams.com

Idealist
> TEL: 212.843.3973
> FAX: 212.564.3377
> WEB: www.idealist.org

International Research and Exchange Board (IREX)
> TEL: 202.628.8188
> FAX: 202.628.8189
> WEB: www.irex.org

SEC. 601 International Education Program
> WEB: www.ed.gov/legislation/GOALS2000/TheAct/sec601.html

Seton Hall University Grants Watch
> TEL: 201.378.9810
> WEB: www.shu.edu

The Taft Group
> TEL: 800.877.8238
> FAX: 800.414.5043
> WEB: www.taftgroup.com/

U.S. Department of Education
> TEL: 800.USA.LEARN
> FAX: 202.401.0689
> WEB: www.ed.gov/

Modern Languages and Area Studies

(Chapter 7: *Building a Bridge to Liberal Arts*)

Bibliography

Bikson, T.K., and S.A. Law. *Global Preparedness and Human Resources:*

College and Corporate Perspectives. RAND Corporation Social Policy Department Series, Santa Monica, CA: RAND, 1994.

Brenes-García, Ana María. "Teaching Business Culture: Results of a Survey Administered at Thunderbird." *The Journal of Language for International Business,* v. 10, n. 1 (1999): pp. 43-56.

Brod, Richard, and Bettina Huber. "Foreign Language Enrollments in United States Institutions of Higher Education, Fall 1995." *ADFL Bulletin,* v. 28, n. 2 (1997): pp. 56-61.

Burn, Barbara. "Study Abroad and Foreign Language Programs." *International Education Forum,* v. 16, n. 1 (Spring 1996): pp. 20-31.

Fixman, C.S. "The Foreign Language Needs of U.S.-Based Corporations." *National Foreign Language Center Occasional Papers Series.* Washington D.C.: National Foreign Language Center, 1989.

Grandin, J.M., and E.W. Dehmel. "Cross-Cultural Issues in Educating Engineers for the Global Workplace." *Journal of Language for International Business,* v. 8, n. 2 (1997): pp. 1-15.

Grosse, C.U. "Corporate Recruiter Demand for Foreign Language and Cultural Knowledge." *Global Business Languages* (1998): pp. 1-22.

Guntermann, G., and B. Fryer, eds. *Spanish and Portuguese for Business and the Professions.* Lincolnwood, IL: National Textbook Company, 1998.

Herberger, Roy. "New Corporate Global Strategies and the Impact on Specialized Language Instruction." Keynote address presented at the Eighth Annual CIBER Conference on Language for Business and Economics, Anderson Graduate School of Management, University of California Los Angeles, February 13, 1998.

The Journal of Language for International Business. Glendale, AZ: Department of Modern Languages, American Graduate School of International Management, Semiannually. TEL: 602.978.7291; FAX: 602.439.1435; WEB: www.t-bird.edu/research/journals/jolib/current.asp

Lambert, Richard. "Foreign Language Use among International Business Graduates." *Annals of the American Academy of Political and Social Science* 511 (September 1990): pp. 47-59.

Loughrin-Sacco, S. J. "Redefining the Role of the Foreign Language Department Chair: The Chair as Fundraiser, Program Developer, and Entrepreneur." *ADFL Bulletin*, v. 27, n. 2 (1996): pp. 39-43.

Machan, D. "Ici On Parle Bottom-Line Responsibility." *Forbes*, v. 141 (1998): pp. 138-140.

Proficiency Guidelines. Yonkers, NY: American Council on the Teaching of Foreign Languages, 1986.

Scott, James Calvert. "Developing Cultural Fluency: The Goal of International Business Communication Instruction in the 21st Century." *Journal of Education for Business*, v. 74, n. 3 (January/February 1999): pp. 140-3.

Turley, L.W., Richard Shannon, and J. Mark Miller. "International Marketing: Student Attitudes and Behavior." *Marketing Education Review 3.1* (Spring 1993): pp. 52-57.

Vande Berg, C.K. "Corporate versus Academic Perceptions of the Need for Language Fluency." *Journal of Language for International Business*, v. 8, n. 2 (1997): pp. 16-21.

Organizations & Online Resources

African Studies Center, University of Pennsylvania
TEL: 215.898.6971
FAX: 215.573.8130
WEB: www.sas.upenn.edu/African_Studies/AS.html

American Council on the Teaching of Foreign Languages (ACTFL)
TEL: 914.963.8830
FAX: 914.963.1275
WEB: www.actfl.org

Asian Studies Network Information Center
    WEB: asnic.utexas.edu/asnic/index.html

Asian Studies WWW Virtual Library:
    WEB: coombs.anu.edu.au/WWWVL-AsianStudies.html

Center for Language Education and Research (CLEAR), Michigan State University
    TEL: 517.432.2286
    WEB: clear.msu.edu/

The Center for Middle Eastern Studies
    TEL: 512.471.3881
    FAX: 512.471.7834
    WEB: link.lanic.utexas.edu/menic/

The Council for European Studies
    TEL: 212.854.4172
    FAX: 212.854.8808
    WEB: www.columbia.edu/cu/ces

ERIC Clearinghouse on Languages and Linguistics (ERIC/CLL)
    TEL: 800.LET.ERIC
    WEB: www.cal.org/ericcll

Languages Across the Curriculum (LAC)
    WEB: www.language.brown.edu/LAC/

Latin American Network Information Center (LANIC)
    WEB: lanic.utexas.edu

MLA on the Web: The Modern Language Association of America
    TEL: 212.475.9500
    FAX: 212.477.9863
    WEB: www.mla.org

National Capital Language Resource Center
    TEL: 202.739.0607
    FAX: 202.739.0609
    WEB: www.cal.org/nclrc/

National Foreign Language Center
    TEL: 202.637.8881
    FAX: 202.637.9244
    WEB: www.nflc.org/

National Foreign Language Resource Center, University of Hawaii
    TEL: 808.956.8041
    FAX: 808.956.9685
    WEB: www.cba.hawaii.edu/ciber/home.htm

National Foreign Language Resource Center, Ohio State University
    TEL: 614.292.4361
    FAX: 614.292.2682
    WEB: www.cohums.ohio-state.edu/flc/

Russian and East European Network Information Center
    TEL: 512.471.7782
    FAX: 512.471.3368
    WEB: www.reenic.utexas.edu/reenic.html

San Diego State University: Language Acquisition Resource Center (LARC)
    TEL: 619.594.6177
    FAX: 619.594.0511
    WEB: larcnet.sdsu.edu

Virginia Commonwealth University Trail Guide to International Sites & Language
    Resources
    WEB: www.fln.vcu.edu/

Yale Africa Guide InterActive
    WEB: swahili.africa.yale.edu/links/

Outreach

(Chapter 9: *The Far Reach of Outreach*)

Bibliography

Background Notes. U.S. Department of State, Washington, DC: Superintendent of Documents, U.S. Government Printing Office. TEL: 202.512.1800; FAX: 202.512.2250; WEB: www.state.gov/www/background_notes/

Bikson, Tora K., and Sally Ann Law. *Global Preparedness and Human Resources: College and Corporate Perspectives.* Santa Monica, CA: Rand, 1994.

Breaking Into the Trade Game: A Small Business Guide to Exporting Washington, DC: U.S. Small Business Administration, 1993. TEL: 800.U.ASK.SBA

Culturgrams: The Nations Around Us, Volume 1, The Americas and Europe. Chicago, IL: Ferguson Publishing Company, 1999. WEB: www.culturgram.com

Culturgrams: The Nations Around Us, Volume 2, Africa, Asia, and Oceania. Chicago, IL: Ferguson Publishing Company, 1999. WEB: www.culturgram.com

Export Yellow Pages. Washington, DC: Venture Publishing, Annually. (Free from DOC and SBA); TEL: 800.288.2582

Exporters' Encyclopedia. Bethlehem, PA: Dun and Bradstreet, 1998.

International Trade Reporter. Washington, DC: Bureau of National Affairs, Inc., 2000.

McCue, Sarah S. *Trade Secrets: The Export Answer Book.* Detroit, MI: Michigan Small Business Development Center, 1998.

Nash, Bernard A. "Internationalizing the Business School—Responding to the Customer's Needs." *Journal of Teaching in International Business,* v. 9, n. 1 (1997): pp. 73-85.

Preparing for Global Marketing. Columbia, MO: Extension Publications. TEL: 800.292.0969; WEB: www.muextension.missouri.edu/export/

Sizoo, Steven L., Joseph M. Bearson, and Naveen K. Malhotra. "Partnering for Success—Using Retired Multinational Executives to Assist in Teaching

Business Strategy." *Business Education Forum*, v. 52 (October 1997): pp. 28-29.

Woznick, Alexandra, and Edward G. Hinkelman. *A Basic Guide to Exporting, 3rd Edition.* San Rafael, CA: World Trade Press, 2000.

The UNZ & Company Sourcebook 2000 (A How-To Guide for Exporters and Importers). Jersey City, NJ: UNZ & Company, 2000.

Organizations & Online Resources

Association of Small Business Development Centers (ASBDC)
    TEL: 703.271.8700
    FAX: 703.271.8701
    WEB: www.asbdc-us.org/index.html

BISNIS Reports and Publications
    TEL: 202.482.4655
    FAX: 202.482.2293
    WEB: www.bisnis.doc.gov/bisnis/bulletin.htm

Bureau of Export Administration
    TEL: 202.482.4811
    FAX: 202.482.3617
    WEB: www.bxa.doc.gov

Bureau of National Affairs
    TEL: 202.452.4200
    WEB: www.bna.com

Center For Global Education
    WEB: www.usc.edu/dept/education/globaled/

Central and East European Business Information Center (CEEBIC)
    WEB: www.itaiep.doc.gov

Central Intelligence Agency—The CIA Factbook
    WEB: www.cia.gov/cia/publications/factbook/index.html

Clear Freight
>TEL: 310.726.0400
>FAX: 310.726.0420
>WEB: www.clearfreight.com/clear_internet_trc/trade.htm

District Export Council
>WEB: www.dec.interactiveinc.com/

Economic Development (Agencies) Directory
>WEB: www.ecodevdirectory.com/

Europages
>WEB: www.europages.com/

Europeonline
>WEB: www.europeonline.com/

Export-Import Bank of the United States
>TEL: 800.565.3946
>FAX: 202.565.3380
>WEB: www.exim.gov

ExportNet
>WEB: www.exporttoday.com

FedWorld
>WEB: www.fedworld.gov

Foreign Agricultural Service, USDA
>WEB: www.fas.usda.gov

For World International Business Web Center: Business Organizations
>WEB: www.forworld.com/organization.htm

Global Electronic Commerce Opportunity
>WEB: www.ecplaza.net/

Inter-American Development Bank
>TEL: 202.623.1000
>WEB: www.iadb.org

International Bureau of Chambers of Commerce
TEL: 33(1)49.53.29.44
FAX: 33(1)49.53.29.38
WEB: www.icc-ibcc.org

International Business Directory
TEL: 801.378.6495
FAX: 801.378.2411
WEB: www.marriottschool.byu.edu/ciber/ibd/index.htm

International Chamber of Commerce World Business Organization
WEB: www.iccwbo.org

International Monetary Fund
WEB: www.imf.org

International Trade Administration (ITA)
WEB: www.ita.doc.gov

International Trade and Business Bookstore U.S. Department of Commerce
TEL: 202.482.3465
FAX: 202.482.3471
WEB: tradecenter.ntis.gov/

International Trade Desk
WEB: www.users.aol.com/tradedesk/trade.htm

International Trade Division of the World Bank
WEB: www.worldbank.org/research/trade/

Mexico NAFTA Resources
WEB: www.lanic.utexas.edu/la/Mexico/nafta/index.html

National Export Offer Service (NEOS)
WEB: www.exportservices.com/

National Trade Data Bank (NTDB) available through STAT-USA.
WEB: www.stat-usa.gov

Organization for Economic Cooperation and Development (OECD)
WEB: www.oecd.org

Service Corp of Retired Executives (SCORE)
TEL: 800.634.0245
WEB: www.score.org

Small Business Administration (SBA), Office for International Trade
TEL: 800.8.ASK.SBA
WEB: www.sbaonline.sba.gov/OIT/info/links.html

STAT-USA/Internet
TEL: 800.STAT.USA
WEB: www.stat-usa.gov

Strategis
TEL: 800.328.6189
WEB: www.strategis.ic.gc.ca/engdoc/main.html

Tradeport
WEB: www.tradeport.org/

Trade Compass
TEL: 202.783.4455
FAX: 202.783.4465
WEB: www.tradecompass.com

Trade Events, Shows and Exhibitions
WEB: www.expoguide.com/

Trade Show Central
WEB: www.tscentral.com/

United Nations
WEB: www.un.org

United States Commercial Service
WEB: www.ita.doc.gov/ita_home/itausfcs.html

United States Council for International Business
    TEL: 212.354.4480
    WEB: www.uscib.org

United States Department of Commerce
    TEL: 800.288.2582
    WEB: www.doc.gov
    Economic Bulletin Board
    TEL: 202.482.1986
    TEL: 800.288.2582
    FAX: 202.482.2164

United States Export Assistance Center
    WEB: www.sba.gov/oit/txt/export/useac.html

United States State Department
    WEB: www.state.gov/

United States Trade Representative
    TEL: 888.473.USTR
    WEB: www.ustr.gov

The Universal Currency Converter Home Page
    WEB: www.xe.net/currency/

University of Missouri Outreach and Extension, Export Development Program
    WEB: www.muextension.missouri.edu/export/

World Bank
    WEB: www.worldbank.org

World Trade Centers
    WEB: www.wtca.org/

World Trade Organization
    WEB: www.wto.org

International Opportunities

(Chapter 10: *Developing International Relationships*)

Bibliography

Academic Year Abroad 1999/2000: The Most Complete Guide to Planning Academic Year Study Abroad. New York, NY: Institute of International Education, 1998.

Altbach, P. G., and P.M. Peterson. "Internationalize Higher Education." *Change*, v. 30, n. 4 (1998).

Bell, Arthur. *Great Jobs Abroad.* New York, NY: McGraw-Hill Publishers, 1997.

Craighead's International Business, Travel, and Relocation Guide to 84 Countries 2000-2001. Detroit, MI: Gale Research, 1999.

Daniels, John D. "Relevance in International Business Research: A Need for More Linkages." *Journal of International Business Studies*, v. 22, n. 2 (1989): pp. 177-186.

Davis, Todd M., ed. *Open Doors 1998/99: Report on International Educational Exchange.* New York, NY: Institute of International Education, 1999.

Folks, W. R. Notes, *Administrative Strategies for International Business Programs*, April 16-18. Atlanta, GA, 1999.

Green, Robert T., and Linda V. Gerber. "Linkages with Overseas Business Schools: Keys to Success." *Internationalizing Business Education: Meeting the Challenge.* S. Tamer Cavusgil, ed. East Lansing, MI: Michigan State University Press, 1993.

Green, Robert T., and Linda V. Gerber. *Strategic Partnerships for Global Education: Linkages with Overseas Institutions.* Austin, TX: Center for International Business Education and Research, The University of Texas at Austin, 1995.

Guidelines for College and University Linkages Abroad. Washington, DC: American Council on Education, 1997.

Halloran, Edward J. *Careers in International Business.* Lincolnwood, IL: VGM Career Horizons, 1996.

Harlow, Victoria, and Edward W. Knappmann, eds. *American Jobs Abroad.* Detroit, MI: Gale Research, 1994.

Highham, Matthew T., and Hilary Berkey, eds. *The ACCESS Guide to International Affairs Internships, 5th ed.* Washington, DC: Access, 1997.

International Exchange Locator: A Resource Directory for Educational and Cultural Exchange, 1998. New York, NY: Institute of International Education, 1999.

Kanet, Roger E. "Internationalization, Constrained Budgets, and the Role of International Education Consortia." *International Education Forum* v. 16, n. 1 (Spring 1996): pp. 59-70.

Kashlak, Roger J., and Raymond M. Jones. "Internationalizing Business Education: Factors Affecting Student Participation in Overseas Study Programs." *Journal of Teaching in International Business,* v. 8, n. 2 (1996): pp. 57-75.

Lay, David, and Benedict A. Leerburger. *Jobs Worldwide.* Manassas Park, VA: Impact Publications, 1996.

Organizations & Online Resources

College Consortium for International Studies (CCIS)
TEL: 800.453.6956
FAX: 202.223.0999
WEB: www.ccisabroad.org/

Council for International Exchange of Scholars (CIES)
TEL: 202.686.4000
FAX: 202.362.3442
WEB: www.iie.org/cies/

Council on International Educational Exchange (CIEE)
    TEL: 800.40.STUDY
    FAX: 212.822.2779
    WEB: www.ciee.org/

Deutscher Akademischer Austauschdienst
    WEB: www.daad.de

Educational Credential Evaluators (ECE)
    TEL: 414.289.3400
    FAX: 414.289.3411
    WEB: www.ece.org

GlobaLink International Business Educational Exchange Directory
    WEB: www.bus.utexas.edu/~ciber/services/studexch.htm

The Internationalist—The Center for International Business & Travel
    WEB: www.internationalist.com/

Institute of International Education (IIE)
    TEL: 212.984.5400
    WEB: www.iie.org/

International Research & Exchange Board (IREX)
    TEL: 202.628.8188
    FAX: 202.628.8189
    WEB: www.irex.org/

Overseas Academic Opportunities
    TEL: 516.632.7030
    FAX: 516.632.6544
    WEB: www.sunysb.edu/studyabroad/main.html

Petersons.com
    WEB: www.petersons.com/stdyabrd/sasector.html

Study Abroad Links
    WEB: www.studyabroadlinks.com/

Studyabroad.com
     WEB: www.studyabroad.com/

Syracuse University Abroad
     TEL: 800.235.3472
     WEB: sumweb.syr.edu/dipa/

University Studies Abroad Consortium (USAC)
     TEL: 775.784.6569
     FAX: 775.784.6010
     WEB: www.usac.unr.edu/

World Education Services, Inc. (WES)
     TEL: 212.966.6311
     FAX: 212.966.6395
     WEB: www.wes.org

Technology

(Chapter 11: *Welcome to Virtual Business Education*)

Bibliography

Brugger, Esrey. *Challenges for the New Millennium in Latin America.* TM
     Editors, 1998.

Crawford, Richard. *In The Era of Human Capital.* New York, NY:
     HarperCollins Business, 1991.

Díaz, Karen R., ed. *Reference Sources on the Internet: Off the Shelf and onto
     the Web.* New York, NY: Haworth Press, 1997.

Driscoll, Margaret. *Web-Based Training.* San Francisco, CA: Jossey-
     Bass/Pfeiffer, 1998

Fairness, Access, Multiculturalism, & Equity (FAME). The GRE, FAME Report
     Series (Vol. 1), Educational Testing Series, USA, 1998.

Flaherty, M. Therese. *Global Operations Management.* New York, NY: McGraw-Hill, 1996.

Galvis, A. *Ingenieria de Software Educativo.* Ediciones Uniandes, Universidad de Los Andes, Colombia, 1992.

Karakeya, Fahri, and Kaynak, Erdener. *Utilizing New Information Technology in Teaching of International Business: A Guide for Instructors.* New York, NY: International Business Press, 1993.

Karakaya, Fahri, and Kaynak, Erdener. *How to Utilize New Information Technology in the Global Marketplace: A Basic Guide.* New York, NY: International Business Press, 1995.

Kotabe, Masaaki. *Global Sourcing Strategy.* New York, NY: Quorum, 1992.

LaBonty, Dennis, ed. *Integrating the Internet into the Business Curriculum.* Reston, VA: National Business Education Association, 1998.

May, Bruce E. "Curriculum Internationalization and Distance Learning: Convergence of Necessity and Technology." *Journal of Teaching in International Business*, v. 9, n. 1 (1997): pp. 35-50.

Newsline. Volume 28, Number 1, AACSB. The International Association for Management Education, 1998.

Oblinger, Diana G., and Sean C. Rush, eds. *The Learning Revolution.* Bolton, MA: Anker Publishing Company, 1997.

Sauer, Christopher, and Philip W. Yetton. *Steps to the Future.* San Francisco, CA: Jossey-Bass, 1997.

Schon, D. *The Reflective Practitioner.* Basic Books, 1983.

Schreiber, Deborah A., and Zane L. Berge. *Distance Training.* San Francisco, CA: Jossey-Bass, Inc, 1998

Stacey, Ralph D. *Complexity and Creativity in Organizations.* San Francisco, CA: Berrett-Koehler Publishers, 1996.

Vaughan, T. *Todo el Poder de Multimedia*. New York, NY: McGraw Hill, 1995.

Organizations & Online Resources

Computer Assisted Language Instruction Consortium (CALICO)
TEL: 512.245.1417
FAX: 512.245.8298
WEB: www.calico.org

Integrating Internet Into International Management Education
WEB: www.csun.edu/~mli/iii.html

Interactive Internet-Based Language Learning
TEL: 541.346.4319
FAX: 541.346.3917
WEB: www.babel.uoregon.edu/yamada/interact.html

Language Learning & Technology
WEB: llt.msu.edu

San Diego State University: Language Acquisition Resource Center: LARC
TEL: 619.594.6177
FAX: 619.594.0511
WEB: larcnet.sdsu.edu

SyllabusWeb
TEL: 800.773.0670
FAX: 408.261.7280
WEB: www.syllabus.com/

UVA Foreign Languages & Cultures: Teaching Technologies
WEB: www.virginia.edu/~asmedia/flitig.html

Program Evaluation

(Chapter 12: *Evaluating Your Program*)

Bibliography

Boulmetis, John, and Phyllis Dutwin. *The ABCs of Evaluation: Timeless Techniques for Program and Project Managers.* San Francisco, CA: Jossey-Bass Publishers, 2000.

Fink, Arlene, and Jacqueline Kosecoff. *An Evaluation Primer.* Beverly Hills, CA: SAGE, 1978: pp. 4, 71-74.

Fitz-Gibbon, Carol Taylor, and Lynn Lyons Morris. *How to Design a Program Evaluation.* Newbury Park, CA: SAGE, 1987: pp. 9, 56-62.

Gredler, Margaret E. *Program Evaluation.* Englewood Cliffs, NJ: Merrill, 1996.

A Guide to Planning and Evaluating Performance. Washington, D.C.: U.S. Department. of Health and Human Services, 1990: p. 2.

Morris, Lynn Lyons, and Carol Taylor Fitz-Gibbon. *How to Plan an Evaluation Report.* Beverly Hills, CA: SAGE, 1978: pp. 16-26, 19, 27-41, 38-46.

New, Cheryl C., and James A. Quick. *Grant Winner's Toolkit: Project Management and Evaluation.* New York, NY: John Wiley & Sons, 2000.

Orlich, Donald C. *Designing Successful Grant Proposals.* Alexandria, VA: Association for Supervison and Curriculum Development, 1996: pp. 72-74.

Owen, John M. *Program Evaluation: Forms and Approaches.* London; Thousand Oaks: Sage Publications, 1999.

Popham, W. James. *Educational Evaluation.* Englewood Cliffs, NJ: Prentice Hall, 1988: pp. 14, 178, 323.

Rossi, Peter H., and Howard E. Freeman. *Evaluation: A Systematic Approach.* Beverly Hills, CA: SAGE, 1985: pp. 19, 38.

Smith, Helen, Michael Armstrong, and Sally Brown, eds. *Benchmarking and Threshold Standards in Higher Education.* London: Kogan Page, 1999.

Stark, Joan S., and Alice Thomas, eds. *Assessment and Program Evaluation.* Needham Heights, MA: Simon & Schuster Custom Publishing, 1994.

Stecher, Brian M., and W. Alan Davis. *How to Focus an Evaluation.* Newbury Park, CA: SAGE, 1987: p. 16.

Steffy, Betty E., and Fenwick W. English. *Curriculum and Assessment for World-Class Schools.* Lancaster, PA: Technomic, 1997: pp. 97, 99-100, 117.

Torney-Purta, Judith, ed. *Evaluating Global Education: Sample Instruments for Assessing Programs, Materials and Learning.* New York, NY: American Forum for Global Education, 1987.

Tuckman, Bruce Wayne. *Evaluating Instructional Programs.* Boston, MA: Allyn and Bacon, 1985: pp. 3, 41, 189-92.

Wholey, Joseph S., Harry P. Hatry, and Kathryn E. Newcomer, eds. *Handbook of Practical Program Evaluation.* San Francisco, CA: Jossey-Bass, 1994: pp. 2, 15, 549-51, 553-72.

Worthen, Blaine R., James R. Sanders, and Jody L. Fitzpatrick. *Program Evaluation: Alternative Approaches and Practical Guidelines.* New York, NY: Longman, 1997.

International Trade

(General Reference: *Books, Periodicals*)

Books

Axtell, Roger E. *The Do's and Taboos of International Trade: A Small Business Primer.* New York, NY: J. Wiley, 1994.

Axtell, Roger E., Tami Briggs, Margaret Corcoran, and Mary Beth Lamb. *Do's and Taboos Around the World for Women in Business*. New York, NY: J. Wiley, 1997.

Colas, Bernard, ed. *Global Economic Co-operation: A Guide to Agreements and Organizations*, 2nd ed. Didcot, England: Management Books, 2000.

Curry, Jeffrey E. *A Short Course in International Economics: Understanding the Dynamics of the International Marketplace*. Novato, CA: World Trade Press, 2000.

Czinkota, Michael R., Ilkka A. Ronkainen, and Michael H. Moffet. *International Business*. Fort Worth, TX: Dryden Press, 1999.

Dunkel, Arthur. *Key Words in International Trade: ICC's Unique Business Language Handbook*. Paris: ICC Publishing, Inc., 1996.

Epping, Randy C. *A Beginner's Guide to the World Economy: Seventy-one Basic Economic Concepts That Will Change the Way You See the World*. New York, NY: Vintage Books, 1992.

Fatouros, A. A., ed. *Transnational Corporations: The International Legal Framework*. London: Routledge, 1994.

Foley, James F. *The Global Entrepreneur: Taking Your Business International*. Chicago, IL: Dearborn, 1999.

Friedman, Thomas L. *The Lexus and the Olive Tree*. New York, NY: Anchor Books, 2000.

Gelder, Alice A., and Rudy Yuly. *World Business Desk Reference: How to Do Business with 192 Countries by Phone, Fax and Mail*. Burr Ridge, IL: Irwin Professional Publishers, 1994.

Guy, Vincent, and John Mattock. *The International Business Book: All the Tools, Tactics, and Tips You Need for Doing Business Across Cultures*. Lincolnwood, IL: NTC Business Books, 1995.

Hinkelman, Edward G. *Dictionary of International Trade: Handbook of the Global Trade Community Includes 12 Key Appendices.* San Rafael, CA: World Trade Press, 2000.

Incoterms 2000: ICC Official Rules for the Interpretation of Trade Terms. Paris: ICC Publishing, Inc., 1999.

International Banking: A Legal Guide. London: Euromoney Publications, 1991.

Jimenez, Guillermo. *Export-Import Basics: The Legal, Financial & Transport Aspects of International Trade.* Paris: ICC Publishing, Inc., 1997.

Johnson, Thomas E. *Export/Import Procedures and Documentation.* New York, NY: Amacom, 1997.

Jonnard, Claude M. *International Business and Trade: Theory, Practice, and Policy.* Boca Raton, FL: St. Lucie Press, 1998.

Joyner, Nelson T. *How to Build an Export Business.* Reston, VA: The Federation of International Trade Associations, 1995.

Karamally, Zak. *Export Savvy: From Basics to Strategy.* New York, NY: International Business Press, 1998.

Mahony, Stephen. *The Financial Times A-Z of International Finance: The Essential Guide to Tools, Terms and Techniques.* London: FT Pitman, 1997.

Mohammadi, Ali, ed. *International Communication and Globalization: A Critical Introduction.* London: Sage Publications, 1997.

Morrison, Teresa C., et al. *Dun & Bradstreet's Guide to Doing Business Around the World.* Englewood Cliffs, NJ: Prentice Hall, 1997.

Munger, Susan H. *The International Business Communication Desk Reference.* New York, NY: Amacom, 1993.

Neipert, David. *A Tour of International Trade.* Upper Saddle River, NJ: Prentice Hall, 2000.

Nelson, Carl A. *Import/Export: How to Get Started in International Trade.* New York, NY: McGraw-Hill, 1995.

Official Export Guide. Hightstown, NJ: Primedia Directories, 1999.

Pagell, Ruth A., and Michael Halperin. *International Business Information: How to Find It, How to Use It*, 3rd ed. Phoenix, AZ: Oryx Press, 1998.

Pencak, Rich. *Pencak's Guide to Importing Purchases into These United States of America.* Port Jervis, NY: Pencak & Company, 1999.

Pilditch, James. *I'll Be Over in the Morning: A Practical Guide to Winning Business in Other Countries.* London: Mercury Books, 1992.

Reif, Joe, et al. *Services: The Export of the 21st Century: A Guidebook for U.S. Service Exporters.* San Rafael, CA: World Trade Press, 1997.

Reuvid, Jonathan. *The Strategic Guide to International Trade.* London: Kogan Page Publishers, 1997.

Rosenberg, Jerry M. *Dictionary of International Trade.* New York, NY: J. Wiley, 1993.

Ryans, Cynthia C. *Building a Foreign Trade Library: A Compilation of Basic Resources for Small- to Medium-sized International Business Firms.* Cleveland, OH: World Trade Education Center, 1983.

Ryen, Dag. *The ABCs of World Trade: A Handbook for State Officials on International Trade and Export Promotion.* Lexington, KY: Council of State Governments, 1997.

Schreiber, Mae N. *International Trade Sources: A Research Guide.* New York, NY: Garland, 1997.

Stanat, Ruth. *Global Gold: Panning for Profits in Foreign Markets.* New York, NY: Amacom, 1998.

Tuller, Lawrence W. *Exporting, Importing, and Beyond: How to "Go Global" with Your Small Business.* Holbrook, MA: Adams Media Corporation, 1997.

United Nations Development Education Directory: Economic and Social Development in the United Nations System: A Guide for NGOs, 8th ed. Geneva: United Nations Non-Governmental Liaison Service, 1995.

U.S. Customs House Guide. Hightstown, NJ: Primedia Directories, 1999.

U.S. Customs Service Department of the Treasury, Compiler. *A Basic Guide to Importing.* Lincolnwood, IL: NTC Business Books, 1995.

U.S. International Trade Administration. *The Big Emerging Markets: 1996 Outlook and Sourcebook.* Lanham, MD: Bernan Press, 1995.

U.S. Small Business Administration, Office of International Trade. *Exporter's Guide to Federal Resources for Small Business.* Washington, DC: U.S. Government Printing Office, 1992.

Weiss, Kenneth D. *Building an Import/Export Business.* New York, NY: J. Wiley, 1997.

Wells, L. Fargo. and Karin Dulat. *Exporting: From Start to Finance.* New York, NY: McGraw-Hill, 1995.

Wild, John J. *International Business: An Integrated Approach.* Upper Saddle River, NJ: Prentice Hall, 2000.

Wilfong, James. *Taking Your Business Global: Your Small Business Guide to Successful International Trade.* Franklin Lakes, NJ: Career Press, 1997.

Zuckerman, Amy, and David Biederman. *Exporting and Importing: Negotiating Global Markets.* New York, NY: Amacom, 1998.

Periodicals

Business Week. New York, NY: McGraw-Hill. Weekly. TEL: 800.635.1200; WEB: www.businessweek.com

The Economist. New York, NY: The Economist Newspaper, NA, Inc. Weekly. TEL: 212.541.0500; FAX: 212.541.9378; WEB: www.economist.com

Export Today's Global Business. Washington, DC: Trade Communications, Inc. Monthly. TEL: 202.737.1060; FAX: 202.783.5966; WEB: www.globalbusinessmag.com

The Exporter. New York, NY: Trade Data Reports, Inc. Monthly. TEL: 212.587.1340; FAX: 212.587.1344; WEB: www.exporter.com

Far Eastern Economic Review. Hong Kong: Review Publishing Company Limited. Weekly. TEL: 852.2508.4338; FAX: 852.2503.1553; WEB: www.feer.com

The Journal of Commerce. New York, NY: Journal of Commerce, Inc. Daily. TEL: 800.331.1341; FAX: 908.454.6192; WEB: www.joc.com

Latin Trade. Coral Gables, FL: Freedom Magazines International. Monthly. TEL: 800.799.6895; FAX: 818.760.4490; WEB: www.latintrade.com

World Trade. Troy, MI: Business News Publishing. Monthly. TEL: 248.362.3700; FAX: 248.362.0317; WEB: www.worldtrademag.com

CIBER Sites (*Center for International Business Education and Research, Individual Contact Information*)

Note that a central CIBER directory is provided at:
WEB: ciber.centers.purdue.edu/local_cibers/main.html

Brigham Young University
TEL: 801.378.6495
FAX: 801.378.2411
WEB: www.marriottschool.byu.edu/ciber/

Columbia University
TEL: 212.854.3413
FAX: 212.316.9219
WEB: www.sipa.columbia.edu/cibe.html

Duke University
    TEL: 919.660.7836
    FAX: 919.660.7769
    WEB: faculty.fuqua.duke.edu/ciber/

Florida International University
    TEL: 305.348.1740
    FAX: 305.348.1789
    WEB: www.fiu.edu/~ciber/

Georgia Institute of Technology
    TEL: 404.894.1463
    FAX: 404.894.6625
    WEB: www.ciber.gatech.edu/

Indiana University
    TEL: 812.855.1716
    FAX: 812.855.9006
    WEB: www.bus.indiana.edu/ipweb/ciber.htm

Michigan State University
    TEL: 517.353.4336
    FAX: 517.432.1009
    WEB: www.ciber.bus.msu.edu/

The Ohio State University
    TEL: 614.292.0845
    FAX: 614.688.3688
    WEB: www.cob.ohio-state.edu/ciber

Purdue University
    TEL: 765.494.4463
    FAX: 765.494.9658
    WEB: www.mgmt.purdue.edu/centers/ciber/

San Diego State University
    TEL: 619.594.6023
    FAX: 619.594.7738
    WEB: www.rohan.sdsu.edu/dept/ciber/

Texas A&M University
    TEL: 979.845.5234
    FAX: 979.845.1710
    WEB: cibs.tamu.edu

Thunderbird
    TEL: 602.978.7716
    FAX: 602.978.7729
    WEB: www.t-bird.edu/research/ciber/

University of California at Los Angeles
    TEL: 310.206.5317
    FAX: 310.825.8098
    WEB: www.anderson.ucla.edu/research/ciber/

University of Colorado at Denver
    TEL: 303.556.4738
    FAX: 303.556.6276
    WEB: www.cudenver.edu/public/inst_intl_bus/main.html

University of Connecticut
    TEL: 860.486.5458
    FAX: 860.486.5497
    WEB: www.sba.uconn.edu/ciber/index.htm

University of Florida
    TEL: 352.392.3433
    FAX: 352.392.7860
    WEB: bear.cba.ufl.edu/centers/ciber/index.htm

University of Hawaii at Manoa
    TEL: 808.956.8041
    FAX: 808.956.9685
    WEB: www.cba.hawaii.edu/ciber/home.htm

University of Illinois at Urbana-Champaign
    TEL: 217.333.8335
    FAX: 217.333.7410
    WEB: www.ciber.uiuc.edu/

University of Kansas
TEL: 785.864.3125
FAX: 785.864.3768
WEB: www.bschool.ukans.edu/kuciber

University of Memphis
TEL: 901.678.2038
FAX: 901.678.3678
WEB: www.people.memphis.edu/~wangctr/

University of Michigan
TEL: 734.936.3917
FAX: 734.936.1721
WEB: www.umich.edu/~cibe/

University of North Carolina
TEL: 919.962.7843
FAX: 919.962.8836
WEB: www.kenanflagler.unc.edu/ip/CIBER/ciber.html

University of Pittsburgh
TEL: 412.648.1509
FAX: 412.648.1683
WEB: www.pitt.edu/~ibcmod/

University of South Carolina
TEL: 803.777.3600
FAX: 803.777.3609
WEB: www.business.sc.edu/ciber2001/

University of Southern California
TEL: 213.740.2852
FAX: 213.740.2858
WEB: www.marshall.usc.edu/cibear/cibear.html

University of Texas at Austin
TEL: 512.471.1829
FAX: 512.471.7556
WEB: www.bus.utexas.edu/ciber/

University of Utah
> TEL: 801.585.5560
> FAX: 801.581.7214
> WEB: www.business.utah.edu/ciber/

University of Washington
> TEL: 206.685.3432
> FAX: 206.685.4079
> WEB: www.depts.washington.edu/ciberweb/

University of Wisconsin
> TEL: 608.262.3819
> FAX: 608.265.3121
> WEB: www.wisc.edu/ciber

Field Notes, a Guide to Planning

This section is intended as a resource for planning the internationalization process. The checklist on the first page provides an overview of nine major aspects of IB education. The following checklists further break down those aspects. Users of this information should feel free to modify the various forms to fit their situations and add additional checklists as necessary.

Project/Issue	Start Date	Target Completion Date	Person(s) Responsible	Status	Notes
1. Plan Your Strategy					
2. Solicit and Gain Support					
3. Design the IB Curriculum					
4. Collaborate with Modern Language and Area Studies					
5. Identify and Seek Funding					
6. Develop Outreach Programs					
7. Develop International Relationships					
8. Utilize Virtual Business Education					
9. Evaluate Your IB Program					

1. Plan Your Strategy

Project/Issue	Start Date	Target Completion Date	Person(s) Responsible	Status	Notes
1. Identify past and present internationa-ization experiences					
2. Identify competitive position					
3. Identify key objectives					
4. Identify IB team members					
5. Assess resources					
6. Prepare project proposals for funding					
7. Develop an evaluation process					
8. Prepare a timetable for implementation					

2. Solicit and Gain Support

Project/Issue	Start Date	Target Completion Date	Person(s) Responsible	Status	Notes
1. Identify and deal with obstacles					
2. Articulate internationalization vision and develop goals and objectives					
3. Identify an IB champion or champions					
4. Gain administrative support					
5. Gain faculty support					
6. Sustain and institutionalize the IB program					

3. Design the IB Curriculum

Project/Issue	Start Date	Target Completion Date	Person(s) Responsible	Status	Notes
1. Form an interdisciplinary undergraduate curriculum team					
2. Conduct a needs assessment					
3. Apply business, culture, and language framework					
4. Articulate curricular goals					
5. Determine educational objectives					
6. Select curriculum inter-nationalization methods					

4. Collaborate with Modern Language and Area Studies

Project/Issue	Start Date	Target Completion Date	Person(s) Responsible	Status	Notes
1. Approach modern language and area studies faculty to discuss collaboration					
2. Discover common professional interests and focus on relationship building					
3. Develop collaborative activities that are *win-win* for all involved					
4. Be a guest speaker in each others' classes					
5. Sponsor regularly-scheduled international forums					
6. Apply together for external funding					

5. Identify and Seek Funding

Project/Issue	Start Date	Target Completion Date	Person(s) Responsible	Status	Notes
1. Identify potential funding sources					
2. Identify and contact the program officer					
3. Identify and contact other grantees					
4. Develop a proposal					
5. Engage other individuals to review and revise the entire proposal					
6. Submit proposal for review					
7. Review feedback and funding from granting agency					

6. Develop Outreach Programs

Project/Issue	Start Date	Target Completion Date	Person(s) Responsible	Status	Notes
1. Evaluate what others have done in outreach programs					
2. Identify other international assistance providers and market needs					
3. Identify potential client base					
4. Develop outreach program portfolio					
5. Integrate IB program into business community and client base					
6. Assess educational service delivery system					

7. Develop International Relationships

Project/Issue	Start Date	Target Completion Date	Person(s) Responsible	Status	Notes
1. Assess home institution's strategic objectives, financial resources, and human resources					
2. Research what other institutions have done					
3. Evaluate international linkage options					
4. Identify participant issues					
5. Develop exchange programs and agreements					
6. Recruit faculty, staff, and students to participate in programs					

8. Utilize Virtual Business Education

Project/Issue	Start Date	Target Completion Date	Person(s) Responsible	Status	Notes
1. Form a virtual IB team					
2. Rethink the teaching-learning process					
3. Develop virtual business education objectives					
4. Assess resources and options					
5. Acquire needed technology					
6. Evaluate technological tools and needed upgrades					

9. Evaluate Your IB Program

Project/Issue	Start Date	Target Completion Date	Person(s) Responsible	Status	Notes
1. Identify what to evaluate					
2. Set evaluation objectives					
3. Identify measurement tools					
4. Plan when the evaluation will occur, who will conduct it, and what it will cost					
5. Determine the format of the evaluation report					
6. Prepare report					
7. Carefully review the report					
8. Carefully consider ways to accommodate the report's findings and recommendations					

Notes on Authors, Editors, and Contributors

M. Fall Ainina is Professor of Finance in the Department of Finance, Insurance, and Real Estate and at Wright State University. He holds a Ph.D. in Finance from Arizona State University. He served as the ambassador extraordinary and plenipotentiary of Mauritania to the U.S., Brazil, and Mexico from February 1992 to September 1994. He was the past president of the Economic Group of the African Diplomatic Corps in Washington, D.C., and participated in all the negotiations with the World Bank and the International Monetary Fund on the economic adjustment program for Mauritania. He has published in the areas of corporate finance, leveraged buyouts and investments in journals such as the *Journal of Business, Finance and Accounting,* the *Journal of Risk and Insurance,* the *Journal of Applied Business Research,* and the *Academy of Management Executive.* He coauthored Managerial Finance Using Lotus 123 (Harper & Row, New York). He was a visiting professor at the Universidad de La Frontera in Temuco, Chile, at Ecole Supérieure des Sciences Commerciales d'Angers, Angers, France, and the H. L. Stoutt Community College, Tortola, British Virgin Islands. He has codirected three U.S. Department of Education, Business and International Education grants and a National Security Education Program grant. He is fluent in Arabic, French, English, and Spanish.

Sarah T. Beaton has been involved in international business education for a decade at the U.S. Department of Education. She previously administered the Business and International Education (BIE) program and currently oversees the BIE program, the Centers for International Business Education, and the Undergraduate International Studies and Foreign Language program, two other Title VI programs, and two Fulbright-Hays programs as the Branch Chief of the International Studies Team. She designed and implemented several international faculty development conferences with both U.S. and foreign institutions of higher education. Her background includes the study of economics, liberal arts, and business—both at home and abroad. She is an enthusiastic internationalist and uses her talents to help develop sustainable and creative international programs at universities and colleges throughout the United States.

Joop Bollen teaches at Northern State University in Aberdeen, South Dakota. He is a native of Eindhoven, Netherlands, and came to the United States as a high school student to Los Angeles—where, at the University of California, he also earned his B.S. in Economics and Business. He earned his M.S. from the American Graduate School of International Management. As the director of the South Dakota International Business Institute, a nonprofit organization designed to support state and federal agencies in their efforts to enhance international business throughout the upper Midwest, Bollen has developed, implemented, and managed more than fifty workshops and seminars. In addition, he has organized two international academic business conferences, received two Title VI grants, successfully negotiated and entered into contracts with the South Dakota Governor's Office of Economic Development and the North Dakota Department of Economic Development & Finance, and has developed an international lab which provides export counseling and international trade services to the business community in the upper Midwest.

Claire D. Cornell is the director of External Grants for the University of South Carolina, College of Science and Mathematics and College of Education. In this capacity she and her staff research funding sources and develop proposals. They pursue public and private funding and develop collaborations with colleges, universities, government offices, and businesses throughout the state. Until the spring of 1999, Ms. Cornell ran a grant office for the University of Iowa's College of Liberal Arts, College of Business, and Graduate College. Since 1981, she has also operated a private grants consulting practice. While working for the University of Iowa, Ms. Cornell collaborated with business faculty to develop successful grant applications to the Business and International Education (BIE) program (two awards), the Department of Education Fund for the

Improvement of Post-Secondary Education (FIPSE) program, the Ewing Marion Kauffman Foundation, and other business funders. Her grant development efforts have consistently generated more than $5 million per year.

William R. Folks, Jr. is Professor of International Business and Director of the Center for International Business Education and Research of the Darla Moore School of Business at the University of South Carolina (USC). Professor Folks has also served as a Visiting Professor at Université Catholique de Louvain (Belgium), the Helsinki School of Economics and Business Administration (Finland), and Xiamen University (People's Republic of China), and has taught in numerous executive education programs in the United States, Brazil, and Finland. Professor Folks received his D.B.A. from the Harvard Business School in 1970, and is the author of over forty research papers in journals such as *Financial Management, Management Science, The Journal of Financial and Quantitative Analysis,* and *The Journal of International Business Studies,* and is the coauthor of the text *International Dimensions of Managerial Finance.* Professor Folks helped develop and serves as academic director of the Masters of International Business Studies (MIBS) program at USC.

Joseph Ganitsky is a native Columbian who received a B.S. in Industrial Engineering from the Universidad de Los Andes, Bogotá, a M.S. in Industrial Management from the Georgia Institute of Technology, Atlanta, and a D.B.A. in Business Administration from Harvard. He has taught at the Central American Institute of Management, Managua, Universidad de Los Andes, Bogotá (where he was the first dean of its Business School); the Jerusalem Institute of Management, Tel Aviv, Tulane University, New Orleans, the Instituto de Empresa, Madrid, the Instituto de Estudios Superiors de Administración, Caracas, and the China-Europe International Business School, Shang Hai. He presently teaches both at the Instituto de Empresa and Loyola University. He coordinates Loyola's IB area and has led four International Business research/community development projects funded by the U.S. Department of Education and the State of Louisiana. His current research interests focus on the strategic evolution of Spanish investments in Latin America and in global entrepreneurship. His recent publications focus on the role of businesses and investors in promoting Latin America's growth, human resource management, and marketing strategy issues of international joint ventures. He is the current president of the Business Association of Latin America Studies (BALAS).

Brian Gauler has developed and coordinated three university export outreach programs in Oklahoma, Arkansas, and Missouri over the past thirteen years. He currently serves as the director of the University of Missouri Extension Export Development Program. He is an experienced global marketing manager, having held international management positions with the Monsanto Company, Mercury Marine, and Zebco. He has authored two international training manuals used nationally by the USDA; a field guide for export service providers; and an export training manual. His book, *Preparing for Global Marketing,* was published last year. He has authored numerous export related articles, and was named the Tulsa World Trade Association "Achiever of the Year" in 1993 in recognition of his outstanding contributions to international commerce.

Linda V. Gerber, received her B.B.A. and Ph.D. from the University of Texas at Austin, where she also now teaches. Dr. Gerber has served as the director of Academic Programs for the Center for International Business Education and Research (CIBER), where her responsibilities included overseeing graduate study abroad programs, the M.B.A./M.P.A. Language Track, and the development of commercial language programs for business students. Dr. Gerber regularly serves as a speaker at professional meetings and conferences related to language education in business. Along with Robert T. Green, she coauthored "Linkages with Overseas Business Schools: Keys to Success" in *Internationalizing Business Education: Meeting the Challenge* (Michigan State University Press, 1993) and "Strategic Partnerships for Global Education: Linkages with Overseas Business Schools" (*Journal of International Marketing,* 1996).

Jaime Alonso Gómez is the dean of the Graduate School of Business Administration and Leadership, and Professor of International Management and Operations, at the Instituto Tecnológico y de Estudios Superiores de Monterrey, Mexico. Dr. Gómez has been a consultant for companies and institutions in the Americas, Europe, and Asia, and is a member of editorial boards of academic and business journals including the *Latin American Business Review and Revista Expansión.* He participates as a member of the board of several multinational organizations in the Americas. As an international scholar, Jaime Alonso has been a visiting professor/speaker at the Massachusetts Institute of Technology, Carnagie Mellon University, Georgia Institute of Technology, the University of California at Los Angeles, the University of Texas at Austin, and McGill University in Canada. His research interests include strategic management, socio-technical systems, and business applications of the chaos/complexity theory.

Lourdene Huhra is executive dean of Workforce and International Development at Bunker Hill Community College in Boston. She holds an M.M. degree in International Business and Marketing from the Kellogg Graduate

School of Management at Northwestern University. Huhra served as project director for four Business and International Education Program grants and one Undergraduate International Studies and Foreign Language Program grant. She coauthored two books on international business education: *Training for Trade: Community College Programs to Promote Export* and *Strengthening America's Competitiveness: Profiles of Leading Community College International Trade Centers*, published by the American Association of Community Colleges. Huhra is past-president and continues as a member of the board of the North American Small Business International Trade Educators (NASBITE).

Lorraine A. Krajewski received her Ph.D. from Arizona State University and is Professor of Management at Louisiana State University in Shreveport, where she teaches undergraduate and graduate courses in International Business, International Studies, International Business Communication, and Managerial Communication. She has served in several positions related to international studies and international business, was director of two Title VI projects, and has been a panel reviewer for Title VI programs. She has also worked as a consultant and external evaluator for international business projects. Dr. Krajewski's primary region of focus is Asia. In 1994 she was awarded a Fulbright-Hays Seminars Abroad Fellowship to study in Indonesia and has received three fellowships to study and travel in China. She has also been the recipient of two fellowships to study at the East-West Center in Honolulu under the auspices of the Asian Studies Development Program.

Rishi Kumar is the dean of the Raj Soin College of Business at Wright State University, and holds a faculty appointment as Professor of Economics. Dr. Kumar earned an M.A. from the University of Delhi, and another from Vanderbilt University. Dr. Kumar came to the United States on a Fulbright-Smith-Mundt Fellowship and received his Ph.D. from Wayne State University. Dr. Kumar has over forty years of academic experience and has written numerous articles in professional journals on economics and international topics. Dr. Kumar is very active in various community organizations. He is currently on the Board of Directors of the India Foundation of Dayton, the National Conference for Community and Justice, the Dayton Council on World Affairs, the Asian-Indian American Business Group, and various other Hindu community organizations. He has been the recipient of numerous awards for community service and academic excellence including the Wright State University Presidential Award for Outstanding Faculty Member.

Steven J. Loughrin-Sacco is the codirector of San Diego State University's Center for International Business Education and Research (CIBER), is chair of the International Business Program, and a Professor of French. For sixteen years, he has collaborated with business and engineering faculty to develop cutting edge international education curricula. Since 1988, he has been awarded forty grants totaling $3 million, most of which involved collaboration with business schools. These awards include nine U.S. Department of Education grants from five different funding programs and grants from four countries: Canada, France, Japan, and Mexico. He has served as a consultant to over twenty business schools and foreign language departments, and is a recognized authority in the teaching of foreign languages for business and economic purposes and is the author of two books, *Quebec Inc.*, and *Making Business French Work*, as well as over fifteen articles. He has also served as the editor of the newsletter *French for Business and International Trade* since 1997.

Zaida L. Martínez is Associate Professor of International Business, and associate director on a Business and International Education (BIE) grant at St. Mary's University. Prior to 1993, she was Associate Professor of Management and Chair of the Business Administration Department at South Carolina State University. Her teaching is in the areas of cross-cultural management, international human resource management, and international strategic management. Her research is multidisciplinary and has recently focused on the training and development practices of international companies. She reviews for several academic journals such as *Management International Review* and *Journal of International Management*. She was responsible for a Title VI-B grant while at South Carolina State University and a Title VI-A grant while at St. Mary's University.

Jeffrey F. Meyer is currently serving as the executive director of the Van Andel Global Trade Institute located at Grand Valley State University in Grand Rapids, MI. The institute serves as the central clearinghouse for international trade training, education, consulting, and resources for the Western Michigan business community. Previous to this position, Meyer served as director for International Trade Programs at Wright State University and simultaneously served as the Executive Director of the North American Small Business International Trade Educators (NASBITE). Meyer has experience teaching international marketing, management, and trade in the U.S. and abroad. He brings to his new position experience in grant writing, academic program development, and program implementation. Meyer has made presentations at conferences on various international topics, both in the U.S. and abroad. Meyer also has experience in sales, marketing, and research on U.S. and overseas markets.

Kelly Jett Murphrey is associate director of the Center for International Business Education and Research (CIBER) and the Center for the Study of Western Hemispheric Trade (CSWHT) in the Lowry Mays College and Graduate School of Business at Texas A&M University. He frequently speaks—nationally and internationally—on topics related to internationalizing business education, distance education, and electronic commerce. He is currently involved in the development of a series of bilingual educational modules on international trade that will be delivered via CD-ROM and the Internet. He is a member of the Academy of International Business, the North American Small Business International Trade Educators, and Phi Beta Delta, the Honor Society for International Scholars. Dr. Murphrey holds a master's degree from Thunderbird, the American Graduate School of International Management, and a doctoral degree from Texas A&M University.

Eugenio Oblitas Díaz currently serves as an assistant professor of Organizational Communication in the Department of Social Communication, College of Social Sciences, at the Universidad de Concepción in Concepción, Chile. He is also Professor of Communication at Universidad del Desarrollo in Concepción, and has been a Visiting Professor of Management at Wright State University. He holds a bachelor's degree in Journalism from the Universidad de Concepción, a master of arts in Communications from the University of Dayton, and a doctorate in Information Sciences from the Pontificial Universidad de Salamanca, Spain. He has consulted with a variety of public and private sector organizations on communication and human performance issues. He has authored or coauthored both scholarly and practitioner publications, including two books, *Conversations About Creativity* and *Creativity in the Classroom*.

Germán Otalora is a professor, researcher, and consultant at the Instituto Tecnológico y de Estudios Superiores de Monterrey (ITESM), Graduate School of Business, where he was dean for eleven years. Before, he taught at Universidad Iberoamericana in Mexico City and worked for GRUPO ICA, the largest Mexican engineering and construction firm. His Ph.D. in Organizational Sociology is from the University of Pennsylvania. He has been a visiting professor at the National University of Honduras, at ESADE in Barcelona, Spain, at the Escuela Militar de Ingeniería in La Paz, Bolivia, and at several Mexican universities. He has done research on industrial relations, the impact of organizational hierarchy on the behavioral system of the organizations' members, family structures of juvenile delinquents, strategic changes in small and medium size enterprises during the Mexican crisis of 1982, and profiles of Mexican executives in the context of NAFTA. His research has been published in books and professional journals. Professor Otalora is one of the four Mexican fellows of the International Academy of Management.

Margarete M. Roth is Professor of International Business and Economics and Director of the Center for International Studies at Benedictine University. Her doctorate in Economics is from the University of Cologne in Germany. She was in charge of the East and South Africa desks of Misereor, the German Bishops' Commission against Hunger and Disease in the World. She has developed international programs including majors in International Studies, International Business, and Economics, and exchange agreements with universities in Denmark, Germany, Japan, and Mexico. She has done fieldwork in Tanzania and Uganda, and research in Peru, which resulted in publication, several articles, and a book. She has been the recipient of many grants, including a research grant from the German Thyssen Foundation, grants from the National Endowment for the Humanities (NEH), three U.S. Department of Education Title VI grants, and a Fulbright Scholar in Residence grant. She served as a Danforth Associate, and is a consultant/evaluator and a reader's panel member of North Central Association, the regional accreditation association for universities and colleges.

Robert F. Scherer is Professor of Management and associate dean for Community Relations in the Raj Soin College of Business at Wright State University (WSU), in Dayton, Ohio. He holds a Ph.D. in business administration from the University of Mississippi and is certified as a Senior Professional in Human Resources (SPHR). He has published more than 100 scholarly and professional works including journal articles, conference papers, edited editions, and book chapters and reviews, in the areas of business education, performance, occupational stress and safety, entrepreneurship, international management, and gender issues in the workplace. Currently, he is directing WSU's collaborative program with the British Virgin Island's H. L. Stoutt Community College, which offers an M.B.A. to students in Tortola. He collaborated with the Universidad de La Frontera in Temuco, Chile, in the design of their Masters of Management degree program. He served as a Fulbright Senior Scholar in Chile, at the Universidad de Concepción during the 1998-1999 academic year. While in Chile he also taught at Universidad de Magallanes and Universidad del Desarrollo. Dr. Scherer serves or has served on the boards of more than ten public, nonprofit, or professional organizations. He is currently an executive editor for the *Journal of Social Psychology*. For nine years prior to entering a university career, he held managerial positions in the insurance and magazine publishing industries. He has received over $2 million in grant funding for international and domestic projects since 1994.

James Thomas is a professor, writer, and editor. He received his Ph.D. in English from the University of Utah, Salt Lake City, where he also founded *Quarterly West*, a literary magazine, and directed Writers @ Work, a summer writers' conference. He has taught fiction writing at Bowling Green State University, Baylor University, Wright State University, and Antioch College. For his own fiction, Thomas has received two National Endowments for the Arts (NEA) grants, a Stegner Fellowship from Stanford University, and a James Michener Fellowship from the University of Iowa. His stories have appeared in numerous literary magazines and in *Esquire*, and have been read on National Public Radio (NPR). His collection of stories—*Pictures, Moving*—was nominated for a Pulitzer Prize. He has edited nine anthologies of fiction for W. W. Norton & Co. and other publishers, and served for several years as a senior trade editor for Gibbs M. Smith, Peregrine Books.

Brian Toyne is the Emil C. E. Jurica Professor of International Business and Director of the Center for Global Studies at St. Mary's University in San Antonio. Prior to 1993 he was Professor of International Business and Coordinator for the International Ph.D. Program at the University of South Carolina. He currently teaches in the areas of international marketing and international strategic management. His recent research has focused on the paradigms and theories underpinning international business inquiry. He is the author, coauthor, or editor of ten books such as *Global Marketing Management* and *International Business: An Emerging Vision* and numerous articles dealing with international management, marketing, and business education issues. He has served as associate editor for the *Journal of International Business Studies*, as well as the vice president, for the Academy of International Business and as the chair, for International Management Division, Academy of Management. He has received three Title VI-B grants and one Institute of International Public Policy grant while at St. Mary's University.

Todd Trickler holds an M.B.A. from Wright State University. He has worked for three years in WSU's International Trade Counseling Program. In this capacity, he has assisted students, professors, and the local business community with issues related to international business and education. He has participated in Project CHILE, an international study abroad/internship program, where he assisted a Chilean company with their efforts to do business with companies in the United States. He was also a participant in the Free Market Development Advisors Program, a program sponsored by the U.S. Agency for International Development. In this program he spent a year working in Panama for a nongovernmental organization that was involved in small business development. His undergraduate degree is from Wright State University in International Studies.

Sara D. Tucker is associate director of the Center for International Business Education and Research (CIBER) at the Anderson School at the University of California at Los Angeles. Previously, she was special projects coordinator at the J. Paul Getty Conservation Institute in Los Angeles where she developed and monitored a number of conservation projects in the U.S., Africa, China, Latin America, and Eastern Europe. Prior to her work with the Getty, she founded her own consulting company which specialized in helping U.S. companies entering the Korean and Asian markets. She also helped start the International Management Fellows (IMF) Program at the Anderson School by serving as its first internship coordinator, assisting in developing corporate internships in Asia, Europe, and Latin America for IMF Students. Sara Tucker speaks Mandarin Chinese, Russian, Korean, Spanish, and has studied and worked in China, Japan, Korea, and the former Soviet Union. She has a B.A. from Yale University in East Asian Studies and an M.B.A. from the Anderson School at the University of California at Los Angeles.

A Glossary
of Acronyms

Note: see *Organizations* in **Chapter Reference Notes and Additional Resources** for Telephone, FAX, and NET (Internet, World Wide Web) contact information on many of the organizations listed here.

AACC, American Association of Community Colleges

AACSB, The International Association for Management Education

ACE, American Council on Education

ACIIE, American Council on International Intercultural Education

ACTFL, American Council on the Teaching of Foreign Languages

ACUNS, Academic Council on the United Nations System

AIB, Academy of International Business

AIESEC, Association Internationale des Etudiants en Sciences Economiques et Commericale

AIFS, American Institute for Foreign Study

ALA, American Library Association

ASCD, Association for Supervision and Curriculum Development

AWB, Action Without Borders

BALAS, Business Association of Latin American Studies

BIE, Business and International Education (Title VI-B grant program of the US/ED)

BISA, British International Studies Association

C4, CIBER Cross-Cultural Collegium

CALICO, Computer Assisted Language Instruction Consortium

CALL, Center for the Advancement of Language Learning

CCIS, College Consortium for International Studies

CDC, Citizens Democracy Corps

CEEBIC, Central and East European Business Information Center

CEO, Chief Executive Officer

CF, Council on Foundations

CFR, Council on Foreign Relations

CIA, Central Intelligence Agency

CIBER, Center for International Business Education and Research (Title VI-B grant program of the US/ED)

CIE, The Coalition for International Education

CIEE, Council on International Educational Exchange

CIES, Council for International Exchange of Scholars

CLEAR, Center for Language Education and Research

DACUM, "developing a curriculum"

EAC, Export Assistance Centers (extensions of the USEAC)

EAIE, European Association for International Education

ECE, Education Credential Evaluators

EFRC, Education Funding Research Council

EMBA, Executive M.B.A.

EMC, an export management company

ERIC, Educational Resources Information Center

ERIC/CLL, ERIC Clearinghouse on Languages and Linguistics

ESL, English as a second language

ETC, an export trading company

EU, European Union (formally the EEC, European Economic Community)

EWCP, Export Working Capital Program (arm of the SBA)

Ex-Im, Export-Import Bank

FAS, Foreign Agricultural Service

FDIB, Faculty Development in International Business (programs offered by CIBERs)

FEMBA, a fully-employed M.B.A.

FIPSE, Fund for the Improvement of Postsecondary Education (grant program of the US/ED)

FLIE, foreign language and international economics (as an academic major)

FTE, full-time equivalent

GARNET, Global Applied Research Network

GBN, Global Business Network

GPRA, Government Performance and Results Act of 1993

HRM, human resource management

IADB, Inter-American Development Bank

IB, international business

IBE, international business education

IBS, international business seminars

ICC, International Campus Consortium (sponsored by Thunderbird, The American Graduate School of International Management)

ICC, International Chamber of Commerce

ICCWBO, International Chamber of Commerce World Business Organization

ICIE, Illinois Consortium for International Education

IGL, Institute for Global Communications

IIE, Institute of International Education

IIO, Institute of International Opportunity

IISD, International Institute for Sustainable Development

IMF, International Monetary Fund

IONet, International Organization Network

IPNet, International Political Economy Network

IREB, International Research and Exchanges Board

IREX, International Research Exchange Scholars Program

ISA, International Studies Association

IT, information technology

ITA, International Trade Administration

ITESM, Instituto Tecnológico y de Estudios Superiores de Monterrey (Monterrey Institute of Technology and Higher Education in Mexico)

LAC, languages across the curriculum

LANIC, Latin American Network Information Center

LARC, Language Acquisition Resource Center

LSP, languages for special purposes

MERCOSUR, Mercado Común del Sur (Southern Common Market)

MEXUS, Project Mexico-U.S., a transnational dual-degree program at San Diego State University

MIBS, Masters of International Business Studies

MIMLA, Masters of International Management for Latin America

MLA, Modern Language Association of America

MNE, multinational enterprises

NAFSA, Association of International Educators

NAFTA, North American Free Trade Agreement

NASBITE, North American Small Business International Trade Educators

NBEA, National Business Education Association

NCLIS, National Council for Languages and International Studies

NCOLCTL, National Council of Organizations of Less Commonly Taught Languages

NDEA, National Defense Education Act

NEH, National Endowment for the Humanities

NEOS, National Export Offer Service

NFLC, National Foreign Language Center

NGO, nongovernmental organization

NRC, National Resource Centers

NSF, National Science Foundation

NTDB, National Trade Data Bank

OECD, Organization for Economic Cooperation and Development

OSAD, Online Study Abroad Directory

PRIME, Pacific Rim Education Program

RFP, request for proposals

RFQ, request for quotations

SBA, Small Business Administration

SBDC, Small Business Development Center

SCORE, Service Corps of Retired Executives

SWOT, strengths, weaknesses, opportunities, and threats (also known as **TOWS**)

TESOL, teaching English to speakers of other languages

TOEFL, Test of English as a Foreign Language

TOWS, see **SWOT**

UISFL, Undergraduate International Studies and Foreign Languages (Title VI-A grants program of the US/ED)

UN, United Nations

UNESCO, United Nations

Educational, Scientific, and Cultural Organization

USAC, University Studies Abroad Consortium

USAID, U.S. Agency for International Development

US/ED, U.S. Department of Education

USEAC, U.S. Export Assistance Centers (agency of the U.S. Department of Commerce)

USIA, U.S. Information Agency

VU, "virtual university"

WB, the World Bank

WES, World Education Services, Inc.

WTCA, World Trade Centers Association

WTO, World Trade Organization

WWI, World Resources Institute

WWW, the World Wide Web

Index

PRINTER: Ginny's Printing & Copying

COVER PAPER: Natural Karma Cover

TEXT PAPER: 60# Accent Opaque,

Warm White

TYPE: Futura, Eurostile

COLOR: CMYK, Black

DESIGNER: Tammy Brazel